OCCUPATIONAL HEALTH AND SAFETY
International Influences and the "New" Epidemics

Edited by

Chris L. Peterson and Claire Mayhew

POLICY, POLITICS, HEALTH AND MEDICINE SERIES
Vicente Navarro, Series Editor

CRC Press
Taylor & Francis Group
Boca Raton London New York

CRC Press is an imprint of the
Taylor & Francis Group, an informa business

First published 2005 by Baywood Publishing Company, Inc.

Published 2018 by CRC Press
Taylor & Francis Group
6000 Broken Sound Parkway NW, Suite 300
Boca Raton, FL 33487-2742

First issued in paperback 2018

ISBN 13: 978-0-415-78389-7 (pbk)
ISBN 13: 978-0-89503-303-1 (hbk)

Visit the Taylor & Francis Web site at
http://www.taylorandfrancis.com

and the CRC Press Web site at
http://www.crcpress.com

Library of Congress Catalog Number: 2005041013

Library of Congress Cataloging-in-Publication Data

Occupational health and safety : international influences and the "new" epidemics / edited by Chris L. Peterson and Claire Mayhew
    p. cm. -- (Policy, politics, health, and medicine series)
  Includes bibliographical references and index.
  ISBN 0-89503-303-8 (cloth)
    1. Occupational diseases--Epidemiology. 2. Communicable diseases--Social aspects. 3. Epidemics--Social aspects. 4. Epidemics--Political aspects. I. Peterson, Chris L., 1949- II. Mayhew, Claire III. Series.

RC964.O254 2005
616.9'803--dc22

                                                       2005041013

Contents

PREFACE

OCCUPATIONAL HEALTH AND SAFETY EPIDEMICS AND
GLOBAL CHANGE—REVEALING THE NEW FORMS OF
RISK AT WORK AND THE DANGER OF IGNORING THEM

Work has always entailed health risks. "Through work, man transforms nature but also himself" (Karl Marx). As with other animals, prehistoric women and men faced risks of accidents and bodily wear and tear in their toil for food and shelter. As they started to master natural resources they were also exposed to hazardous materials. In historical times, the various health risks have been repeatedly described, notably by Ramizzini (1700). Lead, poor working postures, noise, and other harmful conditions caused diseases through the same biological mechanisms as now.

However, the form of exposure to these "eternal" risks vary as the organization and technology of production change. To develop effective prevention, we need to know the more precise risks of various machines, chemicals, work organizations, etc. Large funds have been allocated to accumulate and disseminate such preventive oriented knowledge, especially since the major Occupational Health and Safety (OHS)/Occupational Safety and Health (OSH)[1] reforms of the 1970s and 1980s. At least in the Western world, the main cause of work-related ill health is therefore lack of action, not lack of knowledge. Those who control the organization and technology of production do much too little of what they know should be done to prevent occupational injuries and diseases. If they don't personally know the right thing to do, they can find adequate advice if they only look for it.

Many of us think that we know what should be done and "only" have to improve its implementation. The outstanding achievement of this book is to lift a self-delusive veil from our eyes. Employers' and managers' lack of preventive measures remains a fundamental cause behind why workers are injured or fall ill from work. Yet Mayhew, Peterson, and their colleagues demonstrate how increased globalization, flexibility, and other related changes in the organization of production create new, more complex, and too often ignored patterns of risks at work. These risks become so prevalent that they can truly be called

---

[1] OHS and OSH are used interchangeably.

v

occupational epidemics. The various chapters of the book discuss the mechanisms behind these changes, such as international migration of hazardous production, precarious work, the shift toward service work and weakened worker resistance. On the other hand, they analyze the epidemic outcomes, e.g., the continuous growth of violence and stress.

All writers come from the Anglo-Saxon world, notably Australia. Yet their outlook is international and so is the relevance of the problems they describe. Even in Scandinavia—with a comparatively strong labor movement and active OSH policies—the same mechanisms result in the same health problems. The commuters of Stockholm recently both endured and supported a bus strike. The drivers' grievance of not even having time to pee was something everybody could understand. This, and many other problems, was the result of privatization and competitive tendering which had continuously squeezed resources and timetables. We too have, and will have, increasing work environment problems due to the flexibilization of production. This book offers a wealth of explanations to help understand the roots of epidemics and their forms.

One recurring theme of the book is especially important, that is, how risks are perceived. We can only act on our socially constructed perceptions of reality, not on any theoretically "true reality." How occupational risks are noted or not is therefore fundamental for how all involved—workers, politicians, employers, OSH researchers, and others—react to them. These actors have varying interests in OSH prevention and thus in getting information about OSH risks but they all base their actions on how they view the situation. Many chapters discuss how our understanding of the relation between risk causes and health effects is becoming more diffuse with the increased flexibilization of production. For example, when workers move between different jobs and are exposed to some materials at one workplace and to others at the next, the etiology of long latency diseases may be very difficult to trace. And when you have a precarious situation on the labor market, you are less prone to register injuries or compensation claims.

Both a reduced reporting and the obscuration of causes and effects makes official OHS statistics even more unreliable than they are today as indicators of occupational risks. Much governmental OSH prevention in practice boils down to minimization of workers' compensation figures. The longer and more complex causal chains described in this book may give ample excuse for further reductions in the acceptance of compensation claims. The gap between OSH politics and figures on the one hand, and work related ill health on the other, may therefore get even wider. Though workers themselves bear the worst part, the lack of recognition of the OSH risks may also increase the general societal costs of destroying the productivity of labor. Those who defend workers' health—as a human right but also as a societal resource—do well to learn about the more complex nature of risks as described in this book.

The book mainly describes and analyzes the changing nature of the OSH risks and of the mechanisms behind them. However, it also touches upon how new structures of production affect various actors ability to promote prevention. For example, Peterson (Chapter 7) discusses how weaker unions have less clout to defend workers against ever increasing production demands, and the resulting stress. Messing et al. (Chapter 8) try to understand why even feminist researchers don't take much interest in the pain and possible serious health risks of standing work, mainly by low-skilled women in service jobs. And Quinlan (Chapter 4) describes how workers in temporary and other precarious jobs not only are exposed to worse risks, but also have even less power to demand improvements.

In all, the book presents a fairly grim picture of the development of occupational health and safety, even in the Western world with our OSH reforms and rhetoric. But the writers also give us some hope and point to possible ways forward. Mayhew (Chapter 11) analyzes and gives advice on early warning systems for new, large scale OSH risks. In his overview (Chapter 2), Walters sees some positive trends, not the least a growing public interest in participation in risk regulation, expressed, for example, in EU's directive on OSH management. Quinlan notices that a better enforcement of employers' general duty of care, including to third parties, could curb some of the OSH problems of precarious work. And Leigh (Chapter 5) discusses alternative hazard surveillance strategies, when connections between exposure and diseases become more complex.

Yet the main purpose and effect of the book is to be an important alarm signal. This is the way the nature of work is changing and these are some of the major health risks it creates. The major hope that Mayhew, Peterson, and the other excellent writers offer us is that by recognizing the warning signals, and understanding what is happening, we are better equipped to resist and instead promote the safe and decent work advocated by the ILO.

Kaj Frick
National Institute for Working Life
Professor of Work Environment at Lulea Technical University, Sweden

Introduction to Occupational Health and Safety: International Influences and the "New" Epidemics

Chris L. Peterson and Claire Mayhew

The industrial revolution brought together large numbers of workers under supervision in a single worksite for prolonged periods of time to conduct mechanized work for the first time in history. Since then, occupational health and safety (OHS) has been an important concern of organized labor and social-justice activists. Early testimonies to unsafe practices were recorded by writers who identified the squalor of the work and living condition of miners and their families in Manchester, Britain, as well as widespread injuries, morbidity, and mortality associated with work. Engels (1), his colleague Marx (2), and many of the early epidemiologists, including Snow, detailed a range of horrors that accompanied work in these early factories and mines, as well as the risks attendant to living in the shoddy housing and suburbs where the new industrial proletariat existed outside of their hours of labor (3). These risks and outcomes have also been well identified elsewhere, including in Mayhew (4) and in various works by Charles Dickens (5). Many of these "old" hazards and risks identified by the writers charting the course of the industrial revolution in Britain still remain, although the potency of these "epidemics" has been diminished by legal protective interventions and the work of OHS professionals and trade-union activists.

The endemic risks associated with work in these early factories spawned legislation which was initially aimed at protecting child workers and the morals of working women, but subsequently spread to cover most working men. From this early beginning in Britain, legislative interventions and other protective practices spread across the industrialized world. As a result, the proportion of workers who are killed, maimed, or suffer a chronic and disabling illness from work have decreased significantly. Nonetheless, even in an advanced industrialized country such as Australia, around 2,900 workers each year still die from a work-related injury or illness (6–8). Yet barely a quarter of these fatalities—let alone short-term injuries or illnesses—are formally reported to workers' compensation authorities. The reasons why official databases are incomplete are complex, including lack of coverage for the self-employed (who are an increasing proportion of the labor force), because penalties result which influence the reporting behaviors of financially stressed employers (e.g., loss of no claim bonuses), restrictions on coverage (for example, with long-latency diseases where cause-effect relationships are unclear), and/or fear of reporting (e.g., if punitive sanctions are placed on the precariously employed workers) (9). That is, all the available evidence indicates that a significant number of known injuries and illnesses are not formally reported, recorded, or compiled.

In addition to these under-reported—but *known*—negative occupational health and safety incidents, as "new" forms of work-related injuries and illnesses emerge, their distinct signs and symptoms, risk factors, and causal pathways may be poorly recognized. Such emerging conditions are also likely to be subjected to intense suspicion and may even be "blamed on the victim" until such time as there are sufficient cases with clear objective cause-effect correlations for all facets of the new epidemic. For example, in the 1980s, Occupational Overuse Syndrome (also known as RSI) was almost universally denigrated as a psychosomatic condition until a more full-blown "epidemic" was extant with well-documented and widespread pre-condition work characteristics—such as excessive fine-motor movements required over an extended time period (10).

In this book, we argue that there are a range of similar nascent epidemics that are emerging across industrialized countries in this new century, the majority of which have their roots in the changing employment contract/labor process. That is, as the labor market and the organization of work change in a post-industrial society, the risks for new forms of epidemics rise. Unfortunately, these new epidemics are generally hidden because the shifts that have occurred in employment structures/the labor process over the past decade shield the extent of work-related injuries and illnesses from public view.

In this book, the key facets of these "new" epidemics are explored. Each of the different chapters was written by an author who was requested to illuminate the quite-specific risk factors associated with an emerging OHS threat. Many of these "new epidemics" were unknown a century—or even a decade—ago. The editors conclude that new forms of preventive interventions will be needed to reduce the potency of the "new epidemics." Further, because these new risks are poorly controlled by existing OHS protective mechanisms, we believe that new forms of social contracts will need to be devised that permeate all working relationships and diverse forms of worksites if the widespread morbidity associated with modern labor processes are to be avoided. The founding principle behind this book was to chart these emerging risks associated with changing patterns of employment.

GLOBALIZATION AND
THE INTERNATIONALIZATION OF OHS

Globalization is now an established phenomenon. The term refers to the opening up of nation state borders, the dropping of some international trading regulations, the concept of "free trade," deregulation of markets, and the exploitation of cheaper labor from developing countries. All these factors have fuelled the rapid growth of a globalized economy. The integration of stock markets within these international marketplaces, together with the continually rising power of cross-national conglomerates, has resulted in smaller economies and companies having far less influence on their financial futures. As a result, continual change in products, skill-demand shifts, downsizing of workforces, increasingly precariously employed workers, and the reduction of union coverage have become trademarks of the globalized economy. Thus, globalization poses threats and challenges, but cannot be disentangled from neo-liberal economic and social policies. Where open-market forces are allowed to dictate the terms of development, dominant corporations may use practices such as downsizing, shifting to locations where OHS regulation is less stringent, and restriction of social investment in communities where they operate. Overall, the consequences of globalization tend to be beneficial for those nations that are strong and dominant, and may result in increased impoverishment for poorer communities.

Concomitant with globalization has been increased pressure to deregulate many aspects of the OHS protections developed over the past two centuries—in line with the dominant neo-liberal economic ideology. While resistance to deregulation of OHS protections has been somewhat muted in countries such as the U.S., in many other industrialized countries (such as the European Union), there have been substantial paradigm shifts that have enhanced protection. For example, member states of the European Community are, over time, adopting the same regulatory and policy guidelines. As a result, nation states bordering the Mediterranean have begun to move toward acceptance of guidelines initiated in Scandinavia which are, arguably, of superior OHS protective value.

Mitchell (11) argues that "globalization" is likely to increase the number of work-related diseases and injuries during the 21st century because of pressures to deregulate protective standards, and because hazardous work processes have been rapidly relocating to the Third World. For example, the International Labour Organisation (ILO) has estimated there are 250 million incidents per year, 335,000 fatalities, and approximately one million fatalities from illnesses caused by pollution and toxic materials (12). Further, approximately 350 carcinogenic chemicals and 3,000 allergenic chemicals are used in workplaces worldwide.

However, the increased economic competition associated with globalization means that greater resources are concentrated in the hands of fewer people and organizations (13). A number of multinational corporations have adopted a policy framework of downsizing in the industrialized world as a way of maintaining profitability, and of encouraging reduced union involvement in their workforces. These trends, coupled with the ability to manage and manipulate large volumes of capital, make it easier to exploit international labor and contribute less in social capital to the communities where they employ cheaper workers. Thus, the increased OHS risks are likely to be exacerbated in developing countries where most people are involved in mining and agriculture, do work that is physically demanding, and are exposed to parasites and infectious diseases in addition to "industrial" work-related risks. According to Mitchell (11), developed economies have undermined OHS protections at work in order to lower production costs and to win contracts from transnational corporations.

Within industrialized countries, Coburn (13) argues that globalization, as a real force and as ideology, has reinforced the dominant class position of business at both national and international levels. This business dominance of the market and the state has led to attacks on working class and social-citizenship rights. For example, the welfare state enacted in most of the Anglo-American nations has been undermined in ways that reinforce privately owned business power. Similarly, neo-liberal policies are increasingly restricting free access to healthcare, which is a basic tenant enacted during the post World War II years.

INTERNATIONAL CONTROLS AND DEVELOPMENTS

Walters (14) argues that the European Community (E.C.) represents a converse force to globalization, with improving OHS protective policies emerging over recent times in a number of member states. Overall, there appears to have been an emphasis on process rather than prescription, which reflects the changing political and economic landscape over the last few decades (14). However, this move is encapsulated within a paradigm shift away from setting prescribed OHS regulatory standards to one where duty holders are required to engage in risk identification, assessment, and control. For example, in Scandinavia there are strong labor protective standards that play a powerful role in the implementation and operation of OHS protection. In Britain, Scandinavia, and France there is a single central authority, and a relatively low level of autonomy for regional and local administrations. In corporatist systems such as Germany, co-determination (as well as local factors such as federalism in Germany and a dual system for making and enforcing law in the Netherlands) has a strong influence on OHS regulation. In France, OHS is heavily regulated with significant state involvement and a lower level of union association with policy making. Italy is quite different again, with significant overlap between the responsibilities of different authorities and a lot of conflict and debate between labor and capital. While OHS in Britain is much more deregulated than in many other parts of Europe, there is extensive guidance on risk control. To some extent, the British focus followed concern about widespread costs to the public purse. However, the E.U. *Directive 89/391 Introduction of Measures to Encourage Improvement of Safety and Health of Workers at Work* has been a watershed in ensuring OHS management systems were adopted across member states of the E.C. (15).

The implementation of international standards formulated by the International Labour Organisation (ILO) can counteract the negative outcomes from globalization. However, many countries have not yet become signatories to the core *Conventions and Recommendations* established by the ILO, including Australia and the U.S. The editors of this book believe that the ILO *Conventions and Recommendations,* as well as the guides produced through the SafeWork program of the ILO, provide the basis for effective policies and strategies to enhance OHS protection. There are also other international developments that assist with protection of OHS, such as the Social and Economic Council of the U.N. that promotes a consistent world-wide system for Classification and Labelling of Chemicals (16).

CHANGING PATTERNS OF EMPLOYMENT AND MOVE TO SERVICE INDUSTRIES

New "at-risk" groups of workers are being identified as employment patterns shift. In both the industrialized and developing world, new forms of labor employment are emerging, including home-based businesses, mobile worksites, and a range of forms of precarious short-term employment. At the same time, the industry-sector basis of much employment is changing. Both these shifts in employment have effects on OHS.

First, in terms of the labor-market changes associated with globalization, Quinlan (17) argues that labor-market restructuring is having a significant impact on occupational safety and health. Increasing use of short-term employment contracts, the unpicking of award structures, growth in precarious employment, decreasing levels of unionization, under-funding of state OHS authorities, and dispersion of workers across more—but smaller—organizations has resulted in increasing difficulty in enforcement of basic OHS standards (18).

Second, while employment in traditional industry sectors such as farming and manufacturing continues, the working population is increasingly concentrated in the "services" sector in nearly all industrialized countries, including in tourism, hospitality, healthcare, and recreation. Employment in the services industries is also commonly associated with smaller and more scattered worksites with higher turnover ratios. Further, the hazards and risks associated with work in the services industries are distinct from those in, for example, manufacturing or farming. Because the hazards and risks are different in the services industry, the OHS threats are distinct—and the most appropriate prevention strategies vary.

Third, the *mobility* of labor in the precarious labor force—particularly those in the services industry sectors—also means that exposure to hazards and risks may be short-term and there may be multiple exposures from different worksites, and hence tracking effects to causative agents will be very complex (particularly for long-latency diseases). But, because the *labor process* increasingly relies on a precariously employed workforce, the flow-on effects from exposure to hazards and risks may not be recognized as rapidly as those injuries and illnesses experienced by more traditional workers. Thus, interventions to reduce the potency of these "new" epidemics may not be sufficiently timely, and there are also likely to be fewer opportunities for researchers to conduct studies based on clear-cut cause-and-effect relationships.

BURDEN OF WORK-RELATED INJURY
AND DISEASE THAT IS
UNDER-REPORTED

In some Third World nations such as Latin America, less than 5 percent of cases are reported. Mitchell (11) argues that there is inadequate access to appropriate health care in developing countries, with only 5-10 percent of the workforce having adequate access. Many non-reported fatalities result from clinicians not being aware that these deaths should be reported to coroners. These problems are not unique to developing countries; for example, workers in small-scale industries are not always adequately protected, and in the U.S. only 10 percent of workplaces have regular inspectorate visits.

In many countries, there is an under-reporting of occupational illnesses and injury. For example, there are approximately 2,900 Australian deaths resulting from traumatic injury and longer-term diseases that can be directly tracked to work (9). Yet official figures are approximately one-fifth of the total, reflecting inadequate reporting mechanisms, the difficulties in recording work-related diseases, and the exclusion of the self-employed from official data sources. Similarly, Mitchell (11) cites under-reporting to the Health and Safety Executive (HSE) in Britain; for example, the self-employed are generally not included. Since implementing the HSE in 1974, there have been over 18,000 deaths, yet an average prosecution result in a fine of only U.K. 4,000 pounds. The majority of these fatal incidents are not investigated, although many are due to illegal employer actions. Figures on work-related illnesses are particularly unreliable, with the HSE only including those resulting from asbestos exposures and similar diseases. Other research suggests that the figures from work-related deaths may be as high as 10,000 to 20,000 per year (11). The restrictions on recording also reflect a conservative approach to the reporting of OHS incidents.

THEORETICAL MODELS RELEVANT
TO NEW EPIDEMICS

When developing models about OHS epidemics, it is evident that a multidisciplinary explanation needs to be provided that encompasses several theoretical levels of analysis. Throughout history there have been a number of different models adopted that explain epidemics, and those provided in the public health literature provide a useful insight. Epidemics were initially explained through biological approaches, with immunology and virology being important disciplines adopted while evaluating the passage of an epidemic and identifying plans for dealing with the threats (3). This biological approach was later developed into a risk-factor model. Subsequently, a socio-psychological explanation was adopted where characteristics of populations and individual susceptibility to disease were considered important, and social and behavioral psychologists examined group behavioral traits (and, occasionally, the behaviors of their employers). Medical sociology began to provide a more holistic theoretical framework for explaining the incidence and spread of disease that incorporated cultural, social, political, and legal dimensions and looked at the interplay between professional groups from each of these disciplines (3).

In examining OHS epidemics, there are three perspectives that could be considered during the emergence of a new form of an "OSH epidemic": (a) biological and biopsychological models; (b) psychosocial risk factors; and (c) socio-political explanations.

(a) The biological and biophysiological model has historically had the most pervasive influence on OSH. It is based on the premise that biological explanations, based on scientifically verified premises, provide the basis for explaining the emergence of epidemics in OHS. Biological explanations can focus on the nature of disease and its spread (such as changes in lung and pleura tissue caused by mesothelioma), and explain the emergence of disease in terms of biological cause-effect mechanisms. At best, the biological and biophysiological models provide a basis for developing the epidemiology of a disease; at worst, they provide a "no fault" explanation for the development of ill health or death. Nevertheless, this approach has been extremely important in developing an acceptable "scientific validity" for a number of OHS conditions, such as the etiology of RSI (repetitive strain injury or occupational overuse syndrome). However, the biological approach does not adequately explain the processes during the early stages of an epidemic when there are few "cases."

(b) The psychosocial risk factors perspective provides a broader explanation of the causes and consequences of OHS epidemics. This approach focuses on individual workers and group characteristics, the fit between them, and the demands of the particular job-task environment. A psychosocial perspective, for example, can help to explain the emergence of issues such as work-related stress and violence in the workplace by examining characteristics among perpetrators, changes in work organization, and individual endurance in the context of changing work demands. Such analyses can also identify the needs of individuals for supportive work environments in the context of increasing competition and more demanding work schedules. Karasek's (19, 20) demand-control model is an example of a psychosocial explanation of a person-environment fit where individual characteristics may not be able to match conditions of excessive demand. However, there is little explanation of why some conditions become compensatable, and therefore documented "epidemics," and why some do not.

(c) A socio-political model is the clearest in providing an explanation for how risk factors for an epidemic emerge as a result of poor labor relations, inadequate work practices, stringent financial constraints on safety spending, or derisory enforcement. A socio-political model can also indicate how an OHS issue becomes acceptable to medical and legal authorities, or how a particular epidemic becomes a compensatable condition. Figlio (21), Navarro (22, 23), and Willis (24) provide good examples of this approach.

In 1986, Quinlan (25) argued that it was characteristic in many cases of OSH injury and illness for a "blame the victim" approach to be used. Little has changed since this time, with those who report an *unusual* or *sentinel* occupational illness or injury still commonly being blamed for their conditions, being accused of trying to "rort" the system, or attention being paid to the worker's personal shortcomings. As work intensification has increased over the past decade—associated with the pressures of globalization—it appears that managerial willingness to accept responsibility for the consequences of poor OHS has diminished. Stress is a good example, where tests have been proposed to filter out people prone to stress during pre-employment screening, presumably to divert attention away from stress-inducing tasks and to place the onus on individuals.

In sum, there have been marked shifts in employment structures in industrialized countries over the past decade. At the same time, there has been a shift in the industry basis of much employment. Inevitably, there has been significant change in the OHS hazards and risks faced by workers in all industrialized countries. Hence, the pattern of work-related injuries and diseases has also changed: there have been improvements in the OHS profile of some jobs, stasis in others, and in a few industry sectors/employment situations, new "epidemics" have emerged.

In this book, the authors argue that emerging or "new" epidemics are manifested in quite different ways to the plagues of the past, but are equally debilitating. As in the past, some injuries and diseases are invariably fatal. It is clear that in each of the "new" epidemics discussed in this book, quite different pathways between causative agents, contributing risk factors, and outcomes occur. These unfolding epidemics are complex, and hence prevention may require much more sophisticated responses than did the epidemics of the past, which may have had much more clear-cut cause-effect relationships. Thus, the evidence indicates that the most appropriate preventive strategies can be quite different for the distinct "new epidemics" compared to historical risk management techniques. The remainder of this book is focused on elucidating these "new epidemics."

ORGANIZATION OF THE BOOK: PAST AND EMERGING OHS EPIDEMICS

In Chapter 2, David Walters presents the important international issues affecting OHS. Some of these international issues are related to the effects of globalization, but issues that were pressing during the end of the 20th century, such as deregulation of working conditions and of OHS, are still important issues today. He argues that the reasons for the development of epidemics are multifactorial, but that the organization and structure of OHS has been extensively affected by the processes of deregulation, and that the union movement, for example, has diminished in its effects.

In Chapter 3, Claire Mayhew provides an overview of occupational violence. She argues that the jobs at risk for violence at work are similar across industrialized countries. However, the incidence varies because patterns of employment (and hence exposure) and other structural factors (such as access to firearms) are diverse from one place to another. The core argument in this chapter is that the incidence of occupational violence is increasing to the point that, in high-risk jobs, aggression against workers is at epidemic levels.

In Chapter 4, Michael Quinlan provides a detailed analysis of the OHS consequences from precarious employment. In this chapter, he brings together evidence from more than 180 pieces of research published internationally since 1966, and analyzes the effectiveness of regulatory responses. Quinlan argues that the growth of precarious employment has undermined the ability of OHS preventative and workers' compensation/rehabilitation regulatory regimes to fulfill their objectives, and that responses to the emerging pre-conditions for the new epidemic are fragmented and partial. Thus the "epidemics" experienced by precariously employed workers remain largely unreported, uncompensated, and pose a long-term threat to the viability of social-security support mechanisms unless preventive interventions are rapidly implemented.

In Chapter 5, Jim Leigh argues that some of the "old" diseases due to occupational exposures remain endemic in industrialized societies. He argues that the effects of chemical and physical agents such as dusts, fumes, and vapors have largely been brought under control in large-scale plants, although workers in the informal sectors of the economy face a significant level of risk. In essence, it is the *labor process* that now creates the pre-conditions for a prolonged extension to the long-standing epidemics.

In Chapter 6, Claire Mayhew analyses the OHS consequences of adolescent and child labor in industrialized countries. She provides evidence that young people working outside of the formal system are at high risk, particularly those in family businesses, on farms, and sometimes completing illegal and/or dangerous tasks. The fast-food industry, garment manufacturing, and farming are used as case studies. The author concludes by arguing that the work-related injuries and illnesses experienced by working adolescents in industrialized countries are extensive, but these data are not fully reflected in the official databases. Thus, this epidemic remains largely non-reported and hidden.

In Chapter 7, Chris Peterson argues that stress is at epidemic proportions due to the effects of neo-liberal policies associated with work intensification and deregulation. Stress in many countries has become part of the OHS agenda, and consequently compensation is accessible, although management tends to deny the existence of this epidemic. The stress debate and focus of research has moved from biomedical models, psychological approaches, and the nature of stressors in the workplace to issues such as downsizing, decisions about work stress and retirement, and the relationship between work- and home-induced stress. Some newer ideas such as global best practice production techniques are assessed for their impact on stress levels. The author argues that participative work practices and widespread downsizing have strained the coping capacities of workers and managers and have led to significant increases in stress. Peterson concludes by presenting some "best-practice" approaches to stress management, but maintains that there is a paucity of models in the literature.

In Chapter 8, Karen Messing, Katherine Lippel, Ève Laperrière, and Marie-Christine Thibault investigate scientific evidence for the links between illness/injury and standing at work. They report that while the proportion of workers who stand on the job varies between countries, those who do risk a far higher incidence of back pain. The authors argue that epidemiological studies have not been successfully applied to workstation redesign for workers affected by standing, and that the current OHS policy frameworks allow an epidemic of pain to be inflicted on workers who have to stand throughout their work shifts.

In Chapter 9, Joan Eakin focuses on the epidemic associated with the discourse of blame for those on return-to-work programs. She presents a case study from Ontario (Canada) of a recent return-to-work policy that has reduced government involvement and increased liability and responsibility for return to work on employers and injured workers. She argues that many of these workers are subject to abuse, particularly those who are not able to make the transition back to work.

In Chapter 10, Greg Murphy presents an evaluation of rehabilitation. He argues the inability to contain costs and provide speedier return to work and reduced absences for individual workers threatens the viability of some rehabilitation programs. He presents the Australian case where responsibility for compensation has shifted from employers to external professionals such as doctors, rehabilitation providers, and insurance companies, and argues that this leads to a lack of cost containment.

In Chapter 11, Claire Mayhew proposes that the internationalization of the business environment has resulted in significant changes to the hazards and risks faced by workers. She argues that completely new morbidity and mortality patterns can result from radically changed working environments. As a result, "new" epidemics can rapidly emerge, and hence the risk factors need to be quickly identified so that interventions can be rapidly implemented. In this chapter, the author analyzes scenarios where baseline OHS empirical studies in industry are warranted, and provides detailed guidance on how to go about conducting such "grounded" OHS research when the first "sentinel" cases of a possible new epidemic are identified.

In Chapter 12, Chris Peterson summarizes the various approaches to identifying epidemics discussed in this book. He argues that the concept of epidemics can be constructed from a number of different perspectives, including legal-litigation, government policy, trade-union approach, management orientation, and the lay person's understanding. Peterson argues that three different approaches are important for understanding the development, identification, and acceptance of an epidemic. The first is the biological and biophysiological perspective; the second a psychosocial approach; and the third the interpretation through a socio-cultural and socio-political perspective. Finally, the author of this chapter assesses the efficacy of each approach.

REFERENCES

1. Engels, F. *The Condition of the Working Class in England.* Panther, London, 1892 (reprinted 1969).
2. Marx, K. *Capital Volume 1.* Pelican, Middlesex, 1867 (reprinted 1976).
3. Daly, J., Kellehear, A., and Gliksman, M. *The Public Health Researcher.* Oxford University Press, Melbourne, 1997.
4. Mayhew, H. *Mayhew's London: Being Selections From "London Labour and The London Poor."* Spring Books, London, 1851.
5. Dickens, C. *The Adventures of Oliver Twist.* Oxford University Press, London, 1838.
6. Driscoll, T. Mitchell, R. Mandryk, J. Healey, S., and Hendrie, L. *Work-Related Traumatic Fatalities in Australia, 1989 to 1992.* National Occupational Health and Safety Commission, Ausinfo, Canberra, Australia, 1999.
7. National Occupational Health and Safety Commission. *Compendium of Workers' Compensation Statistics, 1999-2000.* NOHSC, Canberra, Australia, 2001.
8. Mayhew, C., and Peterson, C. (eds.). *Occupational Health and Safety in Australia: Industry, Public Sector and Small Business.* Allen and Unwin, Sydney, 1999.
9. Driscoll, T., and Mayhew, C. The extent and costs of occupational injury and illness. In *Occupational Health and Safety in Australia: Industry, Public Sector and Small Business,* edited by C. Mayhew and C. Peterson, pp. 28–51. Allen and Unwin, Sydney, 1999.
10. Willis, E. RSI as a social process. *Community Health Stud.* 10(2): 210–210, 1986.

11. Mitchell, P. The impact of globalisation on health and safety at work. Report issued by the World Health Organization and International Labour Organisation, 1999. www.wsws.org/articles/1999/jul1999/who-j23 shtml.

12. Paddon, M., Ewer, P., and Skliros, K. *The Other Face of Globalisation: An Alternative Report on Major Companies at the World Economic Forum.* ACTU, Melbourne, 2000.

13. Coburn, D. Globalisation, neo-liberalism, inequities and health: Beyond the income inequalities hypothesis. Paper presented to the International Sociological Association, Brisbane, June, 2002.

14. Walters, D. (ed.). *Regulating Health and Safety Management in the European Union: A Study of the Dynamics of Change. SALTSA Joint Program for Working Life Research in Europe.* Peter Lang Presses Interuniversitaires Europeennes, Brussels, 2002.

15. *European Community Framework Directive 89/391 Introduction of Measures to Encourage Improvement of Safety and Health of Workers at Work.* Accepted 12 June 1989, to be implemented by Member States by 1 January 1994, Brussels.

16. Stewart-Crompton, R. Globalisation and OHS. *Labour Rev. 2001.* counil.net.au/labour_review/73/update7311.html.

17. Quinlan, M. The implications of labor market restructuring in industrialised societies for occupational health and safety. *Econ. Soc. Democracy* 20: 427–460, 1999.

18. Johnstone, R. Mayhew, C., and Quinlan, M. Outsourcing risk? The regulation of OHS where subcontractors are employed. *Comp. Labor Law Policy J.* 22: 351–393, 2001.

19. Karasek, R. A. Job demands, job decision latitude and mental strain: Implications for job redesign. *Admin. Sci. Q.* 24: 285–308, 1979.

20. Karasek, R. A. Job socialization and job strain: The implications of two related psychosocial mechanisms for job design. In *Working Life: A Social Science Contribution to Work Reform,* edited by B. Gardell and G. Johansson, pp. 75–94. John Wiley and Sons, New York, 1981.

21. Figlio, K. How does illness mediate social relations: Workmen's compensation and medico-legal practices 1890-1940? In *The Problem Of Medical Knowledge: Examining the Social Construction of Medicine,* edited by P. Wright and A. Treacher, pp. 174–224. Edinburgh University Press, Edinburgh, 1982.

22. Navarro, V. The labour process and health: A historical materialist interpretation. *Int. J. Health Serv.* 12: 5–29, 1982.

23. Navarro, V., and Shi, L. The political context of social inequalities and health. *Int. J. Health Serv.* 31: 1–21, 2001.

24. Willis, E. The industrial relations of occupational health and safety: A labour process approach. *Labour Industry* 2: 317–333, 1989.

25. Quinlan, M. Psychological and sociological approaches to the study of occupational illness: A critical review. *Aust. N.Z. J. Sociol.* 24: 189–207, 1988.

CHAPTER 2

International Developments and Their Influence on Occupational Health and Safety in Advanced Market Economies

David Walters

This chapter outlines some of the characteristic features of change and their consequences for occupational health and safety (OHS) evident in developed western countries today. Many of these features are the subjects of more detailed treatments in other chapters. What is undertaken here is an overview that suggests some connections between the various threats to, and opportunities for, future improvements in the work environment and workers' well-being. It addresses some of the issues that have contributed to causing or exacerbating emerging epidemics in OHS in advanced market economies, as well as considering policies aimed at their prevention and amelioration. Its thesis is that such epidemics are largely the consequence of a constellation of features of change in modern economies. As well as structural changes occurring in work and the labor market, these include continuing deregulation and the withdrawal of the state from inspection, control, and resourcing roles in preventive OHS and are also largely the result of the pressures of globalization.

However, two caveats are especially important. The first concerns the need for an appropriate theoretical framework. The chapter begins by asking what are the significant international developments that impact on occupational health and safety? But to understand these developments and their consequences properly, it is essential they are located within a framework that allows for a proper analysis of cause and effect. Increasingly in modernity, such a framework must draw upon disciplines that range far wider than those normally found in health and safety studies. Clearly, most of the changes that are currently experienced in the work environment are not only the result of technological, scientific, engineering, or regulatory developments (or the absence of them), but also the political and economic uses and control of such developments. These changes also concern the distribution of power and authority within societies and markets, which has major

13

implications for the way work is organized, structured, and regulated, including impacts on labor markets and on how work is done, where, and by whom. Such issues cannot be explained solely within national boundaries. The international dimensions of their causes and effects must also be accounted for. Proper analysis of all this requires at the very least an integrated application of sociological and economic paradigms with those more traditionally associated with studying OHS.

The second caveat leads from this. The focus of the pages that follow concerns experiences in advanced market economies. Attention is drawn to some of the consequences of developments occurring in these countries for the work environments of millions of people who do not live within their developmental territorial/regulatory boundaries. The wider consequences of globalization—in the form of the multitude of direct threats to well-being in parts of the world that do not share the benefits of advanced capitalist states—is also mentioned, but it is acknowledged that, overall, the analysis offered here is limited by concentration on the experience occurring largely within, or created by, advanced market economies. This is only one rather limited perspective, and alternative analyses are possible. Analyses might, for example, be located within parameters and dependencies dictated by life in the so-called developing world. Or they might take an integrated approach, in which rich and poor, north and south, market and non-market economies are examined in ways seeking to balance cause and effect in occupational health and safety across rich and poor countries, thus offering yet another perspective on emergent threats and opportunities for global health and safety. Such analyses are beyond the scope of the present chapter. It is recognized, therefore, that it represents an incomplete picture of the true extent of the international consequences for health and safety of current economic, regulatory, and political policies and trends.

INTRODUCTION AND BACKGROUND

Over the last decade the context of productive activities in advanced market economies of Europe, North America, and Australasia has undergone momentous change, both within these regions and in international markets. There have been inevitable OHS consequences, both positive and negative. Negative consequences have included the rapid growth in importance of the health effects of psychosocial aspects of work intensification and the shift from manufacturing to service-based economies as well as growth in significance of musculoskeletal disease (MSD). At the same time, risks from more traditional chemical, physical, and biological hazards have by no means disappeared. Hazardous work processes have been increasingly imposed on more vulnerable workers. This has occurred both in rich, regulated countries as a result of the trends in the structure and organization of work and labor markets, and in less regulated economies when multi-national business interests have gone off-shore to reduce labor costs and avoid regulation, resulting in workers in developing and newly industrializing countries being exposed to noxious production processes. In advanced market economies the impact of economic liberalism has continued to promote deregulation, arguably resulting in decreased protection for workers in these countries.

Positive consequences may be harder to discern. The long-term trend of reduction in injury and fatality rates continues in most developed countries, although increased awareness of the probable full extent of work-related ill health tends to place such improvement in perspective. Moreover, in many advanced economies of Europe and Australia, the rate of such reduction is perceived to have slowed, stimulating discussion of a change to more effective preventive strategies. Similarly, the negative OHS consequences of the rapid rate of change in communication technologies probably outweigh the positive ones. However, positive consequences do exist, not least being the increasing internationalization of knowledge and action on OHS. Additionally, there has been change in societal perception of risk and in notions of social justice especially in relation to fatalities at work, both of which have been rapidly internationalized as a result of the use of modern communication technologies. Moreover, the model of mandatory OHS management in which the use of appropriate competencies by, or on behalf of employers as well as the participation of workers and their representatives, is now characteristic of regulatory requirements in E.U. member states and widely adopted in other advanced market economy countries such as Australia and New Zealand.[1] Similarly, policy approaches to compensation, retention, and return to work are increasingly internationalized as countries with historically very different systems and strategies in these areas face up to common operational problems.

The chapter considers three broad aspects of international change in OHS in advanced market economies. It begins with an outline of some of the direct effects of change in the organization of work and labor markets on health and safety. The intention is not to provide a detailed analysis but rather to show the extent to which these issues are of international significance and the extent to which they serve to contribute to or ameliorate the negative consequences of OHS at this level. Second, it considers changes in societal perceptions of risk and social justice on OHS issues. Finally, some of the features of national and international OHS policy responses to both these areas of change are addressed. While it is perhaps over simplistic to consider current international trends in terms of their actual or potential positive and negative consequences for OHS *epidemics,* this is the theme around which the discussion in the chapter organized.

---

[1] But not in all—the U.S. still remains outside this regulatory model, with its continued preference for reliance on non-statutory approaches to systematic OHS management and on employers' voluntary adoption of management systems. However, even in the U.S. voluntary approaches there are broadly comparable elements of internationalized trends in OHS management that are in evidence (see Frick and Wren 2000 for a discussion of these international trends).

THE IMPACT OF CHANGE IN THE STRUCTURE
AND ORGANIZATION OF WORK

Although it is perhaps stating the obvious, it is nevertheless important to note that in terms of the measurable negative effects of work on life, health, and well-being, there continues to be a marked difference between patterns in advanced market economies and those in other parts of the world. The overall incidence of work-related mortality and morbidity in advanced market economies is considerably lower than among the economically active populations of the rest of the world. Conservative estimates suggest that in an economically active world population of 2.7 billion, 1.9 to 2.3 million people may have been victims of work-related deaths in the year 2000 (1). Of these, there were some 1.6 million victims of occupational disease and 355,000 fatal occupational accidents (22,000 of which were children). The vast majority of these preventable occurences took place in countries other than the advanced market economies that are the main subject of the present chapter, which accounted for only 6 percent of the total. The nature of work-related disease is also different in different world regions with malignant neoplasms featuring quite prominently in established market economies, while communicable diseases are still of major significance in work-related disease in Africa and India, respiratory disease in China, and circulatory system disease in the former socialist countries of Europe and in the Middle East. There is considerable variation in the frequency of accidents in different economic sectors, with the highest incidence in fishing, agriculture, and construction worldwide. While advances in technology and engineering have been associated with the long-term improvement in occupational fatality rates in established market economies, the fact that globalization encourages the relocation of production to countries in which such benefits are not so apparent and where regulation is far more lax should be of some concern.

Globalization of markets, production, and capital, its consequences for the structure and organization of work and the labor market, and the representation of labor, for states and for whole societies, were among the defining features of the closing decades of the 20th century. Their influence continues unabated during the present time. Indeed it would be surprising if such momentous change did not affect OHS, both in terms of outcomes and responses. Such effects are analyzed in depth elsewhere in this book. Direct effects of the way in which work in affluent societies has been intensified, in which the employer-employee relationship has increasingly given way to more tenuous emerging "networks of production" driven by rapid technological change and deregulation of world markets, have profoundly affected occupational OHS.[2] Moreover, since it

[2] See Frick *et al.* pp. 1–14, for a more detailed discussion of the breakdown of the traditional employer-employee focus of work relations, brought about by current patterns of production and services and its consequences for OHS arrangements.

is increasingly implausible for analysis of the relationship between work and health to ignore the connection between these developments in post-industrialized countries and those affecting workers in the rest of the world, such outcomes and responses take on an inescapable global character. As Loewnson puts it (2):

> While the share of world trade to the world's poorest countries has decreased, workers in these countries increasingly find themselves in insecure, poor-quality jobs, sometimes involving technologies which are obsolete or banned in industrialized countries. The occupational illness which results is generally less visible and not adequately recognised as a problem in low-income countries. Those outside the workplace can also be affected through, for example, work-related environmental pollution and poor living conditions.

As far as outcomes in advanced market economies are concerned, the effects of change in the structure and organization of work are becoming better documented with the results of national and international surveys.[3,4,5] Moreover, it is also widely acknowledged that such evidence of much of the likely consequences of current changed work structure, organization, and practice—the OHS epidemics of the future—remains hidden even in these established market economies. At the same time, the survey evidence, such as that collected in the European Foundation series, demonstrates that traditional occupational health issues have by no means disappeared. In the case of certain past exposures, such as that to asbestos, their negative health consequences continue to exert a mounting toll of mortality and morbidity that is likely to continue well into the present century. Indeed, while regulatory stringency has massively reduced the role of asbestos in most advanced market economies, it continues to be mined and used extensively in poorer countries, suggesting an even longer reach for its latent health effects on these populations.

[3] There have been regular and ad-hoc surveys of the extent of the burden of work-related ill health in many countries in Europe and North America. In addition, there have been cross-country surveys such as those undertaken by the European Foundation for Living and Working Conditions in the European Union (see European Foundation for the Improvement of Living and Working Conditions. *First European Survey on the Work Environment 1991–1992*, EF/92/11/EN. Office for Official Publications of the European Communities, Luxembourg, 1992; and European Foundation for the Improvement of Living and Working Conditions. *Second European Survey on the Work Environment*, Office for Official Publications of the European Communities, Luxembourg, 1997. See also Paoli, P., and Merllie, D. *Third European Survey on Working Conditions 2000*. European Foundation for the Improvement of Living and Working Conditions, Office for Official Publications of the European Communities, Luxembourg, 2001.

[4] Most of these surveys show rising incidence of stress related conditions and MSD. Furthermore, they point to substantial incidence of work-related ill health that is not reported by conventional statutory reporting requirements, leading to estimates such as those in the U.K. where 25,000 people are believed to leave employment each year as a result of a work-related injury and illness (HSE 1999).

[5] Such ill health and injury is responsible for the loss of over 25 million working days annually. See Jones, J. R., Hodgson, J. T., Clegg, T. A., and Elliot, R. C. *Self Reported Work-Related Illness*. HSE Books, Sudbury, 1998.

Large parts of the labor force in advanced market economies currently experience radically different working conditions from those of a generation ago. Decline in manufacturing, heavy engineering, and mining as well as in large, relatively stable enterprises and the growth of the significance of work in small enterprises, contingent and peripheral employment, casualization, and outsourcing has resulted in job insecurity and work intensification in an environment that has become far more difficult to regulate (3). Organizational aspects of these situations are increasingly less defined by individual employment relationships and more by "structured networks of production." As a result, influences from outside enterprises are beginning to have greater impact than employers on what is produced and how it is produced (and the consequent health effects), since production decisions are increasingly removed from the direct control of employers. The so-called supply chain and the role of intermediary processes and actors in the wider economic (and sometimes social) environment in which work takes place are increasingly recognized as important influences on the health and safety of workers. There are also important gender considerations to bear in mind when contemplating the effects of the changing world of work on health. In particular, the "double burden" of work experienced by many women as well as the disruption of work-life balances that is the potential consequence of many new forms of work organization have been further significant consequences of recent changes.

Over decades of struggle, organized labor has played a major role in protecting workers' health and safety through a combination of means, leading a recent reviewer of the history of occupational health to comment: "Organised labour has been the essential factor central to most workplace health and safety improvements from the industrial revolution to the present" (4).

However, one of the more obvious aspects of recent economic and political trends that have reshaped the world of work has been the decline in membership and influence of trade unions in most advanced market economies.[6] This decline has several consequences: not only does it directly affect the extent to which workers have access to representation, but it probably also affects all of the other ways in which trade unions act to protect workers' OHS interests. On a more positive note, there are some recent signs of a slowing and possible reversal of this decline in some countries. There are also signs that trade-union efforts to reshape their identities in attempts to reverse the trend of decline in

[6] Trade union membership in most advanced market economies has reduced substantially since its peak in the 1970s—for example in the U.K., the U.S., and in Australia it has nearly halved. It has declined throughout Western Europe. Indeed, only in countries where the Ghent system operates (i.e., where unions perform functions in the administration of unemployment benefit and social insurance) have trade unions maintained or improved upon levels of unionization of the 1970s (see for example Waddington, J. Towards a reform agenda? European trade unions in transition. In *European Industrial Relations IRJ Annual Review 1999/2000*, edited by B. Towers. Blackwell, London.

some countries is leading to both a more prominent role for health and safety issues in their strategies for renewal and to more effective means of representing the health and safety interests of workers in the fractured labor-relations scenarios that are increasingly typical of the current structure and organization of work, as described above. For example, there have been marked trends toward the achievement of better representation of workers' interests in small enterprises and on multi-employer worksites in recent years, especially in E.U. countries, and there is increasing interest in these approaches in other advanced market economies (5).

SOCIETAL PERCEPTIONS OF RISK AND SOCIAL JUSTICE: THE CHALLENGE OF CHANGE

Changes in the structure and organization of work pose major challenges both to conventional approaches to regulation and to the engagement of stakeholders in preventing unwanted effects on the health of workers. They create difficulties for the organization of prevention in an increasingly fragmented economy and labor market.

While these consequences and their problems for regulation are manifest in all advanced market economies, it is also evident that in the same countries there is a changing public perception of occupational risk, in which, among other things, a shift has occurred in the nature and extent of risks that society is prepared to tolerate. This is further reflected in the marked drop in public confidence in both governmental and expert decision makers' assessment of risk management. Although the public is more widely experienced in relation to environmental and food issues, this shift in public consciousness also increasingly pervades areas of decision-making concerning occupational risks such as, for example, asbestos, nuclear radiation, and working with chemical carcinogens as well as with the uncertainties of the risks of new substances and new technologies.

Social theorists such as Ulrich Beck and Anthony Giddens have argued that these changes are part of a wider and more fundamental transformation in society that is occurring simultaneously across affluent western countries and which is linked to both cause and consequence of many of the global trends previously identified.[7] Beck for example, suggests that a modernity based on nation-state

[7] Space does not permit more than a brief mention of such social theory and the debates with which it is surrounded. For a more detailed introduction to the ideas of its major advocates, see Beck, U. *Risk Society: Towards a New Modernity.* Sage, London, 1992. Beck, U. *World Risk Society.* Polity Press, Cambridge, 1999. See also Giddens A. *The Third Way: the Renewal of Social Democracy.* Polity Press, Cambridge, 1999. From the perspective of occupational health and safety see especially Walters, D. R. Change and continuity: 2 Health and safety issues for the new millennium, *J. Inst. Occup. Saf. Health,* 3:1999. Pearce, F., and Tombs, S. *Toxic Capitalism: Corporate Crime and the Chemical Industry.* Ashgate, Aldershot, 1999; and also Lupton, D. *Risk.* Routledge, London, 1999.

societies in which social relations, networks, and communities are essentially understood in a territorial sense has been undermined by five interlinked processes of globalization, individualization, gender revolution, underemployment, and global risks (environmental and financial, themselves the product of successful modernity). Both he and Giddens, in their different ways, argue that traditional theoretical and social responses to such developments are inappropriate and inadequate largely because they are rooted in ways of thinking about social organization in nation-state societies, when it is new paradigms that are required. The point about this for OHS is that it reinforces the notion that changes in OHS and responses to it—the new epidemics, for example—are not isolated phenomena but closely interlinked with broader changes in society and the way we think about and respond to them. This has long been apparent in the case of environmental risks and, as a consequence, strategic responses to their assessment, regulation, and management are often highly charged political issues in which their wider ramifications and public perceptions of both acceptability and accountability are central concerns. In the case of OHS, there is still often resistance among policy makers, regulators, practitioners, employers' organizations, and even some trade unions to acknowledging these wider dimensions. Their presence is nevertheless characteristic of current discourse on OHS in advanced market economies, and change in the 21st century is inextricably bound up with them.

The same altered societal perceptions of risk and the responsibility for its management are behind demands for more visible social justice for the victims of accidents and disasters and greater retribution against those perceived to be responsible for them.[8] These are demands increasingly made in the wake of disasters in which both workers and members of the public have been victims. In the public outcry that has followed such events, the primary issue is not whether they were occupational or environmental disasters, but that people were placed at unacceptable risk and that once again duty holders, experts, regulators, etc. had failed in undertaking their basic social responsibilities. Also behind such demands are changing perceptions of the nature and meaning of crime in society and in the role played by enforcement and the courts. Thus, a further defining feature of modern times in advanced market economies are debates surrounding corporate criminal responsibilities, the means of extending the effective application of the crime of manslaughter to corporate criminal activity, as well as more generally, issues concerning the form and rigor of the methods with which compliance with the law of health and safety at work may be secured. Indeed, in countries such as the U.K. political and media debates on law reform in OHS are largely dominated

---

[8] They are also evidence of the blurring of the boundaries between work and society, between occupational and environmental risk, and between workers and members of the public—further examples of the consequences of change in the structure and organization of work and the interpenetration of work, public, and domestic life.

by these issues.[9] Arguably these changes and debates are also reactions to deregulation, market liberalization, and the dismantling of social welfare systems that are further features of the state responses to global-market pressures faced by advanced market economies. These issues are considered in more detail in the following section.

JOINED-UP OR WITHDRAWN? THE STATE AND OHS IN THE 21st CENTURY

The third aspect of the development of OHS that is prominent internationally is found in the responses of the state to late modernity in advanced market economies. The developments in the global economy described previously represent enormous challenges to pre-existing notions of nation-state policies for regulating the economy and social welfare, in which occupational health and safety policies are a small but integral part. Such responses are therefore part of the changing economic, health, and social welfare scenarios of the advanced market economies of post-industrial Europe, North America, and Australia. On the positive side, integration between OHS and broader issues of public health, regulation, employment, and social welfare is emphasised, while on negative side are the resource and regulatory implications of state withdrawal, in which it is debatable whether state agencies any longer have sufficient *will or capacity* to aspire to their historical (and necessary) functions of inspection and control in regulating the work environment.

The recent E.U. Strategy on Health and Safety at Work, for example, highlights pan-E.U. concern with such issues as changing forms of employment, the feminised and aging workforce, and change in the nature of risk—with issues of stress, violence, and intimidation at work now accounting for a substantial amount of worker time-off and is particularly prevalent in public services. It is also an important statement on the continuing E.U. struggle to try to balance issues of employment and employability along side those of the well-being of workers and the quality of working life (6). At the same time, its relatively low-key approach to legislating these issues and its apparent desire to advocate the use of social dialogue as a means of developing and

---

[9] In the U.K., for example, reform of the law on corporate manslaughter and on the criminal duties of the directors of companies has been a prominent issue on the Government agenda since the election of New Labour in 1997—despite this and the considerable campaigning that has gone on around these issues, however, new laws are still awaited. See Bergman, D. *The Case for Corporate Responsibility: Corporate Violence and the Criminal Justice System.* Disaster Action, London, 2000. See also Tombs, S., and Whyte, D. Two steps forward, one step back: Towards accountability for workplace deaths? *Pol. Pract. Health Saf.* 1: 9–30, 2003.

implementing strategy is a further reflection of the general withdrawal of state engagement in regulation.[10]

There are related questions that can be asked about whether social insurance and welfare provisions are any longer sufficiently resourced to provide more than minimal support for a limited number of victims of work-related ill health and injury. As a crisis in the financing of compensation systems becomes apparent in many countries, closer administrative and policy links have been forged between regulating prevention and administrating compensation and return-to-work systems. These are changes that have been superimposed upon existing national strategies, so the effect is not necessarily a convergence of practice. Nevertheless, they are currently prominent on social policy agendas in virtually all advanced market economies. There are some positive aspects to them, as greater attention is paid to support for helping people remain economically active. At the same time, their negative aspect is the reduction or removal of welfare support for many who cannot remain in their preferred occupation (or in work at all in some cases) following occupationally related injury or ill health. In such scenarios, it is important that there is an appropriate balance between the support needed to keep workers at work (prevention and retention) and the concentration on economic performance and possible savings to state welfare budgets. All too often it appears that current governmental strategies in advanced market economies are mostly concerned with achieving the latter, while the former receives scant support in the form of tangible resources.[11] One alarming consequence of this is a reduced presence of prevention services in many European countries (7).

Emerging at the same time in governmental policies has been a rise to prominence of the economic case for prevention through self-regulation. This development has strong associations with the promotion of the business case for health and safety as part of the advocacy of market liberalism by governments that have sought to conflate notions of de-regulation with those of self-regulation during the past decade. In the views expressed by governments in most countries, a policy of withdrawal of the state from a central role in regulation is linked with the desirability of taking a more comprehensive view of the economics of work and health. Thus, for example, the stated aim in U.K. governmental strategy is to keep workers "healthy, happy and here," while at the same time it is quite

[10] See for example Owen, 2002; Vogel, L. Long on ideas, short on means. *TUTB Newsletter*; 18: 3–6, 2002; and James, P. Well-being at work: An issue whose legislative time has come? *Pol. Pract. Health Saf.* 2, 2003, for more detailed analysis of the current E.U. approach to OHS.

[11] The disturbing consequences of this are evident in the Netherlands where for example, despite almost universal coverage of workers, government strategies to reduce welfare costs have created a medicalized, individualized approach that focuses on sickness absence rather than the improvement of working conditions. See Popma, J., Schaapman, M., and Wilthagen, T. The Netherlands: Implementation within wider regulatory reform. In *Regulating Health and Safety Management in the European Union*, edited by D. R. Walters. PIE, Peter Lang, Brussels, 2002.

conspicuously reducing the introduction of new OHS regulations (8). This implies a link between prevention, compensation, and rehabilitation, and return-to-work strategies that has long been absent from the traditional pigeon holing of these approaches in the U.K. But the key to the government interest in promoting this link is clearly the economics involved and the desire to improve productivity while at the same time controlling costs associated with work-related injuries and ill health. Again in the U.K., these associations are also seen in governmental restructuring of its own administration of work and health.[12] Strong cross-referencing between prevention systems and those dealing with return-to-work in U.K. government strategies is yet another (albeit belated) example of economically driven policies to improve well-being at work while improving productivity and cutting the costs of sickness-related absence. None of these policy scenarios is an isolated U.K. phenomenon—indeed comparative analysis shows how far the U.K. lags behind many other countries in these policies. For example, the Dutch drive to reduce social welfare costs while placing obligations on employers to use certified prevention services has been a part of national strategy for over a decade, as has the joining of administrative systems for prevention, rehabilitation, and compensation in some Australian and Canadian jurisdictions.

Another international trend is found in preventive OHS regulation, in which regulating the systematic management of health and safety has become its *leitmotif.* A glance at the way regulatory policies in most European countries, Australasia and North America have been heading over the past 20 years shows a strongly converging pattern of increased attention to process regulation in which inspection and control is (at least in theory) more and more focused on the way employers take a systematic approach to managing their health and safety responsibilities. These regulatory approaches are perhaps better adapted to dealing with the rapidly changing world of work described previously than the more prescriptive systems that they replace, which were based on more fixed notions of how and where work is undertaken. In combination with elements of participation and the use of competence in OHS management, they may be one of the features of policy development in advanced market economies that provide some cause for optimism concerning improved OHS outcomes for the future. However, they also need to be seen in the context of the constraints imposed on the resources for inspection and control, which, coupled with trends toward privatization and market testing of services, have been a growing feature of the treatment of state OHS agencies in the hands of public-sector managerialism in many countries in recent years (9).

---

[12] For example, the recent relocation of the HSE to the Department of Work and Pensions is a clear illustration of the desire to achieve a more "joined up" approach to prevention, compensation, and return to work, as indeed is the current national strategy on occupational health.

SOME POSITIVE ASPECTS OF CHANGE AND THE
INTERNATIONALIZATION OF OHS

The preceding pages have painted a picture of current trends in OHS that raise causes for concern. While it is not meant to be overly pessimistic, the intention of this approach has been to draw attention to the fact that there are a range of current issues in the economic, political, and regulatory situation that are common to most advanced market economies and it is these that importantly form the backdrop to the OHS epidemics featured in other chapters. The argument has been that to understand the causes and consequences of such epidemics it is necessary to analyze their wider contexts. It was argued, therefore, that the practice of improving the work environment does not occur in a political or economic vacuum. It is important to understand the position of prevention in relation to these wider determinants. This means relating prevention to changing work structure and organization and labor markets as well as national/international economic issues such as those driving reform of compensation and return to work. Prevention strategies also need to account for the limits of regulation in modern market economies. In addition, they cannot ignore socially determined perceptions of risk and notions of accountability and social justice.

All this suggests the need for a broader focus of discourse on the relationship between health and work—one that embraces its technical, medical, and scientific elements but places them in context. The increasing recognition of the multidimensional nature of cause and effect evident in governmental thinking in advanced market economies, presents significant opportunities to instigate this broader focus. At the same time it enables OHS to be placed in a more central position in national and international discourse on health and social policy and discussion of the development of economic policies. Interpreted positively, these developments suggest an international trend toward widening and raising the level of discourse on improving the work environment, so that it is no longer marginalized as a largely technical issue, peripheral to these debates.

Contributing to this process is the impact of international standards-setting agencies such as the ILO.[13] The influence of other international bodies such as the European Union is also considerable. The impact of E.U. legislative standards are felt in other countries through extension of international trade pressures, resulting in trends of *de facto* adoption of international standards in order to gain access to markets. Directives from the European Union such as the Framework Directive 89/391 on the Introduction of Measures to Encourage Improvement of Safety and Health of Workers at Work have significantly boosted use of formal risk

[13] The ILO's recent intervention in establishing an international OHS management systems standard—ILO-OSH 2001—provides one example of the continued importance of its role. See ILO (International Labour Office). *Guidelines on Occupational Safety and Health Management Systems, ILO-OSH 200*. ILO, Geneva, 2001.

assessment and control procedures in a wide range of countries outside its borders. The Directive, however, is also particularly significant because it presents a conceptualization of systematic OHS management in which representative worker participation and the use of competency is deeply integrated. This means that many of the voluntary OHS management systems widely adopted by employers (and approved by the state) in advanced market economies actually fall outside its basic legislative definition of sound systematic OHS management (10). This requires employers to manage the risks of their endeavors in ways that imply a role for competent professionals through provision of information to workers and their representatives, thus facilitating their involvement in all stages of the risk management process (11). Such a legislative model draws deeply on European traditions in the use of prevention services as well as of representative worker participation (12). Its influence is therefore potentially considerably more significant than simply adding to international pressures to adopt more systematic approaches to OHS management because it implies the adoption of a *particular kind* of systematic OHS management.

This is especially the case in relation to participation. Indeed, this is perhaps one of the most interesting areas for the future of workplace arrangements for health and safety. There is now substantial evidence that the model of participation in systematic OHS management envisaged by requirements such as those found in the *Framework Directive* and implemented in statutory measures in E.U. member states is one that works for improving both workplace OHS arrangements and OHS outcomes. However, there is also little doubt that this model is based on a notion of work organization and labor relations that is no longer the norm. It is therefore a matter of some uncertainty how such known workable models of representation and the supports for it can be applied in the new scenarios of work and labor relations that are increasingly evident in advanced market economies. It has already been pointed out that there are some signs of an increased willingness of trade unions to tackle the challenges presented by current patterns of work organization and structure. There are even suggestions of the use of OHS as an issue around which the renewal of trade unions may occur. However, the evidence for such developments is still limited and sometimes uncertain. What does seem certain, however, is that while participation is clearly important in promoting better OHS standards and in keeping with representing both worker and wider public interest in the control of environmental and occupational risks, there is virtually no evidence to suggest that it can function meaningfully or effectively in the absence of support of organized labor.

The combination of public interest in participating in decision making on environmental as well as work-related risks suggests that some form of autonomous worker participation will remain high on the agenda of risk management associated with work in advanced market economies, despite the changes that militate against traditional models. It has also been suggested in relation to developing countries that such participation will continue to "contain the basis of a profound remodelling of scientific knowledge, of professional action and the role of users and workers in production and consumption" (13).

Another response to the combination of current epidemics and the constraints on government resourcing for their prevention is the way that the growing influence of public-sector managerialism is causing state OHS agencies in some counties to set and pursue performance targets in relation to OHS outcomes. For example, recent policy statements in countries such as the U.K. (14) and Australia (15) lay great emphasis on percentage improvements in measures of OHS performance, such as fatalities, injuries, work-related ill health, and days lost from work as a result of those problems, to be achieved within identified time frames. While there are clearly positive aspects to setting such aspirations, the approach also has some important drawbacks. Not least of these are the well-known problems of measuring OHS outcomes, in which *underestimation* is universally acknowledged. Additionally, measurement tends to focus on the more conspicuous indices of OHS performance. Setting targets based on these measures raises the danger of ignoring less conspicuous but equally important indices of performance. Since many of the current (and likely future) epidemics in OHS generally fall into that latter category, the comprehensiveness, accuracy, and reliability of measurement is especially important. Moreover, it would be wise to be clear about cause and effect in setting and achieving performance targets. For example, it is necessary to distinguish between the known long-term decline in fatalities and serious injuries in affluent post-industrial countries, largely attributed to changes in the nature of work and employment patterns, from the effects of particular prevention strategies aimed at achieving the same ends.

The rapid advances in communications technology that helped to make globalized production and services possible, thereby creating many of the challenges to OHS discussed in the present chapter, have also, of course, helped to change the ways in which regulators, researchers, practitioners, and social interest groups respond to such challenges. They have allowed for an internationalized development in research and scholarship through faster formal and informal reciprocal arrangements facilitated by electronic mail and the Internet. Such development has enhanced links between OHS professionals and made international comparative research studies far more practicable. Increasingly, national OHS research strategies focus strongly on collaboration between researchers and between researchers and users. While traditional emphasis on physical, chemical, and biological hazards remains important, there is a change in the focus of research priorities in national strategies in many countries, and greater attention is being paid to current issues such as OHS management, work organization, the aging workforce, psychosocial issues, and labor market changes (16).

Resulting positive consequences therefore include the increasing internationalization of knowledge about OHS protection strategies, closer links between OHS researchers and standards-setting and policy-making authorities in different countries, and widespread dissemination of OHS knowledge via the Internet.

National and international occupational health and safety agencies have focused greater attention on the collection, collation, and dissemination of information; some, like the European Agency for Safety and Health at Work, have even been created for this express purpose. As state expenditure on original research in OHS has become more and more constrained, international communication opportunities that help bring together and disseminate research findings from elsewhere arguably make for greater efficiency in undertaking an *internationalized* research agenda and avoiding duplication of national efforts. The positive and negative potential effects of such trends are well illustrated in countries like Australia where the importance of international research information has accelerated in parallel with the significant reduction of national OHS research funding over the past 5 years and the emasculation of many OHS Inspectorates, and as generalist knowledge has become preferred to specialist OHS content (17). As a result, standards-setting and policy makers have become increasingly reliant on overseas specialist content and knowledge.

Equally important are the opportunities international communications have created for organizing resistance to practices such as the relocation of hazardous processes to less-regulated countries, global environmental abuse, the exploitation of children, and the suppression or denial of information and representational rights to organized labor. Trade unions, together with other often small and under-resourced interest groups, have been able to operate on an international scale, using international electronic facilities to both revitalize old international networks and to create new networks with both economy and strategic purpose to support worker and public interest in curbing abuses on occupational and environmental health issues. Although they remain a long way behind the organization of international capital that led to such abuses, they are nevertheless indicative that the "network society" can be just as useful to social interest groups that have taken up health and safety and environmental issues or workers' rights on an international scale as it has been to the interests of global capital. Here again, it seems inevitable that such developments will continue to play an important role in shaping future action and debates on OHS epidemics at both the national and international level.

CONCLUSIONS: AN INTERNATIONAL ROUTE
FORWARD OR BACKWARD?

It is abundantly clear that the internationalization of OHS is currently one of its most prominent defining features. This is something it shares with many other aspects of life in advanced market economies in the 21st century—and for similar reasons. It is both directly and indirectly a consequence of the rapid technological change, especially in communications technology, and internationalization of production, services, trade, and culture that, in common parlance, are embraced by the term "globalization." In this chapter an effort has been made to link an understanding of the international development of OHS with these wider economic, political, and technological drivers of globalization. While the chapter has little more than scratched the surface of some of these subjects, its purpose has been to point to the need for a broader and deeper understanding of these issues in order that their significance for developments in OHS may be more fully appreciated.

A large part of strategic development in OHS policy in advanced market economies in recent years can be seen as an aspect of governmental, professional, and trade union responses to the challenges of globalization. This chapter has tried to stress the double-edged nature of much of this development. Especially in the case of governmental responses, there are positives and negatives about almost every aspect. They relate, for example, to efforts on the part of the state to withdraw from its established roles in both resourcing and regulating OHS, including the costs of OHS failure, the cost of inspection and control, and the costs of research and development. At the same time, this encompasses the efforts of states to attract inward investment and promote employment through providing competitive environments for trade, production, and services in global markets, which lead to further deregulatory pressures on OHS. Moreover, these efforts of the state are undertaken within the related rubrics of public-sector managerialism—in which the achievement of cost-saving (sometimes ill-conceived) targets are a dominant mantra—and of public policies that demand more integrated efforts from previously separate government agencies. These efforts are further linked to the advocacy of "partnerships" between the state and labor-market actors (and between individual labor market actors themselves), in which self-regulation in a deregulated environment is regarded as the preferred way ahead. That there are obvious dangers in these approaches should be abundantly clear from the preceding pages.

At the same time, employment and productivity are clearly important. If governmental strategies can link improved worker well-being with improved economic output successfully; if they can achieve targets for OHS prevention and link them to work retention; if they can achieve the self-regulation of OHS management and create a meaningful participatory approach to OHS—these would indeed be positive achievements. Furthermore, if these strategies could create fair, transparent, and workable approaches to accountability for OHS and at the same time put in place necessary checks and balances so that self-regulation is not de-regulation, they would come some way toward satisfying demands for social justice. If they could utilize the network society in ways that prevent duplication of research efforts, they could help direct new R&D economically and efficiently where it is most needed. And if these strategies could achieve all of these things without engaging in social dumping of unwanted OHS problems onto workers in newly industrializing and developing countries, then governmental strategies such as those outlined in the previous pages would certainly have some claim to success in tackling the OHS epidemics that are the subject of this book.

At the end of the day, the achievement of an adequate balance between the tensions inherent in current developments in OHS policies in advanced market economies is likely to be the key to the extent to which they are effective in simultaneously improving workers' well-being while promoting economic improvement and addressing the prevention and amelioration of future OHS epidemics. Fundamentally, this is a political issue and, to this extent, it is indicative that perhaps little has really changed in OHS internationally since politics has always been the real arbiter of its development in industrialized countries.

REFERENCES

1. Takala, J. *Global Strategy on Safety and Health, ILO Standards and Concerted National Action.* Paper presented at the Australian OHS Regulation in 21st Century Conference, Gold Coast, July 21–22, 2003, www.nohsc.gov.au/NewsAndWhatsNew/UpComingConferences/AustralianOHS Regulation.asp.
2. Loewenson, R. Globalisation and occupational health: A perspective from southern Africa. *Bull. World Health Organ.* 79, 2001.
3. Walters, D. R. *Health and Safety in Small Enterprises: European Strategies for Managing Improvement.* Peter Lang, Brussels, 2001.
4. Abrams, H. K. A short history of occupational health. *J. Public Health Pol.* 22: 1, 2001.
5. Walters, D. R. Workplace arrangements for worker participation in OHS. In *OHS regulation for a changing world of work,* edited by L. Bluff, M. Gunningham, and R. Johnstone. Federation Press, Sydney, 2004.
6. Tudor, O. The State of the Union. *Health Saf. Bull.* 300: 21–25, 2002.
7. Vogel, L. Special report: Preventive services. *TUTB Newslett.* 21: 19–37, 2003.
8. Health and Safety Commission/Department of Environment, Transport and the Regions. *Revitalising Health and Safety.* Consultation Document, London, Dept. of the Environment, Transport and the Regions, London, 1999.
9. Frick, K., and Wren, J. Reviewing occupational health and safety management: Multiple roots, diverse perspectives and ambiguous outcomes. In *Systematic Occupational Health and Safety Management,* edited by K. Frick, P. L. Jensen, M. Quinlan, and T. Wilthagen. Elsevier, Oxford, 2000.
10. Frick, K., Jensen, P. L., Quinlan, M., and Wilthagen, T. (eds.). *Systematic Occupational Health and Safety Management.* Elsevier, Oxford, 2000.
11. Walters, D. R., and Jensen, P. L. The discourses and purposes behind the development of the EU framework directive 89/391. In *Systematic Occupational Health and Safety Management,* edited by K. Frick, P. L. Jensen, M. Quinlan, and T. Wilthagen. Elsevier, Oxford, 2000.
12. Walters, D. R. (ed.). *Regulating Health and Safety Management in the European Union.* Peter Lang, Brussels, 2002.
13. Dwyer, T. A study on health and safety management at work: The view from a developing country. In *Systematic Occupational Health and Safety Management,* edited by K. Frick, P. L. Jensen, M. Quinlan, and T. Wilthagan, p. 171. Elsevier, Oxford, 2000.

14. Health and Safety Commission/Department of Environment, Transport and the Regions. *Revitalising Health and Safety: Strategy Statement.* Dept. of the Environment, Transport and the Regions, London, 2000.
15. NOHSC (National Occupational Health and Safety Commission). *National OHS Strategy 2002–2012.* NOHSC, Canberra, Australia, 2002.
16. NOHSC (National Occupational Health and Safety Commission). *International Trends in Strategic Directions and Priorities for OHS Research.* NOHSC, Canberra, Australia, 2001.
17. Quinlan, M. Forget evidence: The demise of research involvement by NOHSC since 1996. *J. Occup. Health Saf. Aust. N.Z.* 16, 213–227, 2000.

CHAPTER 3

Occupational Violence: The Emerging OHS Epidemic of the 21st Century

Claire Mayhew

As highlighted earlier in this book, the increasing internationalization of the business environment and productivity pressures associated with globalization both have flow-on effects on OHS. At the same time, the economies of western industrialized countries are shifting toward increased employment in service-based industries. As a result, the hazards and risks faced by the workforce are changing over time. In addition, the increased productivity pressures from the broader environment exacerbate the demands placed on most chief executive officers (CEOs), managers, and workers. The behaviors adopted by supervisors, workers, and clients/customers in response to these changing pressures are not always "best practice," and on occasion may progress from inappropriate inter-personal communications to bullying or even overt violence.

In this chapter, the author provides an overview of the different scenarios in which occupational violence is most commonly experienced, reviews recent research evidence on incidence patterns, and highlights the risk factors. It is argued that the jobs where workers are at risk of violence are similar across industrialized countries. However, the incidence varies internationally because patterns of employment (and hence exposure) and other structural factors (such as access to guns) are diverse from one country to another. Organizational policies and strategies can also exacerbate or reduce the risks. Nevertheless, the general trend in all industrialized countries is for an increasing incidence of occupational violence to the point that, in high-risk jobs, aggression against workers is at epidemic levels.

First, an introduction is provided on the widely accepted separation of occupational violence into three distinct forms: "external," "client-initiated," and "internal." A fourth form of occupational violence—the threat from terrorism—is then briefly addressed. This discussion is followed by a more detailed exploration of a fifth form of occupational violence, which has become known as "systemic" aggression. This fifth form is, arguably, fuelled

31

by economic threats from the broader environment which leads to excessive production demands placed on workers, and these two pressures together fuel the emergence of widespread bullying and other forms of occupational violence directed at subordinates or co-workers.

INTRODUCTION

Occupational violence is a topic of increasing interest across the industrialized world. There is a range of forms of occupational violence, and these occur along a continuum of severity: homicide, assaults, threats, bullying, initiation rites, verbal abuse, and other deliberately hurtful behaviors.

Internationally, there has been a groundswell of interest in unreasonable work practices, bullying at work, and occupational violence more generally (1–3). This rising tide of interest has led to the commissioning of a series of international research studies and discussion papers, as well as the development of a Code of Practice, *Violence and Stress at Work in Services Sectors,* by the International Labour Organisation (ILO), that was finalized in late 2003. The draft Code of Practice states that (4):

> Any action, incident or behaviour that departs from reasonable conduct in which a person is assaulted, threatened, harmed, injured in the course of, or as a direct result of, his or her work.

Incidents can involve both subtle forms of aggression (e.g., "bullying") as well as more explicit acts of occupational violence (e.g., assaults). Particularly for lower-level forms of aggression, interpretations and imputed meanings can vary between individuals because of subtle variations in perpetrator behaviors, the degree of threat to personal self-esteem or livelihood, and acculturation to "normalized" forms of behaviors at different worksites. Hence, a range of inappropriate behaviors makes up the broad gamut of occupational violence.

VARIATIONS ACROSS COUNTRIES

In the *United States*, violence is a significant contributor to work-related fatalities, a pattern which is distinct from other industrialized countries. During the 5-year period from 1995 to 1999, there was an average of 838 work-related homicides each year, with up to two million workers experiencing non-fatal incidents annually (5). Overall, around 17 percent of all fatal traumatic incidents at U.S. workplaces are due to homicide. Occupational violence perpetrated by "outsiders" for instrumental gain is clustered in the retail sector and services industries, which suggests that access to money or "hot products" is a core motivating factor (6). Further, homicides are the leading cause of death for female workers in the U.S., which is undoubtedly linked with their concentration in the retail industry, with the risks possibly exacerbated by the less-stringent firearm regulations in that country (7).

In *Europe*, substantive research studies conducted by the European Foundation in Dublin indicates that approximately 4 percent of all workers experience physical violence each year, 2 percent are sexually harassed, and 8 percent subjected to bullying or other forms of harassment (8). Workers in the service sector reported increased proportions vis-à-vis those in other industries. The International Labour Organisation has also compiled substantive international data and identified similar variations in the level of risk of occupational violence faced by workers in different countries (9).

In *Britain*, the overall incidence of threats and overt violence at work appears to be steadily increasing, although there are significant fluctuations year by year. Studies conducted jointly by the Home Office and The Health and Safety Executive (10) report that assaults at work increased by 61 percent over the period 1991 to 1995, fell by 28 percent between 1995 and 1997, followed by an increase of 21 percent between 1997 and 1999.

In *Australia*, around 2.8 percent of all traumatic work-related deaths are due to homicide (11), a pattern that is distinctly different to that in the U.S. These work-related homicides are concentrated among taxi drivers, sex workers, police and security guards, and other workers in the services sector.

The variations between industrialized countries are most apparent through reports published by the International Crime Victim Survey (ICVS). This survey is repeated every few years, and is co-ordinated by an international committee with representatives from the Ministry of Justice in the Netherlands, the Home Office in Britain, and the United National Interregional Crime and Justice Research Institute. These surveys are conducted in at least 13 countries using random samples of the population over age 16 who are interviewed about their experiences of at least 13 types of crimes. There is a substantial amount of data produced, with the various types of victimization described for specific countries. Overall, occupational victimization is far less commonly reported than are violent experiences elsewhere in urban areas or near the recipient's own home (3). Nevertheless, 10 percent of all victimizations of females occurred at work. The relative risks across countries, where known and for the most recent year available, are summarized in Table 1.

Overall, the incidence and severity of occupational violence varies across countries and jobs because the risk factors differ.

"At-Risk" Jobs and Workers

Overall, occupational violence is most common in jobs (a) where cash is on hand and (b) which require substantial face-to-face contact between workers and their clients or customers (2, 3). The incidence and severity of violence varies markedly between these jobs and those where workers have little contact with

Table 1

Estimates of violent victimization at work across industrialized
countries (%), per year

	Homicide	Assault	Sexual assault	Threat	Bullying	Other	Overall risk
U.S. (12)	0.07%	4.2%	5.3%	—	—	—	—
Europe (7)	—	4%	2%	—	8%	—	—
Britain (10)	—	1.2%	—	1.4%	—	—	2.5

outside people and where money does not change hands. The ILO has also
identified organizations at increased risk as those that (13):

> . . . provide services in direct contact with members of the public, provide
> services early in the morning or late at night, are located in high crime
> areas, operate from relatively unsecured premises, are small and isolated,
> are understaffed, operate under the strain of reform and downsizing, work
> with insufficient resources, function in a culture of tolerance or acceptance
> of stress and violence, have a poor working climate, are management based
> on intimidation and generation of stress, have a climate of discrimination,
> including gender and racial discrimination, have smoking or drinking
> prohibition/limitation; or do not have such rules, have drugs, alcohol or/and
> weapons available onsite, possess unclear codes of conduct, have inconsistent
> rule enforcement.

There are gender variations (a) among *perpetrators*—males are significantly over-represented and (b) among *recipients*—females tend to experience
higher levels of verbal and sexual abuse, and males tend to receive more
overt threats and physical assaults (3, 14). This variation in risk can be partially explained by the gender division of labor, with women concentrated in
lower status and "caring" jobs with greater face-to-face contact with clients/
customers/patients.

Off-site and isolated work environments are associated with higher risk.
One United Kingdom study of 1,000 workers found that 1 in 3 who went out
to meet their clients had been threatened, and 1 in 7 were assaulted at some
stage of their working life (15). "Off-site" workers who have been victimized
include a British lawyer (16), Australian taxi drivers (17), U.S. community service
workers (18), health workers in car parks (11), and those working alone in
high crime areas (19). Further, those who are precariously employed tend to
have a higher incidence (2).

However, accurate data bases documenting work-related violence are scarce.
Only work-related homicides are reliably reported. At best, between 10 to

20 percent of incidents are formally recorded and, as a result, the official databases significantly under-state the extent of occupational violence (2). There are also overlapping jurisdictional responsibilities between the criminal justice system, the OHS authorities, and individual organizations—all of which record some occupational violence data in different ways. Thus, while the general risk factors and overall patterns of occupational violence are known, the data are poor.

DISTINCT FORMS OF OCCUPATIONAL VIOLENCE

In order to better understand the manifestations of occupational violence (and the motivations of perpetrators), aggression can be separated into five basic categories, based on the relationship of offenders to the organization where the inappropriate behavior occurs (see Table 2).

It is crucial to note that while all these types of occupational violence can occur on the one worksite, the perpetrators of the different forms have distinct

Table 2

A typology of forms of occupational violence

Type 1: "External violence	This form of occupational violence is perpetrated on workers by persons from outside the organization, such as during armed hold-ups at shops and banks (18).
Type 2: "Client-initiated" violence	This form of violence is inflicted on workers by their customers or clients, such as patient aggression toward medical officers (18).
Type 3: "Internal" violence (or bullying)	This type of violence/bullying occurs between workers employed in an organization, such as between a supervisor and employees or workers and apprentices (18).
Type 4: Terrorist attacks on worksites	There are two facets to occupational violence from terrorism: (a) direct assaults on worksites; and (b) workers in "helping" or emergency roles who treat or rescue victims of terrorist attacks (20).
Type 5: "Systemic" violence	Here, broad economic and social pressures provoke widespread pressure. For example, global economic pressures may lead to work intensification, job insecurity, heightened anxieties, and contribute to a workplace culture where threatening behaviors occur and/or are tolerated (21).

characteristics and prevention strategies differ markedly. This typology will be elaborated below.

"External" Occupational Violence

The jobs at highest risk of "external" violence are similar across industrialized countries. Workers in banks, post offices, gambling outlets, armored vehicles transporting cash, taxi drivers, convenience stores, hotels, and service stations (garages) are at high risk (3, 22). Taxi drivers are at very high risk as they have become comparatively easy targets since banks and betting shops have progressively tightened security (23). An exponential rise in "external" violence has also been noted for chemist shops (24, 25). One recent empirical pilot study in the Australian State of Tasmania reported that 4 percent of small retail shop owners/managers experienced a hold-up over a 12-month period (26). However, hold-ups occurred in addition to a range of other forms of crime victimization, including shoplifting (76 percent), intimidation/harassment (58 percent), breaking and entering when shops were closed (42 percent), credit-card or fraud (42 percent), employee theft (36 percent), other fraud (24 percent), and other problems (18 percent) (26). That is, the total burden from crimes against small business owners/managers in high-risk areas can be significant (27). Nevertheless, the rewards to the (often desperate) perpetrators can be quite small.

There are four core business risk factors for "external" (or instrumental) occupational violence: cash or valuables on-site, few workers, evening or night trading, and significant levels of face-to-face communication with customers (2, 3, 6). The level of risk can also be affected by levels of social support in a country, extent of substance abuse in a locality, or ease of access to weapons such as firearms. Repeat and multiple victimizations are common in some localities ("hot spots"), and little violence occurs in others (27). Bellamy (28) explained this phenomenon in terms of "attractive" or "unattractive" targets. "Attractive" targets are situated in high-crime areas, have minimal protection for workers, limited observation from passers-by, allow quick access to highway escape routes, and have a number of possible exits from the site (19).

"Client-Initiated" Occupational Violence

Jobs at particular risk of "client-initiated" violence are those that require workers to: ". . . provide care and services to people who are distressed, fearful, ill or incarcerated" (29). The jobs at highest risk in the U.S., Britain, and Australia are police, security and prison guards, fire service, teachers, health care, and social security workers (2, 3, 30).

There are a number of risk factors that emerge in different scenarios. Clients who are intoxicated or who have used illicit substances pose an increased risk in most workplaces (31). Correctional and juvenile detention workers are at particular risk from young males with a history of violence (32). Younger males who suffer psychosis or a neurological abnormality, and who have a history of violence, are more likely to assault staff (33). Research in the health care sector also indicates that perpetrators of "client-initiated" violence are disproportionately male, younger, affected by substances, or suffering from dementia (34, 35).

While the incidence of "client-initiated" violence appears to be increasing, the causes are complex. Mullen (36) has argued that a high unemployment level with marginalization of some groups provides the backdrop for violence directed at community, health care, and other service industry workers. When cuts in public spending and services lead to a reduction in resources, the clients may respond violently, believing they are being discriminated against or treated unfairly (36). The third type of occupational violence arises from quite different perpetrators.

"Internal" Violence
(including Bullying and Initiation Rites)

Supervisors or co-workers are the perpetrators of "internal" violence. That is, in contrast to "external" and "client-initiated" forms of occupational violence, with "internal" aggression the perpetrators and recipients are known to each other, and may even have daily contact.

Bullying incidents are usually repeated, escalate in intensity over time, and are most common in organizations where dominant/subordinate hierarchical relationships exist (37). When the recipient leaves the workplace, another victim is usually selected (38). An international study estimated ". . . at least 10% can be considered as being currently subjected to bullying" (39). Many of the tactics used by perpetrators are subtle and covert, and sometimes bullying evolves slowly over time and a "culture of denial" where victims are blamed develops (3, 40–42). The perpetrators of bullying can be motivated by envy, personal inadequacy, positive consequences from childhood bullying, narcissistic tendencies, or they may be unable to control their aggressive tendencies (38, 43). Bullying may result in serious emotional consequences for victims (40, 44).

Threats, initiation rites, and physical assaults are often preceded by warning signs such as belligerent or intimidating behaviors (3, 43). Overt violent and degrading initiation rites have been reported in a range of industries (3, 43) and some CEOs—and long-standing employees—have accepted these as "normal" practice (3, 40). (There have been a number of reports of such behaviors from the military and among apprentices.) Many of these initiation rites involve threatening behavior, although *premeditated malice* is uncommon.

Recent or imminent job loss is a high-risk factor for "internal" violence as dismissed employees have committed some of the worst U.S. mass shootings (45). Males in the age range 30 to 50 who are married with families and who have been employed with the organization for some time have been reported to be common perpetrators (46). While young males who are intoxicated have been linked with most forms of violence, perpetrators can also include older men, women, and the elderly (47). Thus, relying on profiles is dangerous.

Organizational structure and management style are of central importance. A quasi-military hierarchy with a rigid management style, marked supervisor/ employee divisions, and a highly competitive business environment increases the probability. Additional risk factors include management toleration of initiation rites and bullying, cultures where practical jokes are normalized, and job insecurity (34, 38).

There are a range of strategies to avert this behavior. First, CEOs can commit firmly to "zero tolerance" of occupational violence. Second, the evidence is overwhelming from both OHS and from criminology that the *certainty* of sanction has greater deterrence than the *severity* of a penalty (48, 49). Since most rational people make decisions after they have weighed the risks, perpetrators are likely to alter behavior if sanctions inevitably follow inappropriate activities. Third, workers and supervisors need to internalize the belief that pressure is not a valid excuse for people to behave inappropriately or violently. A few CEOs in larger organizations have devised codes of conduct for staff and enforced these. A few have explicitly recognized that appropriate behavioral standards positively contribute to productivity, organizational reputation, and well-being.

Terrorism at Work as a Form of Occupational Violence

Prior to September 11, 2001, the spectre of a terrorist attack at work was virtually unthinkable for those working in industrialized countries. Since that time, terrorism has become a real possibility, and criminologists, OSH professionals, and public policy makers now routinely engage in risk minimization planning, particularly for workers and buildings in some high-risk environments (50). While at this stage the need for strict anti-terrorism precautions at all worksites within industrialized countries may not be necessary, wise administrators in larger organizations will be reviewing access arrangements and emergency plans, considering the implementation of weapon-screening devices, and instituting controls over vehicles and parcel deliveries. One of the core limitations for anti-terrorist planning is that many organizations operating in democratic countries are routinely open to a wide range of members of the public in the course of conducting their business—for example, shopping centers or hospitals. Further, on a number of sites, materials are stored that can be relatively easily accessed via illegal means and utilized by terrorists—for example, chemicals or petroleum (51).

Service sector workers such as police, fire service, and health care employees (including ambulance officers) are often secondary victims as they provide emergency treatment to the injured and ill victims of terrorists. The Centers for Disease

Control in Atlanta drew up a classification system for bio-terrorist agents based on four criteria: (a) propensity to cause widespread death or disease; (b) transmissibility; (c) infrastructure needed to achieve preparedness; and (d) public perception of harm potential (52). The highest risk category identified includes smallpox, anthrax, plague, Ebola, tularaemia, and botulinum toxin. The second (and considerably lower) risk factor category includes three toxins (ricin, clostridial, and staphylococcal) and three diseases (Q fever, brucellosis, and glanders) (52).

Homeland protection authorities in all industrialized countries have now developed coordinated disaster plans to deal with this potential for chemical, biological, and other terrorist attacks. Of necessity, many aspects of these contingency plans remain confidential, although budget allocations to authorities are often cited in budget papers to the respective parliaments in the U.S., Britain, and Australia. In addition, significant resources may flow confidentially from other departmental budget allocations. For example, in Australia the 2002 federal budget allocated $A11.4 million for the purchase and stockpiling of a range of vaccines, antibiotics, and chemical antidotes in case members of the population were subjected to a terrorist incident (53). Examination of other government papers reveals that the "surge capacity" of the health care system to deal with the consequences of a terrorist incident is under active consideration (54). This form of occupational violence is distinctly different to that experienced as "systemic" aggression.

"Systemic" Occupational Violence

"*Systemic*" occupational violence arises out of broader economic forces in society that place inordinate production demands on managers and result in the encouragement of inappropriate behaviors, some of which come within the ambit of occupational violence. Essentially, "systemic" violence arises and is sustained where global market capitalism is transformed internally into an organizational culture where aggression is rewarded and any protocols that mitigate such activities are devalued. Foucault (55) describes this type of dynamic as a "contour of power" through which rampant economic and cultural forces flow unimpeded into workplaces. Further, in cultures where the pursuit of wealth is valued and violence in sport is normalized, an organizational culture that tolerates lower-level aggression is nurtured (56). The underlying pressures are complex and are derived from global market capitalism and post-modern culture. Yet, arguably, external economic pressure supported by a societal value system that lauds excessive competitiveness and aggression are not sufficient on their own to *inevitably* result in violence at work. These values must be inculcated within organizations to unleash individual's violent tendencies.

Of central importance, it must be remembered that only individuals can perpetrate direct aggression (57). Thus, Liefooghe and Davey (58) have argued that both *pathological organizations* and *pathologized individuals* are essential preconditions to the development of pathological workplace cultures.

In this chapter, it is argued that systemic violence is manifest only when two essential pre-conditions exist:

1. A highly pressurized—and violence conducive—external environment; and
2. An internal *conduit* person who accepts these excessive pressures as legitimate, and adopts aggressive strategies while transmitting these demands onto other workers.

(1) An intensely competitive *economic environment* presents a number of challenges to CEOs, including changing skill needs and innovative product designs. Often restructuring of the organization will be needed, along with downsizing of the workforce and changed production systems, all of which can create a range of negative stresses which are exacerbated when organizational survival is on the line. In such an environment, difficult decisions may have to be made. Whatever strategies are adopted (apart from firm closure), excessive workload increases are likely to result. This fundamental point is often overlooked.

(2) The second pre-requisite for the emergence of *structural* occupational violence is that a supervisor transmits excessive demands onto the workforce in an inappropriate manner. In essence, the perpetrators become *conduits* passing external pressure onto subordinates. While the behaviors adopted by these supervisors are usually aimed at enhancement of productivity, the uncertain environment may allow perpetrators with malevolent leanings to act inappropriately with impunity. The remainder of this chapter is focused on elaborating this process.

HOW EXTERNAL ENVIRONMENTAL PRESSURES ARE TRANSLATED INTO "SYSTEMIC" OCCUPATIONAL VIOLENCE

As with other forms of occupational violence, the inappropriate behaviors adopted by perpetrators of "systemic" violence occur on a *continuum,* ranging from verbal abuse, ridicule, bullying, and threats to assaults. That is, the violent activities range from insensitive verbal interactions or unreasonable demands to criminal acts (2). As with the bullying form of occupational violence, the behavior adopted as a consequence of systemic pressures are also usually repeated and escalate in intensity over time, particularly when the external pressures on perpetrators are sustained.

For many *conduits* of systemic violence, patterns of behavior are thrust upon perpetrators who become more or less complicit because they need to maintain their employment and income. For example, senior staff members (or co-workers) may adopt strategies that coerce subordinates to increase their productivity. Only some of these behavioral adaptations to external pressures lie within generally accepted definitions of occupational violence. Some of the demands placed on workers will be unreasonable in the short-term, some behaviors constitute sustained harassment, others deteriorate progressively over time, and a few perpetrators enjoy enacting sadistic behaviors. Few are likely to be able to resist the pressure to adopt inappropriate behaviors when systemic pressure mounts over time.

In this chapter it is argued that there are eight basic strategies adopted by these perpetrator *conduits* of systemic external pressures which occur along a "continuum of malevolence." At the more humane end are supervisors who merely "look elsewhere" when inappropriate behaviors occur, and at the other extreme are perpetrators who revel in sadistic behavior. The strategies adopted by conduits that are described in this article are "ideal-type" descriptions (59). This typology of behaviors is based on observed colleagues working in the health care, university, and civil service in Britain and Australia. The distinct behavioral types are not static and unchanging. Rather, different behaviors are adopted under distinct circumstances, and individuals may transmute from one form of behavior to another as external pressures intensify, perpetrators move between organizational roles, or as opportunities to enact pathological leanings present themselves. The eight basic "ideal type" behaviors are summarized in Table 3, with detailed descriptions along the "continuum of malevolence" subsequently provided.

The "Missionary" Conduit

This individual is essentially altruistic and focused on performing "good works" in the course of employment. During this process, other issues become secondary considerations, and a rationale may be adopted that is *genuinely believed* which explains away any inequities. Because of the effort devoted to their "good works," missionary conduits may genuinely not have the time to address inequities that arise in any organization from time to time, such as inequitable workloads displaced onto subordinates. Importantly, *malice* is usually totally absent. With "missionary" conduits, inequities or overwork displaced onto subordinates or colleagues is unlikely to ever fall within current definitions of occupational violence.

The "Busy Boss"

"Busy boss" behaviors are usually adopted by hard-working and committed supervisors. In contrast to the motive underlying "missionary" conduit behaviors, business survival is the primary focus of "busy boss" conduits. These production pressures displaced onto subordinates are unlikely to be interpreted as violence by the recipients. Nevertheless, some "busy boss" conduits may develop very poor interpersonal styles, adopt inappropriate coercion when production demands

Table 3

"Ideal-type" behaviors adopted along the "continuum of malevolence" resulting in *systemic* occupational violence

Conduit	Behavioral tactics and strategies
The "missionary"	Altruistic, focused on "good works," but genuinely does not have the time to address inequities.
The "busy boss"	Hard working, decent, but committed to higher order goals.
The "egomaniac"	Focused on personal career or pay advancement, and will not be deflected by excessive demands from the external environment.
The "Lady MacBeth"	Focused on removing potential competitors, usually via covert means.
The "Rottweiler"	Has a very aggressive inter-personal manner, and is often oblivious to the impact on recipients.
The "strategic bully"	Displaces work onto others; may make outlandish claims about personal achievements.
The "career bully"	A practiced bully who enjoys hurting others and who may be hired deliberately by organizations that are downsizing.
The "industrial psychopath"	Enjoys sadistic behavior, may commit criminal acts, thrives in organizations undergoing large-scale change, and is likely to be charming to the CEO (59).

are high, act in a bullying fashion when stressors increase, or develop a mistaken belief that pressure gets the best out of subordinates (2). Some recipients may excuse the perpetrator when aware of the external pressures, and instead blame the conduit's lack of interpersonal skills; for example, it has been reported that 70 percent of recipients blame a manager's poor communication skills (60). Liefooghe and Davey (58) have previously argued that extra-organizational environmental pressures facilitate internal bullying. Mumby and Stohl (61) noted that management *requires* the exercise of power which can inadvertently promote tyranny. Ashforth and Humphrey (62) have also elucidated behavioral strategies that can be adopted in the exercise of petty tyranny. Many of these "busy boss" conduits may be unaware of the impact on recipients. In such scenarios, the CEO may have heard that inappropriate behavior is occurring, delude him/herself that the perpetrator is a very productive employee, may believe that the victim is to blame in some way, or may engage in wishful thinking that this problem will just go away. Arguably, "busy boss" conduits readily drift into bullying.

Yet, because many "busy boss" supervisors are able to recognize the systemic pressures across an organization, they occupy a potentially central position for cohesive resistance. Unfortunately, this unifying role is rarely taken up. Rather, the over-riding mantra of organizational survival is usually widely accepted and they become complicit in a culture of aggression. Hence, power relations are maintained, with perpetrator and recipients becoming pawns of the broader environmental pressures (59).

The "Egomaniac"

Most "egomaniac" conduits are interpersonally skilled, charming, and have high public profiles. However, the "egomaniac" conduit is totally focused on his/her *personal* career and advancement and will not be deflected by increasing pressures from the external environment, the well-being of other workers, or even care for employees in acute distress. While malice is usually absent, deliberate shifting of unattractive tasks and/or gross overwork to others is the norm (59). Only problems that can be manipulated for personal advancement will be addressed. As a result, "egomaniac" conduits will refuse subordinates' leave applications at high-demand times, "forget" to forward information that is advantageous to others, or blame personality conflicts for any difficulties. "Egomaniac" conduits are distinguished from "busy boss" supervisors because *personal* advancement rather than business survival is paramount. While the behavior of "egomaniac" conduits is not likely to lie within any current definition of occupational violence, the strategies adopted are certainly likely to breach ethical norms at many points in time.

The "Lady MacBeth"

The "Lady MacBeth" conduit typically operates in a surreptitious fashion, encourages others to do the "dirty work," and tries to remove potential competitors *before conflict becomes overt.* Hence, when a threat appears on the horizon, the "Lady MacBeth" immediately starts to undermine the potential competitor. Typical strategies adopted include playing on the fears of co-workers, exploiting their vulnerabilities, or quietly supporting prejudices. For example, in university environments co-authors of research studies may not have their contracts renewed to ensure sole intellectual property can be claimed. Character assassinations are also common; for example, through quiet "slips of the tongue" about potential competitor's childcare needs, sexuality, anti- (or pro-) union stance, political affiliations, or, in a male-dominated workforce faced with equal opportunity requirements, fears of compulsory redundancy or skill inadequacies may be played on. Notably, it is usually difficult to track the commissioning of inappropriate behavior directly to the "Lady MacBeth." That is, "Lady MacBeths" are supreme politicians with Machiavellian tendencies, and they are normally *deliberately but covertly* malicious. Again, the behaviors adopted are unlikely to fall within those commonly recognized as constituting occupational violence, although some strategies (e.g., slander) may be subject to criminal charges—if they are caught.

The "Rottweiler"

The "Rottweiler" conduit deliberately develops a very aggressive inter-personal manner, and has typically been hired to fill a role where assertive interactions are prized, such as in industrial relations or the law. Over time, verbally aggressive interactions may become normalized in everyday interactions with competitors and subordinates. Unfortunately, inexperienced/new subordinates may be significantly emotionally harmed, although "Rottweiler" conduits are rarely deliberately malicious. While many "Rottweilers" are oblivious to their own excessive aggression and its impact on recipients, many of their behaviors frequently fall within the "bullying" or harassment categories of occupational violence (59).

The "Strategic" Bully

The core aim of the "strategic bully" is to "look after number one." The "strategic bully" conduit is distinct from the "busy boss," "egomaniac," and "Lady MacBeth" conduits in that overt aggressive behaviors are adopted which are deliberately self-serving and often malicious. "Strategic bully" conduits flourish in environments such as a university where autonomy is prized, and where individuals can avoid increased teaching loads through being grossly objectionable. Notably, the "strategic bully" is likely to have a sympathetic CEO/supervisor.

Such "strategic bully" conduits regularly use a range of weapons as they translate systemic pressures onto subordinates or colleagues. As workload pressures increase, the "strategic bully" will shift work to others, make outlandish claims, attempt to ensure that other potential competitor-workers search for alternative employment opportunities, and personally claim ownership of any successes (59). Overtly aggressive *negative* inter-personal skills are routine, as is denigration of other employees, avoidance of any additional tasks, exaggeration of personal accomplishments, or deliberate assertion of offensive views. As a result, few people wish to work with him/her. Initially, their activities may occur one-on-one and out of sight of others, with belittling masked as "helping" subordinates or co-workers. Over time behaviors become more overtly negative in public, may be in the guise of a joke that denigrates the recipient (or the group/race/gender the victim belongs to), and malicious rumors may be spread. *Repeated* inappropriate behaviors are likely to unsettle recipients so that their productivity declines. The "strategic bully" perpetrator may now provide "evidence" of the victim's incompetency, demand additional resources, promotion, and/or exaggerate their own attributes with impunity. Witnesses and co-workers are likely to be terrified of becoming the next victim, and hence may adopt self-protection strategies such as withdrawing from the recipient. This withdrawal of colleagues from recipients is often extremely hurtful as victims subsequently become isolated (40, 44, 63). In sum, the behaviors of "strategic bully" conduits are likely to include lower-level forms of occupational violence, be quite malevolent, and—as with a "Lady MacBeth" conduit—activities may be subject to charges of slander.

The "Career Bully"

"Career bully" conduits are hired to re-structure organizations and ensure the skills of the workforce better fit the requirements of a changing wider environment. That is, a "career bully" is the public face of the more covert decision-maker. Many are hired to do unpleasant tasks; for example, to encourage a number of staff to accept redundancies, such as in a downsizing civil service department (59). Typical hands-on strategies adopted by "career bullies" include: assignment of meaningless tasks, isolation of recipients, blocking promotion, "game" playing, employment security threats, work overload, or practical jokes (44). In the early stages, it is often hard to prove that inappropriate behavior is occurring, as many of the tactics are *covert,* such as errors of omission when the supervisor "forgets" to provide essential information. The tactics then evolve and may include public demeaning, throwing furniture, stealing files held by others, or repeated abusive e-mails (known as "flaming"). Many of these "career bully" conduits learned their skills over a period of time, beginning as school bullies and finding that it worked for them. Sometimes they will even boast of their "successes" in previous appointments. The recipients are typically better qualified, more popular, or hold political allegiances not appreciated by power holders. Even the most competent recipients with robust self-esteem are likely to feel exasperated when the behaviors are repeated again and again. McCarthy et al. (60) have also argued that restructuring facilitates the emergence of bullying through playing on increased insecurities in the face of changing demands. One important caveat vis-à-vis other conduits is that career bullies generally enjoy their role.

These behaviors are likely to work, and staff will probably resign or accept redundancy packages. Thus, "career bullies" are very useful to unscrupulous employers who need to downsize quickly when faced with a hostile environment. However, in the longer term, a firm is likely to be placed at both financial and legal risk if a "career bully's" lifetime behaviors continue. For example, vicarious liability, criminal charges, or productivity losses are other potential consequences. Further, Sheehan et al. (64) have argued that bullying may contribute to a culture of corruption in large organizations and eventually lead to financial collapse, as occurred at Enron and in the British office of HIH Insurance. That is, after the "career bully" has served his/her immediate purpose, wise employers will ensure that they leave to prevent significant longer-term negative outcomes.

The "Industrial Psychopath"

An "industrial psychopath" conduit is attracted to employment in stressed organizations because these present an opportunity to act out sadistic fantasies with minimal personal risk. Babiak (65) has argued that organizations that are undergoing re-structuring in a hostile external market provide a fertile environment for industrial psychopaths as uncertainties are rampant. In such scenarios, an "industrial psychopath" may be very charming, but lie about his/her technical abilities to address a particular problem, steal key documents, report totally untrue "facts" in order to assassinate competitors, disregard formal organizational policies, sabotage property, engage in patently illegal activity, or exaggerate close links with power holders. A number of the inappropriate behaviors adopted are likely to fall within criminal codes. *Malice* is *invariably* present as a motivating factor, either directed to individuals or even the organization as a whole. Those with sadist leanings may also gain a perverse psycho-erotic thrill from exercising power in ways that result in pain for others (59). Unfortunately, CEOs may discover the truth too late to prevent criminal charges being laid, or to fend off organizational failure.

CONCLUSION

In this chapter it was argued that the incidence of occupational violence varies significantly across jobs, is a predictable accompaniment at work in many jobs, and is in epidemic proportions in a few. Historically, the workers at greatest risk of occupational violence were those who (a) handled cash or valuables in the normal course of their work or (b) had significant levels of face-to-face contact with clients or customers. However, as risk factors alter over time, different vulnerabilities emerge. Because employment in most industrialized countries is increasingly skewed toward the services industries, an increased incidence of occupational violence can be expected because these jobs usually involve extensive face-to-face contact with clients/customers.

The incidence and severity of violent events also varies across industrialized countries because of an array of factors, including societal acculturation to aggression, changing availability of social supports, access to firearms and other weapons, levels of substance addiction in the broader population, and extent of preventive strategy implementation. These risks are being increasingly recognized by OHS professionals, criminologists, and those who develop public policy.

Arguably, to a great extent, the development and implementation of preventive interventions has been reactive and followed media reports, fatal incidents, or documentation of costs. More recently, the ILO commissioned a Code of Practice on *Violence and Stress at Work in Services Sectors* which, if accepted by nation states, will provide an important international regulatory benchmark.

In this chapter it was argued that there are five basic types of occupational violence, based on the relationship of perpetrators to the organization.

- "External" occupational violence which is motivated by instrumental gain and is perpetrated by an offender from outside of the organization; for example, during a hold-up at a corner store.
- "Client-initiated" occupational violence is perpetrated by a client or customer receiving a service.
- "Internal" occupational violence/bullying/initiation rites which are perpetrated by a co-worker or supervisor.
- A terrorist threat or attack on a worksite which results in danger, injury, or death of employees, or where workers treat or assist the victims of such an attack.
- "Systemic" occupational violence which directly results from extreme economic pressures in the wider economic or social environment and which encourages supervisors to behave inappropriately. It was argued in this chapter that "systemic" occupational violence arises when two essential preconditions exist: (a) an excessively hostile economic environment and (b) an internal conduit who adopts inappropriate personal behaviors as s/he transfers these pressures onto less powerful subordinates. A typology of behaviors adopted by such supervisors who translate systemic pressures onto workers was presented. It was argued that there are eight basic "ideal types" of behavior adopted when unremitting excessive pressure from the external environment is experienced. These "ideal types" range from the altruistic "missionary" to the "industrial psychopath" at the other extreme of the continuum of malevolence. Because the pressures that lead to "systemic" violence are becoming endemic in western industrialized countries, more supervisors are likely to be tempted to externalize these pressures onto their subordinates. Hence, economic cost/benefit calculations are needed that quantify the toll of human misery caused by "systemic" occupational violence.

However, these distinct forms may overlap, for example, between the "internal" and "systemic" forms of occupational violence. At the same time, each type of violence can be experienced along a continuum of severity, either as verbal abuse, threats, assaults, bullying, or homicide.

In sum, the risks of "external" occupational violence are well known, and preventive strategies have been widely applied throughout the retail industry. The risk factors associated with "client-initiated" occupational violence are also becoming familiar, although the shift in employment patterns toward the services industries means that an increasing incidence is probably inevitable. "Internal" occupational violence is also increasingly being reported, although preventive measures are being implemented in many larger organizations. Terrorist-related occupational violence has only recently become widely recognized within industrialized countries. However, as the forms of threat and the risk factors become better known, enhanced prevention efforts are being rapidly implemented in most larger and public sector organizations.

By the end of 2004, "systemic" occupational violence remains the only major form of occupational violence that is poorly recognized, and for which few preventive interventions have been implemented and evaluated as effective. Yet all the indicators are that an "epidemic" of "structural" occupational violence is emerging as global market capitalism ramps up the economic pressures and as productivity demands increase. At this stage the only control strategies available are those derived from prevention of "internal" occupational violence, which tend to focus solely on individual behavior and which do not adequately mitigate the externally imposed pressures. As the pressures that fuel "systemic" occupational violence become endemic in western industrialized countries, the risk factors will become more clear-cut. Innovative strategies are required to enable early identification and control of the threats so that the toll of human misery from the emerging epidemic of occupational violence can be stemmed.

REFERENCES

1. Di Martino, V., Hoel, H., and Cooper, C. *Preventing Violence and Harassment in the Workplace.* European Foundation for the Improvement of Living and Working Conditions, Dublin, 2003.
2. Mayhew, C. Occupational violence in industrialised countries: Types, incidence patterns, and "at risk" groups of workers. In *Occupational Violence in Industrialised Countries,* edited by M. Gill, B. Fisher, and V. Bowie, pp. 21–40. Willan Press, United Kingdom, 2002.
3. Chappell, D., and Di Martino, V. *Violence at Work,* Ed. 2. International Labour Office, Geneva, 2000.
4. International Labour Organisation. *Code of Practice on Workplace Violence in Services Sector and Measures to Combat this Phenomenon,* p. 4. An ILO Code of Practice. International Labour Organisation, Geneva, October 2003.
5. Jenkins, E. L. Workplace violence in the USA: From research to prevention. Presented at the Injury Prevention and Control 6th World Conference, Montreal, May 2002.
6. Jenkins, E. L. *Violence in the Workplace: Risk Factors and Prevention Strategies.* National Institute for Occupational Safety and Health, CDC, Washington D.C., 1996.
7. Santana, S., and Fisher, B. Workplace violence in the USA: Are there gender differences? In *Occupational Violence in Industrialised Countries,* edited by M. Gill, B. Fisher, and V. Bowie, pp. 90–113. Willan Press, United Kingdom, 2002.
8. Paoli, P. Presented at the Australian OHS regulation conference, Gold Coast, 21 July 2003. Paper based on data collated at the European Foundation for the Improvement of Living and Working Conditions, Dublin.

9. Takala, J. Global strategy on safety and health, ILO standards and concerted national action. Presented at the Australian OHS regulation conference, Gold Coast, 21 July 2003.
10. Budd, T. *Violence at Work: New Findings From the 2000 British Crime Survey*, p. 4. The Home Office and the Health and Safety Executive, London, July 2001.
11. Driscoll, T., Mitchell, R., Mandryk, J., Healey, S., and Hendrie, L. *Work-Related Traumatic Fatalities in Australia, 1989 to 1992*, National Occupational Health and Safety Commission, Ausinfo, Canberra, 1999.
12. Chappell, D., and Di Martino, V. Op cit, 2000, Table 9, for homicides. Figures for assault and sexual assault are for female workers only and taken from p. 26.
13. International Labour Organisation. *Violence and Stress at Work in Services Sectors*, p. 18. An ILO Code of Practice, second draft of in-progress document, International Labour Organisation, Geneva, February 2003.
14. Mayhew, C., and Quinlan, M. The relationship between precarious employment and patterns of occupational violence: Survey evidence from thirteen occupations. In *Health Effects of the New Labour Market*, edited by K. Isaksson, C. Hogstedt, C. Eriksson, and T. Theorell, pp. 183–205. Kluwer Academic/Plenum Publishers, New York, 1999.
15. Phillips, C., Stockdale, J., and Joeman, L. *The Risks in Going to Work: The Nature of People's Work, the Risks they Encounter and the Incidence of Sexual Harassment, Physical Attack and Threatening Behaviour*. Report for the Suzy Lamplugh Trust, London, 1989.
16. Bibby, P. *Personal Safety for Health Care Workers*. Report commissioned by the Suzy Lamplugh Trust, United Kingdom, 1995.
17. Mayhew, C. Violent assaults on taxi drivers: Incidence patterns and risk factors. *Trends and Issues in Crime and Criminal Justice*, no. 178. Australian Institute of Criminology, Canberra, Australia, 2000a.
18. CAL/OSHA. *Guidelines for Security and Safety of Health Care and Community Service Workers*. Division of Occupational Safety and Health, Department of Industrial Relations, San Francisco, 1998. See www.dir.ca.gov/DOSH/dosh_publications/hcworker.html.
19. Occupational Safety and Health Administration. *Recommendation For Workplace Violence Prevention Programs in Late-Night Retail Establishments*. United States Department of Labor, Washington D.C., 1998.
20. Mayhew, C. OHS in the health industry: Well-known problems and some emerging risks. *J. Occup. Health Saf. Aust. N.Z.* 18: 3–9, 2003.
21. Bowie, V. Defining violence at work: A new typology. In *Violence at Work: Causes, Patterns and Prevention*, edited by M. Gill, B. Fisher, and V. Bowie, pp. 1–20. Willan Publishing, Devon, United Kingdom, 2002.
22. Trades Union Congress. *Protect Us From Harm: Preventing Violence at Work*. A TUC health and safety report by Julia Gallagher, TUC Health and Safety Unit, London, 1999.
23. Mayhew, C. *Violence in the Workplace-Preventing Commercial Armed Robbery. A Practical Handbook*. Research and Public Policy series No. 33. Australian Institute of Criminology, Canberra, 2000.
24. Taylor, N., and Mayhew, P. Robbery against service stations and pharmacies: Recent trends. *Trends and Issues in Crime and Criminal Justice*, no. 223. Australian Institute of Criminology, Canberra, Australia, 2002.

50 / Occupational Health and Safety

25. Perrone, S. Crimes against small business in Australia: A preliminary analysis. *Trends and Issues in Crime and Criminal Justice*, no. 184. Australian Institute of Criminology, Canberra, Australia, 2000.
26. Mayhew, C. Getting the message across to small business about occupational violence and hold-up prevention: A pilot study. *J. Occup. Health Saf. Aust. N.Z.* 18: 223–230, 2002.
27. Fisher, B., and Looye, J. Crime and small businesses in the Midwest: An examination of overlooked issues in the United States. *Secur. J.* 13: 45–72, 2000.
28. Bellamy, L. Situational crime prevention and convenience store robbery. *Secur. J.* 7: 41–52, 1996.
29. Warshaw, L., and Messite, J. Workplace violence: Preventive and interventive strategies. *J. Occup. Environ. Med.* 38: 4, 993–1005, 1996.
30. Fisher, B., and Gunnison, E. Violence in the workplace: Gender similarities and differences. *J. Crim. Justice* 29: 145–155, 2001.
31. Fisher, B., Jenkins, E. L., and Williams, N. The extent and nature of homicide and non-fatal workplace violence in the United States: Implications for prevention and security. In *Crime At Work: Increasing the Risk for Offenders*, edited by M. Gill, p. 8. Perpetuity, Leicester, England, 1998.
32. Flannery, R. Violence in the workplace, 1970–1995: A review of the literature. *Aggression Violent Behav.* 1: 57–68, 1996.
33. Turnbull, J., and Paterson, B. (eds.). *Aggression and Violence: Approaches to Effective Management.* MacMillan, London, 1999.
34. Mayhew, C., and Chappell, D. The occupational violence experiences of some Australian health workers: An exploratory study. *The Journal of Occupational Health and Safety: Australia and New Zealand, 19*(6): 3–43, 2003.
35. Di Martino, V. *Joint Programme on Workplace Violence in the Health Sector: Synthesis Report.* International Labour Organisation, International Council of Nurses, World Health Organisation, and Public Services International joint program, Geneva, 2002.
36. Mullen, E. Workplace violence: Cause for concern or the construction of a new category of fear. *J. Indus. Relat.* 39: 21–32, 1997.
37. McCarthy, P., Sheehan, M., and Wilkie, W. (eds.). *Bullying: From Backyard to Boardroom.* Millenium Books, New South Wales, Australia, 1996.
38. Mayhew, C. *Preventing Violence Within Organisations: A Practical Handbook.* Research and Public Policy series, no. 29. Australian Institute of Criminology, Canberra, Australia, 2000.
39. Hoel, H., Sparks, K., and Cooper, C. *The Cost of Violence/Stress At Work and the Benefits of a Violence/Stress-Free Working Environment.* Institute of Science and Technology, University of Manchester, report commissioned by the International Labour Organisation, Geneva, 2001.
40. McCarthy, P. Workplace bullying: A postmodern experience. In *Bullying and Emotional Abuse in the Workplace: International Perspectives in Research and Practice*, edited by S. Einarsen, H. Hoel, D. Zapf, and C. Cooper. Taylor and Francis, London, 2002.
41. Keashly, L. Interpersonal and systematic aspects of emotional abuse at work: The target's perspective. *Violence Vict.* 16: 233–268, 2001.

42. Workers' Health Centre. *Health and Safety Fact Sheet: Violence at Work.* Workers' Health Centre, Sydney, 1999.
43. Gaymer, J. Assault course. *Occup. Health* 51: 12–13, 1999.
44. Mayhew, C., and Chappell, D. Internal violence (or bullying) in the health care industry. *J. Occup. Health Saf. Aust. N.Z.* 18: 59–71, 2003.
45. Myers, D. A workplace violence prevention planning model. *J. Secur. Admin.* 19: 1–19, 1996.
46. Capozzoli, T., and McVey, R. *Managing Violence in the Workplace.* St. Lucien Press, Delray Beach, FL, 1996.
47. Standing, H., and Nicotine, D. *Review of Workplace-Related Violence.* Report for the Health and Safety Executive, no. 143/1997. Tavistock Institute, London, 1997.
48. Zdenkowski, G. Sentencing trends: Past, present and prospective. In *Crime and the Criminal Justice System in Australia: 2000 and Beyond,* edited by D. Chappell and P. Wilson. Butterworths, Sydney, 2000.
49. Scholz J., and Gray W. OHSA Enforcement and workplace injuries: A behavioural approach to risk assessment. *J. Risk Uncertainty* 3: 283–305, 1990.
50. See, for example, on-line advice by OSHA in the United States.
51. Grantham, D., Wright, J., Golding, G., Lee, G., Wallace, B., and King, G. The need for occupational hygiene in the health care industry. *J. Occup. Health Saf. Aust. N.Z.* 19: 87–97, 1999.
52. Centres for Disease Control and Prevention. Cited in Smallwood, R. *Vaccines to Combat Bioterrorism.* Paper presented at the World Vaccine conference, Sydney, November 27, 2002.
53. Mathews, J. *Australia Can Deal with a Biological Incident.* Statement by acting chief Medical Officer, Canberra, Australia, October 11, 2001.
54. Smallwood, R. *Vaccines to Combat Bioterrorism.* Paper presented at the World Vaccine conference, Sydney, Australia, November 27, 2002.
55. Foucault, M. *Surveiller et Punir* [Discipline and Punishment]. Editions Gallimard, Paris, 1975.
56. Hatcher, C., and McCarthy, P. Workplace bullying: In pursuit of truth in the bully-victim-professional practice triangle. *Aust. J. Commun.* 29, 2002.
57. Zapf, D. European Research on Bullying at Work. In *Bullying: From Backyard To Boardroom,* Ed. 2, edited by P. McCarthy, J. Rylance, R. Bennett, and H. Zimmerman, pp. 11–22. Federation Press, Sydney, 2001.
58. Liefooghe, A., and Davey, K. Accounts of workplace bullying: The role of the organization. *Eur. J. Work Organ. Psychol.* 10: 375–392, 2001.
59. Mayhew, C. Systemic aggression, occupational violence and bullying in global market capitalism. In *Preventing Violence and Bullying at Work: An International Perspective,* P. McCarthy and C. Mayhew. Palgrave/MacMillan, London, 2004.
60. McCarthy, P., Sheehan, M., and Wilkie, W. (eds.). *Bullying: From Backyard to Boardroom,* Ed. 2. Federation Press, Sydney, 2001.
61. Mumby, D., and Stohl, C. Disciplining organizational communication studies. *Manage. Commun. Q.* 10: 5–72, 1996.
62. Ashforth, B., and Humphrey, R. Emotion in the workplace. *Hum. Relat.* 48: 97–125, 1995.

63. Einarsen, S. Harassment and bullying at work: A review of the Scandinavian approach. *Aggression Viol. Behav.* 5: 379–401, 2000.
64. Sheehan, M., McCarthy, P., Barker, M., and Henderson, M. Ethical investment and workplace bullying: Consonances and dissonances. *Int. J. Manage. Decis. Mak.* special edition on workplace bullying, 2002.
65. Babiak, P. When psychopaths go to work: A case study of an industrial psychopath. *Appl. Psychol. Int. Rev.* 44: 171–188, 1999.

CHAPTER 4

The Hidden Epidemic of Injuries and Illness Associated with the Global Expansion of Precarious Employment

Michael Quinlan

INTRODUCTION: THE REVOLUTION AT WORK

One of the most significant changes affecting work globally over the past 25 years has been the growth (both in absolute and relative terms) of more flexible or less-secure forms of work arrangements, now typically labeled precarious employment (a French-derived term) or contingent work (which originated in the U.S.). The term "precarious" captures the insecurity of many of these types of jobs where there is no ongoing presumption of permanency or long-term tenure while the term "contingent" connotes that labor is purchased in a highly variable fashion at the specific times (including duration) it is required. Despite ongoing debate about what constitutes contingent work or precarious employment—or rather definitional boundaries for inclusion or exclusion (1)— there is wide consensus about the inclusion of some categories of work. These include self-employed subcontractors (including many mobile or home-based workers), temporary (including on-call), leased (or labor hire), or short-term fixed contract workers. More problematic inclusions are micro-small business workers (though many of these are subcontractors) and permanent part-time workers. While the terms precarious employment and contingent work are often used interchangeably, the former term has a somewhat wider coverage. However, even precarious employment fails to take account of the changes to employment that are occurring, most notably that repeated rounds of downsizing by large public and private employers (together with changes in industrial relations regulatory regimes in some countries) have meant that even workers holding nominally permanent jobs are experiencing job insecurity.

Leaving the last point aside, the growth of precarious forms of employment has been charted by a series of both official and academic surveys in Europe,

53

North America, and Australasia (see for example (2–4)). Figures combining available data on various categories of contingent work in particular countries illustrate the magnitude of change. In Australia, those holding a casual or temporary job and non-employees (self-employed, subcontractors, etc.) constituted less than 30 percent of the workforce in 1982 but approximately 40 percent in 1999 (4). If permanent part-time workers are added, the figure rises to 48 percent. Similar significant shifts have been identified in some E.U. countries, Canada (5), and the U.S. (where around 30 percent of the workforce holds part-time, temporary, on-call, day-hire, or short-term contract positions or are self-employed) (6).

While truly comparable global data are often difficult to compile or missing entirely (as with regard to home-based work) and the patterns of employment shifts has varied between countries, the general thrust of the evidence has been consistent and unambiguous, with a relative decline in permanent full-time work and an associated increase in more temporary and insecure work arrangements. For example, combining a study by Campbell and Burgess (7) with unpublished OECD statistics indicates that the average proportion of the workforce in temporary employment across Australia and 14 E.U. countries grew from 9.57 percent in 1983 to 13.75 percent in 1999, an overall increase of 43.68 percent in 16 years (7). In some E.U. countries, notably Belgium and Finland, there has been a rapid expansion of temporary employment in the last 5 years. Unpublished OECD (2001) data for several other countries indicates that Iceland (11.1 percent in 1999), Norway (10.12 percent), Switzerland (11.84 percent), Canada (12.09 percent), and Japan (11.91 percent) had levels of temporary employment roughly comparable to the E.U. average. The level of temporary employment was lower in Hungary (5.2 percent) and the Czech Republic (8.67 percent), but higher in two developing countries, Mexico (21.1 percent) and Turkey (20.73 percent).

In relation to the last point, it should be noted that the growth of precarious employment has not been confined to developed countries. In developing countries there has been a growth of temporary work arrangements within the formal sector of the economy where some form of employment regulation applies. However, it also needs to be noted that these countries also have a substantial informal economy (including backyard factories, street sellers, etc.) outside the cover of any employment regulation and that this sector, which may account for as much as half the economically active workforce (including many women and children), is growing too (for studies of OHS of the informal workforce see 8 and 9). Even developed countries have an informal sector (sometimes called the black economy) and while this is relatively small (at least in comparison to developing countries), it appears to be growing—something not unconnected to the growth of precarious employment (as retrenched workers are forced to find alternative forms of support, by the employment of illegal immigrants in small businesses like restaurants, and by the capacity/pressure to use children in home-based work). As has been argued elsewhere (10), these changes are connected to global changes in business practices (including international supply chains), and all have potentially serious implications for occupational health and safety.

PRECARIOUS EMPLOYMENT AND OHS: GROWING EVIDENCE OF A HIDDEN EPIDEMIC

There is now a large and rapidly growing body of research examining the health and safety effects of job insecurity and contingent work arrangements. In 2001, with several colleagues I published the first review of this research (11) based on a search of relevant journals along with more selective searching of books, research monographs, and government reports (where this involved detailed scientific analysis). The review, covering more than 90 studies (mostly undertaken in Europe, North America, and Australasia, though with some studies from Asia, Africa, and South America), found a clear adverse association between precarious employment and OHS, with over 80 percent of studies finding these work arrangements were associated with inferior OHS outcomes. Later, more specialized reviews of available research on the OHS effects of job insecurity and the safety effects of contingent work largely served to confirm the initial findings (1, 12). Over the past 3 years we have been able to more than double the number of studies in our database (covering the period 1966–2003), in part reflecting both studies missed from the initial review and also studies published after the first review was completed. Of these 188 studies, 53 were undertaken in the U.S., 25 in the U.K., 21 in Sweden, 19 in Australia, 18 in Canada, 16 in Finland, 12 in France, 5 in Germany, 5 in Denmark, 4 in Brazil, 2 each in Norway, the E.U., Spain, and South Africa, and 1 study each in Belgium, Ireland, China, Poland, Egypt, Japan, Netherlands, Switzerland, and Zimbabwe. Along with population-based studies, there were a number of industry-specific studies, including 38 covering manufacturing, 29 in healthcare, 23 in the public sector, 10 each in financial/personal services and construction, 9 in transport, 7 in retail/hospitality, 5 in post/telecommunications/media, 4 in mining/oil, 2 in power generation, and 1 in maritime/fishing.

The reviewed studies used a range of methodologies and OHS indices. Thirty-nine used secondary data analysis, 62 were longitudinal studies, 75 were cross sectional surveys, 9 were qualitative case studies, and a further 9 used some other method. The range of OHS indices used by these studies included injury rates, blood pressure, self-reported injury and health (such as the General Health Questionnaire or GHQ), sickness absence, and knowledge/compliance with OHS law and policies. In grouping these indices it was found that 57 used objective health measures, 105 used subjective health measures, 17 measured sickness absence (using either or subjective measures), 14 measured legal knowledge/compliance, and 10 measured organizational policies/training.

This total exceeds 188 because some studies covered more than one country or used multiple categories, methods, or indices.

Of the 188 studies examined, 29 were deemed to be indeterminate because they lacked a control or benchmark or the results were too ambiguous to interpret. Of the remainder (159), 141 or 88.6 percent of determinate studies (and 77.9 percent of all studies) linked precarious employment to inferior OHS outcomes in terms of higher injury rates, hazard exposures, disease, and work-related stress. Turning specifically to the latter, it can be noted that 74 of 188 studies used some indicator of work-related stress (such as the GHQ). Four of these 74 studies were deemed indeterminate. Of the remaining 70, 63 (or 90 percent of determinate studies and 85 percent of all studies) linked precarious employment to worse stress outcomes.

As in previous reviews, studies were broken down according to the particular type of precarious employment they examined (some studies examined several categories simultaneously) as well as the more generalized notion of job insecurity. The review identified 96 studies of downsizing/job insecurity. Of these, 81 found adverse OHS effects, 8 had nil/positive results, and 9 were indeterminate. In relation to outsourcing and home-based work, the review identified 36 studies. Of these, 27 studies found adverse OHS outcomes while the remaining 9 were indeterminate. Of the 36 studies of temporary or leased workers included in the review, 19 found adverse OHS outcomes, 6 were nil/positive, and 11 were deemed indeterminate. The review included 16 studies of small business (mainly micro-small business) and of these, 8 found adverse OHS outcomes while the remaining 8 were indeterminate.

The review separated out tele-call centers and tele-workers not because they represent a distinct category of contingent work but because they represent a relatively new and significant area of employment often associated with contingent work arrangements (most notably temporary/leased employees and home-based subcontract workers). Only five studies measuring OHS among tele-work/tele-call workers could be identified, and all but one were indeterminate because of the lack of a control group (the exception did identify significantly inferior health outcomes for tele-call workers compared to those completing the same tasks in a more conventional work setting).

The review also included studies measuring OHS outcomes among permanent part-time workers, although whether these workers could be categorized as precarious or contingent is questionable. In the end, the review identified 10 studies, all but 1 of which found OHS outcomes that were nil/positive in comparison to control groups of permanent part-time workers. Hence, this was the only category of workers in the review where the findings did not match those of the overall results.

In sum, the updated review reinforced the results of earlier reviews. While this was a narrative rather than meta-review and no attempt was made to exclude methodologically weaker studies, the vast majority of those studies reviewed were substantial pieces of scholarship published in leading international journals. The research database does help to identify areas of relative neglect. More research is needed on the service sector (e.g., hospitality, tele-call centers), outsourcing/home-based work (especially health effects and hazard exposures), temporary work, leased labor, micro-small business, part-time work, multiple jobholding, and the safety (as opposed to health effects) of downsizing. There is also a need to explore the relationship between contingent work and gender, work/life balance, and shiftwork/long hours. Further, we also need research on the wider social implications of precarious employment for cost externalities, regulatory frameworks, and occupational health management systems. Finally, it should be recognized that the growth of precarious employment poses some major challenges to conventional data sources and research methods. The rapid job churning associated with temporary employment in some industries (like hospitality, road transport, or food processing) will make cohort studies virtually impossible, make epidemiological studies very difficult, and is likely to render official data sources (like workers' compensation claims, death certificates, and the like) less accurate. Control groups may be difficult to establish where, for example, an industry is largely casualized and permanent workers undertake different tasks. Not least of all, in some industries the intense competition between different categories of workers (such as employee and subcontract truck drivers) will tend to diminish OHS outcomes overall, thereby partly obscuring the effects that are due to changes in work arrangements (and indeed understating such effects).

Notwithstanding these caveats, it must now be accepted that there is a large and compelling body of evidence that a number of pervasive flexible work arrangements pose a serious threat to the maintenance of existing standards of OHS. Such an overwhelming result is unusual for a large review of scientific research. It is also important to note that methodology, indices used, or country where the research was undertaken exerted no discernible influence on these results.

OHS Data

An obvious question is why these problems were not identified in official OHS statistics some time ago. Official OHS statistics for most developed countries (often based on workers' compensation/work-related social security claims) would, at first glance, provide no inkling that the changes in work arrangements over the past 25 years pose any real concerns in terms of OHS. These statistics generally indicate an overall downward trend (at least until recently) in the incidence of work-related morbidity and mortality at the same time as use of these work arrangements has grown. There are a number of reasons why the problem has remained hidden.

First, official data were (and still are) seldom organized or presented in a way that enabled comparison of outcomes in terms of job security/tenure or employment status. Associated problems include gaps in reporting (especially in relation to self-employed and home-based workers), the masking effects of gender and inter-industry shifts in employment, and the recent nature of much research into precarious employment. Further, there was little impetus to rectify these deficiencies until recently because, while studies of the health and safety effects of job insecurity and contingent work arrangements can be identified as early as the 1960s, a rapid escalation of published research only occurred from the mid 1990s. It is still often difficult to use even disaggregated workers' compensation claims data to explore these connections because precise information on employment status is missing, agencies have not tracked the association between downsizing or outsourcing and changes in claims performance, and there can be serious reporting effects. In the U.S., a number of studies have been undertaken using workers' compensation claims data, and these have shown that temporary workers have higher claim rates than their permanently employed counterparts (see for example 13–17).

Second, some key indicators used by researchers into precarious employment (such as psychological distress as measured by the General Health Questionnaire or hazard exposures/disease) are not covered (or not covered well) by workers' compensation claims or other official OHS surveillance data. Hence, these associations are difficult if not impossible to explore using the surveillance data. There is growing recognition of the limitations of official OHS data in many developed countries, leading to the increasing use of surveys (like the five yearly E.U. workforce surveys undertaken by the Foundation for the Improvement of Living and Working Conditions) and other sources. At least as important is the fact that the growth of precarious employment has seriously compromised workers' compensation claims data, making it progressively less reliable in terms of measuring these effects. There has been a decline in formal coverage of workers due to growth in the types of work arrangements (mainly self-employed subcontractors, including some home-based workers) that are either excluded from compensation cover or for whom cover is entirely voluntary (for a detailed discussion see 18 and 19). In Australia, every jurisdiction tends to include special categories of self-employed workers who are deemed to have coverage under workers' compensation (such as clothing outworkers), but these deeming provisions were found to be relatively ineffective, and additional elements of confusion were created by further "innovations" in work arrangements, by workers shifting between categories, and by inconsistent definitions of "worker" under workers' compensation, OHS, and industrial relations statutes. Of possibly greater importance than the decline in formal coverage has been a drop in effective coverage (i.e., the failure to make claims) among eligible workers (such as temporary or leased employees) due to ignorance of their entitlements (which is enhanced where there are genuine ambiguities as referred to above), fears for job security or lost income, job churning (making linking a claim to an episode of employment more difficult), and regular shifts in employment status (18, 19). In Australia, fewer than half of the injured workers make a workers' compensation claim (with many relying on Medicare, social security, or their own resources instead), and the claim rate is substantially lower among part-time workers—the closest surrogate we have for contingent workers (20).

Workers' compensation data does not simply become less comprehensive, but in some cases at least, these changes can contribute to serious distortions in terms of the level or nature of risks (for example, in construction, agriculture, and road transport a significant number of occupational fatalities involve self-employed workers). Moreover, the use of subcontractors and leased workers can affect the overall claims experience of an industry or employer, providing a potentially misleading impression of improved performance (a problem also identified by Swedish research, see 21). It is important to note that the growth of precarious employment is also likely to impact adversely on other surveillance and reporting systems. For example, more volatile or mobile workplaces, job churning in particular industries (like hospitality), and more complicated work histories are not conducive to clinical diagnosis of work-related illnesses, cohort or epidemiological studies, or the accurate recording of occupation on death certificates. Again, these issues have a wide resonance. In her study of the French nuclear industry, Thebaud Mony (22) found that subcontractors received 80 percent of the total workforce radiation exposure and this had significant implications for both the identification of hazard exposures, management responses, and deficiencies in regulatory responses. Whatever the problems precarious employment poses for the recognition and treatment of injuries, they can be multiplied when attention is turned to hazardous substance exposures and the threats to worker health and well-being arising from psychosocial factors.

Broader Effects of Precarious Employment on
Community Health and Well-Being

There is increasing evidence that the growth of precarious employment is imposing an array of externalities on the community. While some contingent jobs are well paid, the vast majority are not and even some of those that are well paid are extremely vulnerable to changes in market demand (see the recent experience of the information technology industry). Job insecurity has wide-ranging direct health effects on various categories of workers (23). Researchers have pointed to other indirect effects on workers and the community, with a number of studies finding adverse spillover effects on family and non-work roles (see 24–26). Others have argued that the workplace and social dislocation associated with downsizing and job insecurity is conducive to an increase in violence both within and outside the workplace (see 27, 28). There is also evidence (29) that a succession of short-term or insecure jobs, or the simultaneous cobbling together of several part-time jobs by workers—what some management spin doctors have labeled as "portfolio employment"—can have adverse implications in terms of poverty/ budgeting, accommodation (purchase or rent), the health and education of these worker's children, and welfare and pension entitlements (especially where these are contribution-based).

Contingent workers are often in a weaker position to take out private health insurance to supplement mandated government cover (where this exists but is inadequate). In the United States, where there is no universal government health insurance scheme, workers and their families rely heavily on employer-provided schemes, but workers holding contingent jobs or in small business are less likely to have access to these schemes, and cost-cutting pressures on employers are reducing coverage more generally (30–32). Consistent with this, immigrants (especially those without citizenship) who are concentrated in these types of jobs also have a low rate of coverage (33). The growth of contingent work has been linked to an overall increase in socio-economic inequality, and there is an already extensive body of international evidence on the health and other adverse consequences of poverty and inequality (see for example 34).

Two arguments used to support flexible work arrangements are that they are more family friendly and enhance the capacity of persons to find jobs, thereby reducing unemployment. (A related argument is that this process also provides a more even spread of income opportunities rather than a more bifurcated divide between the permanently employed and the unemployed.) With the exception of permanent part-time work (and even here there are exceptions due to split shifts or other factors), there is little evidence to justify claims of family friendliness. Rather, there is mounting evidence that the long or unsocial hours, lack of bargaining power, and pressures associated with many contingent jobs have deleterious effects on work/family balance (although changes to permanent full-time jobs are indicating a deterioration in work/non-work balance and highlight the point made earlier about interaction or associated effects, as in the case where permanent workers are called on to supervise temporary workers as part of their routine tasks).

With regard to the second argument (i.e., the alleged unemployment reduction effect), it might be suggested this is a socially beneficial change because of the compelling evidence surrounding the adverse health effects of unemployment. However, as has been noted elsewhere (12), even if we ignore other externalities referred to above and, further, confine our examination to the health effects of job insecurity, the purported overall health advantage of promoting employment at the expense of working conditions is questionable. We now have compelling evidence (i.e., 84 out of 96 studies) that job insecurity has serious measurable and, in many cases, long-term effects on worker health and psychological well-being. These effects may not be—on average—of the same order as those experiencing long-term unemployment, but this presumption needs to be tested, especially in the light of selection effects (35), research on the "skidding" effects of retrenchment and the impact of lengthy episodes of intermittent work and unemployment (36). It has long been recognized that job transfers are stressful for workers and their families even when they don't involve a change of employer but rather a geographic relocation (37). The more volatile labor market associated with the move to flexible employment almost certainly entails more job movements (and geographic relocation), including a large number that are essentially involuntary, but the health effects of this, as far as contingent workers are concerned, is yet to be investigated. Even if the presumption holds, the number of persons experiencing job insecurity is now much larger than the number of unemployed in most if not all industrialized countries. So it is more than likely that any health gains from reduced unemployment have been swamped by the losses associated with job insecurity. What is equally disturbing is that this consideration (or the costs of other externalities for that matter) appears to have been ignored by governments when introducing policies promoting flexible employment; and even as the evidence mounts, neo-liberal policy advocates remain conspicuously silent. For those of us who believe that policy should be informed by evidence, this is a disturbing example of what appears to be a growing disjunction between policy discourse and its effects on the community.

The foregoing debate ignores other social and health costs of downsizing/ restructuring, outsourcing/privatization, and increased used of contingent-work arrangements. While these effects have only been partly investigated, available evidence indicates that the effects may be considerable. Changes to staffing levels by large employers and related changes to work practices may expose clients or other members of the community to increased risk. For example, there is now a significant body of research linking reduced staffing levels in hospitals to increased patient mortality, risks of infection, poor hygiene practices, stress, and burnout among nurses and other medical-care staff (38–45). As in other industries, cost savings have been achieved in healthcare not simply by reducing overall staffing levels but by altering the occupational and qualifications mix of staff to utilize fewer higher-expertise/high-cost personnel. Again, there is evidence linking the level of more qualified staff (such as registered nurses) to the quality of care in hospitals (see for example 46 and 47). It has also been suggested that downsizing and moving some healthcare tasks to the home may also adversely affect the reporting of critical incidents involving patients (48), and staff for that matter. These problems need to be seen in the context of the OHS effects of downsizing/job insecurity and contingent work status on healthcare workers, which include increased psychological distress/burnout and increased risk of occupational violence (see for example 49–53). In combination, these problems could lead to attitudinal and behavioral changes among healthcare staff (reduced job satisfaction, increased labor turnover, and difficulties in recruitment) that may have further long term effects on the quality of healthcare (for a partial discussion of this see 54 and 55).

Although healthcare is perhaps the clearest and best-documented example, there are other industries where there are potentially public health and safety externalities associated with neo-liberal policy inspired organizational restructuring and increased use of contingent workers. Obvious examples include transport, where a breakdown of health and safety is liable to affect passengers or others using or living in close proximity to the transport network. Areas of transport warranting further investigation include the growth of "Flag of Convenience" ships (staffed by contingent crews), the outsourcing of aircraft maintenance (a la ValuJet), the outsourcing of track maintenance and use of leased drivers in rail transport, and the increased use of subcontracting and contingent drivers in long-haul road transport (for a more detailed discussion of these see 10, 19, and 56).

There are yet other externalities or hidden costs of the move to more flexible work arrangements. For example, the drop in coverage of workers under workers' compensation (and claims suppression to the extent it occurred) has resulted in cost shifting to the general health care and social security system (18). The same process could occur even in countries where workers' compensation is integrated into social security if, as is the case in some, a differential level of payment for work-related injuries provides an incentive to shift work injuries into the non-work category of social security. This represents an effective externalization of the costs of work-related injury and disease, placing an additional financial burden on government and the community, putting the families of affected workers at a social disadvantage (due to financial burdens and stress), and entailing a set of socially disruptive incentives (57).

REGULATORY CHALLENGES

In industrialized countries, a complex web of regulatory regimes and government infrastructure exists in relation to safeguarding worker health and well-being (and their dependents in the case of injury or disease). While OHS and workers' compensation legislation is most conspicuous in this regard, minimum labor standards/industrial relations and social security/sickness/disability laws as well healthcare infrastructure and insurance cover also perform critical functions. The legal regimes (including implementation/enforcement) that directly address worker health/compensation and labor standards (and in some countries other laws just referred to) were invariably designed on a presumption of full-time secure employment and as such have proved ill equipped to address the problems associated with precarious employment. Indeed, the growth of precarious employment has undermined the effectiveness of these regimes more generally.

A number of the studies reviewed above as well as other literature identified significant OHS regulatory issues in relation to precarious employment, notably lower knowledge of or compliance with legislative requirements among subcontractors, temporary workers, and those employing them and less willingness to raise OHS issues or access entitlements (like workers' compensation) among contingent workers (see for example 58–60). The problems have also been raised in a number of reports prepared for government agencies in Europe, North America, and Australasia, though often at a generic level or in connection to only one aspect of contingent work such as temporary employment or tele-work (see for example 61–65). In 2001, I was commissioned by an Australian state government OHS agency (the WorkCover Authority of New South Wales) to research and report on the regulatory challenges—with regard to prevention and workers compensation/rehabilitation—posed by changing work arrangements and to assess the strategic solutions being developed to address these challenges. The project covered all state, territory, and federal government OHS jurisdictions in Australia, and received the active cooperation of all relevant government agencies. As part of this process I met with 10 of the 12 tripartite industry reference groups (IRGs) established in New South Wales and conducted both focus group and individual interviews (using a semi-structured questionnaire) with 63 regulatory staff (both policy and operational) in 9 of the 10 jurisdictions and 40 senior employer/industry and union representatives. I also conducted a relatively exhaustive search of relevant government material (legislation/regulations, codes, guidance material, information bulletins, internal and public reports, prosecution reports, and workers' compensation claims data pertaining to several jurisdictions over the past five years). This information was augmented by a more selective collection of employer/industry association and union material and workplace visits. I also obtained and perused a number of reports on the issue prepared by or for government agencies in Europe, Canada, the U.S., and New Zealand.

The report based on this project (19) indicated that precarious employment was creating serious problems for OHS regulatory regimes in Australia. Unlike many other countries (apart from Canada), Australian OHS and workers' compensation legislation is largely state/province based. However, like Canada, the United Kingdom, and many other European countries, the legislative framework uses a mixture of process and prescriptive standards based on general duty provisions that set broad behavioral standards for an array of parties (employers, workers, contractors, designers, manufacturers, suppliers, and others). Effectively, the general duties require employers to undertake risk assessment (like the E.U., this is specifically mandated in NSW), to maintain a safe system of work (including adequate plant and equipment, training of workers, and work organization), and to take into adequate consideration any major change in work process (which could include downsizing). Further, like the European Union and Norway, the legislation mandates worker involvement in OHS through elected employee health and safety representatives, or HSRs (there are well over 50,000 of these in Australia at present), and joint worker/employer OHS committees at the workplace. In short, OHS legislation in Australia is broadly similar to that found in many other industrialized countries (including the recent focus on promoting systematic OHS management) and, in very general terms, the same applies to workers' compensation legislation (with the exception of those countries where this has been integrated into social security). It is important to make this point because the reading of overseas reports and other international evidence indicated that many of the problematic issues identified in relation to Australia are by no means unique. Indeed, there is clear evidence a number of these problems are being experienced in other countries. While we need more research to explore the extent of the similarities and where and how differences arise, I think the Australian evidence provides a template for both research and an emerging policy debate. The problems identified were extensive and can only be briefly summarized here.

Prevention

The general-duty provisions in Australia OHS statutes establish a hierarchy of responsibility (as between the principal and a subcontractor) as well as web of multiple or shared responsibilities (as in the case of a labor-leasing firm and its host and on multi-employer worksites). While this would seem well-suited to meeting the challenges posed by changing work arrangements (and indeed it is certainly superior to a legislative framework that fails to recognize or address these complexities), the evidence uncovered in the course of research indicated that the growth of precarious employment was associated with a fracturing of statutory responsibilities (at least in the eyes of those being regulated) that was undermining the effective implementation of the legislation.

Subcontracting (especially multi-tiered or pyramid subcontracting), labor leasing, and much home-based work (where self-employment or subcontracting is entailed) introduce third parties into the work arrangement as opposed to the relatively simple and direct employer/employee relationship that has been the overwhelming focus of OHS regulatory regimes in the past (66). In two jurisdictions, design flaws in the legislative duties limited coverage of certain subcontracting arrangements (one related to work undertaken by subcontractors outside the employers place of work and another limited the capacity to pursue legislative responsibility for more than one step in the subcontracting chain) though other jurisdictions have used deeming and other special provisions to clarify legislative coverage. However, even where changes to work organization have not exposed gaps in statutory coverage, the introduction of third parties creates more complicated and potentially attenuated webs of legal responsibility that place heavier logistical demands on the inspectorate. For example, monitoring to see if there is an integrated OHS management system becomes more difficult on multi-employer sites or those making extensive use of subcontractors or home-based workers, and there is a commensurately greater risk of instances of "paper compliance" escaping undetected. Further, conducting workplace inspections is nothing short of a logistical nightmare in the case of mobile workers, literally thousands of home-based workers, and temporary workplaces (like a tele-call center established for a marketing campaign that may last only a few months). Finally, where a breach is detected or serious incident occurs, the inspectorate can face greater difficulty in identifying the parties to prosecute (such as the principal contractor) and their legal status (especially where the "corporate veil" of shelf companies is used) or the precise employment status of the worker (and this may have implications for the relevant provision to be used in legal proceedings). Further, the existence of third parties make determining the share of responsibility and who to pursue in legal proceedings (more than one party can be prosecuted) more time consuming.

It should be noted here that, as in the U.S., specialist advice has been provided to some Australian employers by legal firms and others about how to configure their organization or their workforce in order to minimize their "exposure" to a raft of statutory requirements (relating to taxation and industrial relations as well as OHS and workers' compensation). For example, in one case a taxi firm configured itself as a trust and its workers as beneficiaries of that trust. While this represents an extreme case, it highlights the element of calculated regulatory evasion that is at least a partial contributor to the growth of precarious employment. Even where there has been no calculated regulatory evasion, growth of these work arrangements increases the potential risk of ignorance or misunderstandings in terms of meeting legislative requirements. Regulators expressed concern that employers often presumed that outsourcing an activity or leasing a worker diminished their responsibility (it doesn't) and that the short-term nature of temporary employment affected employers' attitudes as to the need to provide adequate induction and training or to ensure these workers were represented by HSRs or on workplace committees.

In relation to the last point, it should be noted that, with some notable exceptions (such as the NSW Risk Assessment Regulation 2001), existing laws and guidance material on worker involvement largely presume a permanent work arrangement between employer and employees and as such take little or no account of the presence of subcontractors or leased or temporary workers. The laws only refer to employees or are worded in ways that provide opportunity for ambiguity (for example, failing to specify when subcontractors should be included in workplace health and safety committees). Further, there has been a failure to recognize that workplace size thresholds for establishing a committee or the appointment of a HSR (both de facto and dejure) represent a more critical limitation on worker involvement as downsizing, outsourcing, and other practices reduce the number of workers in particular workplaces. These shifts have been compounded by declines in union density (because unions provide critical logistical support to HSRs) while also making it more difficult for unions to maintain a presence in existing workplaces (something exacerbated by changes to Australian federal industrial relations legislation since 1996). Perhaps at least as important, the project failed to find one jurisdiction/government agency in Australia that has actively monitored compliance with or enforced regulatory requirements in relation to worker involvement. Regulators recognized the problems posed by extensive use of subcontractors (as have some employers) in terms of obtaining representative input on committees from workers, and examples were also cited where temporary workers were grossly under-represented on committees (there are clear logistical incentives for this situation to arise). Available evidence suggests the problems precarious employment poses for worker representation under existing OHS regulatory regimes just described are by no means confined to Australia. This and other problems associated with precarious employment create a serious limitation for systematic OHS management currently being promoted by many industrialized countries (67, 68).

Further, the lead-time for inspectoral agencies to adapt their guidance material and enforcement practices to meet these challenges has arguably contributed to employer ignorance of their general responsibilities where contingent workers are concerned. Surveying of existing materials revealed major gaps in regulations, codes, and guides/information to parties in terms of clarifying responsibilities in relation to particular work arrangements or categories of workers. At present no Australian agency has produced guidance material on downsizing/restructuring although regulators acknowledged such changes could clearly relate to major changes in work processes (under the general-duty provisions), and that in general, employers failed to consult workers adequately and were aware of instances where changes had led to a serious deterioration in OHS. As in the U.S., staffing levels are being included as a risk factor in some guidance material on occupational violence, but this is the limit of activity thus far. Only one Australian jurisdiction (Victoria) has produced generic information to advise employers of their responsibilities in relation to temporary workers, and their production of generic material on home-based work is also exceptional. Given some recent initiatives, the situation is slightly better in relation to subcontracting, labor leasing, and tele-call center work. Relatively detailed guidance material has been produced in relation to specific industries and sectors (such as government and more notably construction), and references to temporary and leased workers can also be increasingly found in industry-specific documentation (like hospitality and agriculture) or at-risk categories of workers (notably young workers, seasonal harvest workers, and immigrant workers). It is worth noting that, as in a number of E.U. countries, Canada, and the U.S., both young workers and small business have received considerably increased attention from inspectorates (though most of the guidance material still fails to identify the concentration of young workers in temporary jobs or the fact that many small businesses are subcontractors).

Given the pervasive use of contingent workers across many industries, the efforts just described leave substantial gaps. What is needed is a comprehensive array of both generic guidance material and more detailed industry/sector-specific guides (which take account of the particular configurations of work arrangements in that industry). Again, examination of OHS agency Websites in the U.S., Canada, and the U.K. indicated that gaps in guidance material were by no means confined to Australia. The European Union has produced a directive on temporary workers (first drafted almost a decade ago), but, as with attempts at uniform regulation of the working hours of self-employed truck drivers, this has not proved a simple process, suggesting that similar delays will accompany efforts to develop directives on other issues like downsizing, leased workers, sub-contractors, and tele-work.

Enforcement

Turning to the question of enforcement, it can be noted that, notwithstanding the logistical problems already identified, OHS agencies in Australia have increasingly sought to target and publicize their prosecutions in ways that would both clarify legal obligations and have a deterrent effect. With regard to sub-contracting and leased workers in particular, this activity appears to have had some effect (in terms of awareness-raising and the activities of individual employers and industry associations). For example, there are a growing number of cases where both the leasing firm and the host employer have been fined substantial sums as a result of serious incidents. At the same time, this has raised questions about whether large labor-leasing firms can actually undertake adequate risk assessment for the diverse and shifting array of workers they provide. Further, rapid turnover among small leasing firms and contractors in some industries considerably weakens the "learning" effect of these prosecutions. In an admittedly extreme case, a new and small leasing firm managed to help "kill" the first worker it supplied. While both the leasing firm and the host employer were prosecuted and the former went out of business, numerous others will take its place, entering the industry equally ignorant of their OHS responsibilities.

In some areas, such as downsizing, prosecutions are virtually unknown because they had been put in the "too difficult" basket in terms of proving a case (although prosecutions may be launched using other grounds). Some targeted and publicized prosecutions are beginning to occur in relation to directly engaged temporary workers (i.e., as distinct from leased workers discussed above), especially younger workers, and with regard to homecare workers and tele-call centers. But, by and large, home-based work has not been the subject of active enforcement. Overall, enforcement is even patchier in terms of coverage than the production of codes and guidance material. Again, from what could be deduced from an Internet-based search of agency and related Websites, the situation appears to be similar in Europe and North America.

Workers' Compensation/Rehabilitation Effects

The possibility that precarious employment poses serious problems for workers' compensation regimes has received far less attention than is the case with prevention, even though by the late 1990s there was evidence to suggest these challenges were by no means insignificant (18). Investigations revealed a number of problems being experienced by Australian jurisdictions.

As indicated in the earlier discussion on OHS statistics, the growth of precarious employment has reduced both the formal and effective coverage of workers' compensation schemes. This has created a policy dilemma for workers' compensation authorities and an access problem for contingent workers, with flow-on effects to other workers where they compete for work with the former (56). While reduced coverage may mean less agency exposure to potentially costly claims, it also undermines the role and social significance of workers' compensation.

For contingent workers injured or exposed to hazardous substances or work practices, there is not only a question of problematic access but the level of entitlements where benefits are calculated on the basis of prior earnings. Benefit levels may in no way meet the long-term needs of a contingent worker suffering a permanent disability because their income levels are often more volatile or they were employed part-time, with income arising from multiple jobholding or a job/study mix. Benefit levels have been identified as a critical issue with regard to contingent workers in Canada.[1]

Insurance agencies were concerned that the growth of small business, subcontractors, temporary workers, labor leasing, and home-based work was adversely affecting premium collection. This resulted from the failure of these groups to take out coverage and (more importantly) to underinsure (by understating workforce/payroll, outsourcing high-risk groups, or manipulation of occupational categories for premium calculation purposes). Agencies were devoting more resources to targeted efforts to combat this fraud. Again, these problems have been identified in other countries such as the U.S. (18).

The more complicated and fluid nature of work arrangements has also created additional administrative demands on workers' compensation agencies. These include determining whether a worker is eligible for workers' compensation or who their employer is in the case of subcontracting or leasing arrangements (i.e., the third-party issue already raised in relation to prevention). The growing incidence of multiple jobholding also poses additional administrative problems for workers' compensation authorities. Essentially identical problems have been identified in other countries such as Canada and the U.S. (see 18 and 64).

Finally, agencies were concerned that attempts to secure a return to work were being hampered because such measures are more difficult for small business, and it was difficult to get employers to take the same responsibility for temporary or leased workers as could be expected with permanent workers. Australia, unlike many European countries, does not mandate occupational health services, but the growth of contingent work has created difficulties

---

[1] I am indebted to Katherine Lippel for alerting me to this issue and to the benefits problem more generally.

for private health service providers. This finding mirrors the experience of a number of European countries, such as France, where services are mandatory (69).

Other Regulatory Effects

In addition to the problems just identified there are other less apparent but arguably significant regulatory and institutional effects.

The growth of precarious employment poses problems for the maintenance of minimum labor standards (minimum wages, maximum hours, etc.) that set a foundation for OHS and workers' compensation law—a nexus more clearly understood by social and labor reformers 100 years ago than today (10). Self-employed subcontractors in Australia (and many other countries for that matter) do not enjoy the regulatory protections of employees with regard to minimum wages, maximum hours of work, and other conditions (such as annual, long-service, maternity leave, sickness absence, etc.). The WorkCover project (described above) reinforced the evidence that, in industries such as home-based clothing manufacture, road transport, and construction, the absence of mini-mum standards and the consequent competition for work encouraged hazardous work practices (long hours, corner cutting, etc.) and diminished compliance with OHS and workers' compensation legislation. Even for employees covered by minimum labor standards, competition from subcontractors or other contingent workers in some industries (like trucking) can encourage significant compliance problems. Similar problems have been identified in Europe and North America (for examples in trucking see 56), and the inadequacy of these standards, especially in relation to contingent workers in countries like the U.S., can have profound health effects (70). The mismatch in key definitions (e.g., worker) in industrial-relations, OHS, and workers' compensation statutes already referred to above exacerbated these problems by promoting ambiguity among key parties and making it more difficult for inspectorates covering these spheres to integrate their enforcement activities.

CONCLUSION

As the review of international research in this chapter demonstrates, there is now substantial if not compelling evidence that the growth of precarious employment poses a serious threat to the maintenance of OHS standards. For a number of reasons already identified, the epidemic of injury and illness related to contingent work arrangements and job insecurity is not apparent in official OHS statistics. But there can be little if any doubt as to their profound effects on workers, their families, and the community more generally. As noted, the growth of precarious employment has entailed a number of significant externalities, including health and safety risks for those who come into contact with these work arrangements, because they share the work space or rely on services provided by these work arrangements. These work arrangements pose a particular challenge to regulatory agencies because they entail a weakening if not outright evasion of the statutory frameworks upon which the regimes are based. Government agencies are beginning to respond with an array of measures but have nothing approaching a comprehensive or strategic response. There is an urgent need for responses that negate the capacity to evade existing standards and that ensure effective protection of contingent workers. As argued elsewhere, this will entail moving beyond the regulatory spheres of social protection and entering the domain of business and taxation law, industrial relations and labor market law, and policy at the national level to create a close nexus between minimum labor standards and trade policy at international level. More than simply looking to protect workers, governments will need to engage more proactively in shaping the types of jobs they wish their citizens to have now and in the future.

REFERENCES

1. Quinlan, M., and Bohle, P. Contingent work and safety. In *The Psychology of Workplace Safety*, edited by J. Barling and M. Frone. American Psychological Association. In press.
2. De Grip, A., Hoevenberg, J., and Williams, E. Atypical employment in the European Union. *Int. Labour Rev.* 136: 49–71, 1997.
3. Bureau of Labor Statistics. New data on contingent and alternate employment. report 900. *New Survey Reports on Wages and Benefits for Temporary Help Service Workers.* US Department of Labor, Washington D.C., 1995.
4. Burgess, J., and de Ruyter, A. Declining job quality in Australia: Another hidden cost of unemployment. *Econ. Labour Relat. Rev.* 11: 246–269, 2000.
5. Lowe, G. *The Quality of Work: A People-Centred Agenda.* Oxford University Press, Don Mills, ON, Canada, 2001.
6. Hipple, S. Contingent work in the late 1990s. *Mon. Labor Rev.* 124: 3–27, 2001.
7. Campbell, I., and Burgess, J. Casual employment in Australia and temporary employment in Europe: Developing a cross national comparison. *Work Employ. Soc.* 15: 171–184, 2001.
8. Santana, V., Loomis, D., Newman, B., and Harlow, S. Informal jobs: Another occupational hazard for women's mental health. *Int. J. Epidemiol.* 26: 1236–1242, 1997.
9. Loewenson, R. Occupational hazards in the informal sector: A global perspective. In *Health Effects of the New Labour Market,* edited by K. Isaksson, C. Hogstedt, C. Erikson, and T. Theorell, pp. 329–342. Klumer/Plenum, New York, 2000.
10. Quinlan, M., Mayhew, C., & Bohle, P. The global expansion of precarious employment, work disorganisation and occupational health: Placing the debate in a comparative historical context. *Int. J. Health Serv.* 31: 507–536, 2001.
11. Quinlan, M., Mayhew, C., & Bohle, P. The global expansion of precarious employment, work disorganisation, and consequences for occupational health: A review of recent research. *Int. J. Health Serv.* 31: 335–414, 2001.
12. Bohle, P., Quinlan, M., & Mayhew, C. The health and safety effects of job insecurity: An evaluation of the evidence. *Econ. Labour Relat. Rev.* 12: 32–60, 2001.

13. Butler, R., Park, Y., and Zaidman, B. Analyzing the impact of contingent work on workers' compensation. *Empl. Benefits Pract. Q.* 4: 1–20, 1998.
14. Park, Y.-S., and Butler, R. J. The safety risks of contingent work: Evidence from Minnesota. *J. Labor Res.* 22: 831–849, 2001.
15. Foley, M. Flexible work, hazardous work: The impact of hazardous work arrangements on occupational health and safety in Washington State, 1991–1996. In *Research in Human Capital and Development,* Vol. 12, edited by I. Sirageldin, pp. 123–147. JAI Press, Greenwich, CT, 1998.
16. Silverstein, B., Welp, E., Nelson, N., and Kalat, J. Claims incidence of work-related disorders of the upper extremities: Washington state 1987 through 1995. *Am. J. Public Health* 88: 1827–1833, 1998.
17. Silverstein, B., Viikari-Juntura, E., Nelson, N., and Kalat, J. Use of a prevention index to identify industries at high risk for work-related musculoskeletal disorders of the neck, back, and upper extremity in Washington state. *Am. J. Indust. Med.* 41: 146–169, 2002.
18. Quinlan, M., and Mayhew, C. Precarious employment and workers' compensation. *Int. J. Law Psychiatry* 22: 491–520, 1999.
19. Quinlan, M. Developing strategies to address OHS and workers' compensation responsibilities arising from changing employment relationships. Research project commissioned by the WorkCover Authority of New South Wales, Sydney, 2003.
20. ABS. Work-Related Injuries, Australia September 2000. Catalogue No. 6324.0. Australian Bureau of Statistics, Canberra, Australia, 2001.
21. Blank, V., Andersson, R., Linden, A., and Nilsson, B. Hidden accident rates and patterns in the Swedish mining industry due to the involvement of contract workers. *Saf. Sci.* 21: 23–35, 1995.
22. Thebaud-Mony, A. *L'industrie Nucleaire: Sous-tratance et Servitude.* INSERM Universite Paris-XIII, Bobigny, France, 2000.
23. Ferrie, J. Health consequences of job insecurity. In *Labour Market Changes and Job Insecurity: A Challenge for Social Welfare and Health Promotion,* edited by J. Ferrie, M. Marmot, and E. Ziglio. European Series No. 81. WHO Regional Publications, 1999.
24. Mauno, S., and Kinnunen, U. Job insecurity and well-being: A longitudinal study among male and female employees in Finland. *Commun. Work Fam.* 2: 147–171, 1999.
25. Burke, R., and Greenglass, E. Work-family conflict, spouse support, and nursing staff well-being during organizational restructuring. *J. Occup. Health Psychol.* 4: 327–336, 1999.
26. Shannon, H., Woodward, C., Cunningham, C., McIntosh, J., Lendrum, B., Brown, J., and Rosenbloom, D. Change in general health and musculoskeletal outcomes in the workforce of a hospital undergoing rapid change: A longitudinal study. *J. Occup. Health Psychol.* 6: 3–14, 2001.
27. Schwebel, M. Job insecurity as structural violence: Implications for destructive intergroup conflict. *Peace Conflict J. Peace Psychol.* 3: 333–351, 1997.
28. Neuman, J., and Baron, R. Workplace violence and workplace aggression: Evidence concerning specific forms, potential causes and preferred targets. *J. Manage.* 24: 391–419, 1998.
29. Barling, J., and Mendelson, M. Parents' job insecurity affects children's grade performances through the indirect effects of beliefs in an unjust world and negative mood. *J. Occup. Health Psychol.* 4: 347–355, 1999.

30. Long, S., and Rogers, J. Do shifts towards service industries, part-time work and self-employment explain the rising uninsurede? *Inquiry* 32: 111–116, 1995.
31. Nollen, S. Negative aspects of temporary employment. *J. Labor Res.* 17: 567–581, 1996.
32. Case, B., Himmelstein, D., and Woolhandler, S. No care for the caregivers: Declining health insurance coverage for health care personnel and their children, 1988-1998. *Am. J. Public Health* 92: 404–409, 2002.
33. Carrasquillo, O., Carrasquillo, A., and Shea, S. Health insurance coverage of immigrants living in the United States: Differences by citizenship status and country of origin. *Am. J. Public Health* 90: 917–923, 2000.
34. Richardson, J. Poor, powerless and poisoned: The social injustice of childhood lead poisoning. *J. Child. Poverty* 8: 141–157, 2002.
35. Mastekaasa, A. Unemployment and health: Selection effects. *J. Comm. Appl. Soc. Psychol.* 6: 189–205, 1996.
36. Claussen, B., Bjorndal, A., and Hjort, P. Health and re-employment in a two year follow-up of long term unemployed. *J. Epidemiol. Public Health* 47: 14–18, 1993.
37. Brett, J. The effect of job transfer on employees and their families. In *Current Concerns in Occupational Stress*, edited by C. Cooper and R. Payne, pp. 99–136. John Wiley and Sons, New York, 1980.
38. Jarman, B., Gault, S., Alves, B., Hider, A., Dolan, S., Cook, A., Hurwitz, B., and Iezzoni, L. Explaining differences in English hospital death rates using routinely collected data. *BMJ* 318: 1515–1520, 1999.
39. Harbarth, S., Sudre, P., Dharan, S., Cadenas, M., and Pittet, D. *Infec. Cont. Hosp. Epidemiol.* 20: 598–603, 1999.
40. Clark, P., Clark, D., Day, D., and Shea, D. Healthcare reform and the workplace experience of nurses: Implications for patient care and union organizing. *Indust. Labor Relat. Rev.* 55: 133–148, 2001.
41. Aiken, L., Clarke, S., Sloane, D., Sochalski, J., Busse, R., Clarke, H., Giovannetti, P., Hunt, J., Rafferty, A., and Shamian, J. Nurses' report on hospital care in five countries. *Health Aff.* 20: 43–53, 2001.
42. Aiken, L., Clarke, S., Sloane, D., Sochalski, J., and Silber, J. Hospital nurse staffing and patient mortality, nurse burnout and job dissatisfaction. *JAMA* 288: 1987–1993, 2002.
43. West, M., Borrill, C., Dawson, J., Scully, J., Carter, M., Anelay, S., Patterson, M., and Waring, J. The link between the management of employees and patient mortality in acute hospitals. *Int. J. Hum. Resour. Manage.* 13: 1299–1310, 2002.
44. Bittner, M., Rich, E., Turner, P., and Arnold, W. Limited impact of sustained simple feedback based on soap and paper towel consumption on the frequency of hand washing in an adult intensive care unit. *Infec. Cont.Hosp. Epidemiol.* 23: 120–126, 2002.
45. Stegenga, J., Bell, E., and Matlow, A.The role of nurse understaffing in nonsocomial viral gastrointestinal infections on a general pediatrics ward. *Infec. Cont. Hosp. Epidemiol.* 23: 133–139, 2002.
46. Anonymous. Careful facility "downsizing" reduces liability risks: Use of inexperienced or unqualified staff threatens patient safety. *Alaska Med.* 39: 82–84, 1997.

47. Needleman, J., Buerhaus, P., Mattke, S., Stewart, M., and Zelevinsky, K. Nursing-staff levels and the quality of care in hospitals. *New Engl. J. Med.* 346: 1715–1722, 2002.
48. Jones, L., and Arana, G. Is downsizing affecting incident reports? *J. Qual. Improve.* 22: 592–594, 1996.
49. Landsbergis, P. Occupational stress among health care workers: A test of the job demands-control model. *J. Organ. Behav.* 9: 217–239, 1988.
50. Flannery, R., Hanson, M., Penk, W., Pastva, G., Navon, M., and Fannery, G. Hospital downsizing and patients' assaults on staff. *Psychiatry Q.* 68: 67–76, 1997.
51. Snyder, W. Hospital downsizing and increased frequency of assaults on staff. *Hosp. Comm. Psychiatry* 45: 378–380, 1994.
52. Woodward, C., Shannon, H., Cunningham, C., McIntosh, J., Lendrum, B., Ronsebloom, D., and Brown, J. The impact of re-engineering and other cost reduction strategies on the staff of a large teaching hospital: A longitudinal study. *Med. Care* 37: 556–569, 1999.
53. Shannon, H., Woodward, C., Cunningham, C., McIntosh, J., Lendrum, B., Brown, J., and Rosenbloom, D. Change in general health and musculoskeletal outcomes in the workforce of a hospital undergoing rapid change: A longitudinal study. *J. Occup. Health Psychol.* 6: 3–14, 2001.
54. McKenna, H. The "professional cleansing" of nurses: The systematic downgrading of nurses damages patient care. *BMJ* 317: 1403–1404, 1998.
55. Burke, R., and Greenglass, E. Hospital restructuring and downsizing in Canada: Are less experienced nurses at risk? *Psychol. Rep.* 87: 1013–1021, 2000.
56. Quinlan, M. *Report of Inquiry into Safety in the Long Haul Trucking Industry.* Motor Accidents Authority of New South Wales, Sydney, 2001. www.maa.nsw.gov.au/roadsafety36reports.htm.
57. Quinlan, M. The implications of labour market restructuring in industrialised societies for occupational health and safety. *Econ. Indust. Democracy* 20: 427–460, 1999.
58. Aronsson, G. Contingent workers and health and safety. *Work Employ. Soc.* 15: 439–460, 1999.
59. Johnstone, R., Mayhew, C., and Quinlan, M. Outsourcing risk? The regulation of OHS where contractors are employed. *Comp. Labor Law Policy J.* 22: 351–393, 2001.
60. Walters, D. *Health and Safety in Small Enterprises: European Strategies for Managing Improvement,* PIE-Peter Lang, Brussels, 2001.
61. Pennings, F., van Rijs, A., Jacobs, A., and de Vries, H. *Telework in the Netherlands: Labour law, social security and occupational health and safety aspects,* pp. 69–105. Hugo Sinzheimer Institute, Amsterdam, 1996.
62. Synthesis Report. *Temporary Work, Accident Prevention and Security: Social Dialogue and Training Techniques.* Italian Ministry of Labour and Social Insurance, Rome, 1997.
63. EFILWC. *The Social Implications of Telework.* European Foundation for the Improvement of Living and Working Conditions, Dublin, 1997.
64. WCB of BC. Determining Who is a Worker under the Workers' Compensation Act: A Briefing Paper. Report to Royal Commission on Workers' Compensation. Workers' Compensation Board of British Columbia, 1997.

65. European Agency for Safety and Health at Work. Research on Work and Health: Research on Changing World of Work. Unpublished working paper. Bilbao, 2002.
66. Johnstone, R. Paradigm crossed? The statutory occupational health and safety obligations of the business undertaking. *Aust. J. Labour Law* 12: 73–112, 1999.
67. Saksvik, P., and Quinlan, M. Regulating systematic occupational health and safety management: Comparing the Norwegian and Australian experience. *Relat. Indust.* 58: 81–107, 2003.
68. Quinlan, M., and Mayhew, C. Precarious employment, work re-organisation and the fracturing of OHS management. In *Systematic Occupational Health and Safety Management: Perspectives on an International Development,* edited by K. Frick, Jensen, P., Quinlan, M., and Wilthagen, T., pp. 175–198. Pergamon, Oxford, 2000.
69. Rondeau Du Noyer, C., and Lasfargues, G. Aptitude du travail des salaries en situation precaire. *Arch. Mal. Prof.* 52: 105–106, 1990.
70. Bhatia, R., and Katz, M. Estimates of the health benefits of a local living wage ordninance. *Am. J. Public Health* 91: 1398–1402, 2001.

CHAPTER 5

Long-Latency Disease:
The Long-Lasting Epidemics

James Leigh

INTRODUCTION

Occupational diseases that affect large populations of workers usually result from widespread and intensive occupational exposure. If such widespread diseases are followed by decreasing levels of disease when exposures are controlled or eliminated, they can be described as *epidemics*. Although the term epidemic was first used in relation to acute infectious diseases caused by microbiological agents, it is now used more generally for a wider variety of diseases (both acute and chronic) following occupational and environmental exposure.

The discussions in this chapter concentrate on long-latency disease, although much of the discussion is also relevant to diseases of short latency. This chapter attempts to give a socio-historical analysis of the reasons for the continuation of epidemics of occupational diseases and indicate ways by which these can be controlled. Case studies of epidemics due to four occupational agents are provided: asbestos, silica, coal, and vinyl chloride.

BACKGROUND

Epidemics of diseases due to occupational exposures are not a thing of the past. While the effects of chemical and physical agents, including dusts, fumes, and vapors, have largely been brought under control in most of the developed world, control is not by any means complete, especially in informal sectors of the economy. In the developing world, the situation is still poorly controlled throughout, and many people are still being made ill and dying from diseases caused by occupational exposures exported from developed countries, under the process of globalization, as well as exposures from local hazards, still uncontrolled because of ignorance or economics. It is often the case that substances banned in developed countries are exported to developing countries.

75

Epidemiology

Epidemiology is the study of the distribution and determinants of disease. Again, originating in the study of epidemics of infectious disease, it is now the fundamental science of population health and the major method of studying human disease causation from any cause and over any time frame. Because it deals with human populations, epidemiological evidence is often given more weight than studies of disease causation based on animal or cellular level models, even though most studies cannot be based on totally controlled experimental designs and are thus always subject to criticism due to statistical uncertainty and uncontrolled biases. The main types of epidemiological study are cohort studies and case-referent (case-control) studies. In a cohort study, an identifiable group of workers exposed to a disease agent is followed over time and the evolution of disease compared in different exposure groups. Sufficient time is needed to assemble enough cases for appropriate statistical power. Larger numbers give more statistical power to such studies. Identifiable groups were easier to find in the past where continuous employment in one job for long periods was usual. In a case-referent study, diseased individuals are collected in an identified population and their exposure history compared with an appropriately selected referent group from the same population. A well-designed case-referent study will give as much information as the equivalent cohort study much more quickly and cheaply because the study is based on cases already assembled.

Latency

Occupational diseases often have a long latency period (years or decades) between the start of exposure and the detection of clinical disease. Occupational health in relation to both short- and long-latency diseases has historically been a story of attention being drawn to health hazards, efforts to deny or minimize their significance by employers and insurers, brave efforts by isolated medical or scientific investigators to defend their position (often in the face of pressure from their employers or conservative professional associations and funding bodies) followed by acceptance as a legally recognized "occupational disease" regulation, setting of ever tighter "safe" exposure levels, and sometimes ultimately pro-hibition. This trend can be traced from Thomas Arlidge (1822–1899) in the Staffordshire potteries, through Thomas Legge (1863–1932) on white lead, Alice Hamilton (1869–1970) on lead, silica, carbon disulphide, mercury, and other substances, Alice Stewart on ionizing radiation, Case on aromatic amines, Gough on coal dust, Lewinsohn, Doll, Mancuso, Selikoff, and others on asbestos, up to Henry Lai and George Carlo on non-ionizing radiation and Winder and Michaelis on aero toxic syndrome. Typically, a clinical cluster of cases is detected and analytical epidemiological studies initiated. These are then criticized and repeated and backed up by mechanistic animal and cellular level studies. Eventually meta-analyses of all studies are carried out and an agreed position finally achieved.

An unfortunate feature of occupational health research is its intrinsic political nature. Studies are often funded by those desirous of a particular conclusion, and as governments withdraw from the field, industry-sponsored research gains undue influence. Industry can also afford to sponsor further review of government- or worker-sponsored research and delay implementation of preventive measures by asserting continuing uncertainty.

Compensation for occupational disease in various countries is a function of the political and legal systems of the particular country. For example, one is much more likely to be compensated for coal workers' pneumoconiosis in the U.S. or Australia than in India, Brazil, or China. Until recently, a coal miner was much more likely to be compensated for emphysema in Australia than in Britain, and an asbestos-exposed worker who developed lung cancer was much more likely to receive compensation in Germany or Finland than in Australia. These differences can be attributed to a range of factors including differing perceived views of the scientific truth, the legal system and the relative power of employers relative to workers, and the social policy of the government of the day. Moreover, what is compensated in one area can change over time in response to changing local political and economic agendas (1).

IMPACT OF GLOBALIZATION

The world is moving to a system of production dominated by large trans-national companies, many of whom command capital resources exceeding those of many nations. In a sense, the role of the state in determining what happens in the lives of people is being increasingly usurped by the private sector. For example, a decision to locate a major facility in a developing country community will have much more effect on that community than any action by government. The difference is that the community may not be able to express any democratic control over the activities of the managers of the facility, who are responsible only to their shareholders. In some places, we are thus moving into an era of non-democratic private government which may be beneficial, or otherwise, in the sense of providing the greatest good to the greatest number. The effectiveness of modern communications is such that organizations can be run on a global basis from almost anywhere.

In this situation, the world is going to have to rely on the acceptance by industry that occupational health and safety is an integral part of industrial operations and not something to be dealt with by denial and minimization or liability insurance. Industry must be convinced that occupational health and safety can actually increase profits. Furthermore where trans-national industry operates in developing countries, the standards applicable to its workforce must be the same as those applying in the developed world.

Freedom of trade and globalization has two sides. Trade could benefit by exploitation of cheap labor, inadequate information, lack of "know how," poor occupational health and safety services, and inadequate control systems of the weaker trader. On the other hand, free trade agreements could catalyze or accelerate the process of occupational health and safety development in the weaker partners. Potential benefits might be economic growth and healthier workers, development of occupational health services, transfer of know how, training and education of occupational health and safety professionals, and the development of occupational health and safety legislation. What is crucial is that provision of a safe workplace is a priority above economics. In global harmonization of standards among trading partners designed not to discriminate and inhibit free trade, there must be a race to the top, not the bottom. That is, the highest standards should be the common standard, not the lowest.

Where industry and private government fail to do this, the state and international agencies must act. While the global tendency toward deregulation of industry is gathering momentum, there will always be a role for legislation, regulation, and enforcement by the state. Furthermore, the penalties for failures must be real penalties, including criminal sanctions with custodial sentences for individuals in management. Financial penalties in some countries are absurdly low and provide no deterrent whatsoever.

While trans-national companies may have high safety and health standards as a corporate philosophy, the application in developing countries with poor governmental regulation may not always be altruistic. In other words, while it would be desirable if we could rely on private governments in the form of corporations to do the right thing in their operations in developing countries (thus actually raising the standards of occupational safety and health at least in the formal sector, and possibly by dissemination and market forces in the less formal sectors), experience has given many examples of the opposite occurring. For example, trans-nationals have taken advantage of the slack occupational safety and health regulations in countries to spend less on provision of services, with dire consequences. The Bhopal and Seveso disasters and the ok Tedi river pollution tragedy are clear OHS examples which also impinge on environmental issues. The operations of trans-national asbestos companies in Brazil and other parts of South America are another good example.

Unions, too, must take a global outlook. A good example of this is the practice of Australian mining and waterside unions to enlist the support of their international organizations in legally preventing attempts by some Australian companies to import foreign non-union labor.

Four case studies are given below which detail evidence about disease recognition, attempts to obfuscate the evidence, and political-economic pressures bought to bear on scientists and OHS professionals.

CASE STUDIES

Asbestos

Industry, sections of the medical and occupational hygiene professions, and governments stand accused to varying degrees of a conscious attempt to delay, obfuscate, and minimize the recognition of the importance of the asbestos hazard (2, 3). This culpability can be clearly seen from the following chronology.

1900   The hazards of asbestos in causing lung disease were first recognized. The Annual Report of the British Chief Inspector of Factories refers to the "evil effects of asbestos dust" and recommends means of dust control.

1906   Auribault drew attention to an extraordinarily high incidence of death from lung disease in French asbestos textile workers and discusses dust control.

1907   Murray clearly described cases of asbestosis in relation to asbestos exposure.

1918   Hoffman of the U.S. Bureau of Labor Statistics recognized the health hazards of asbestos to the lung. U.S. and Canadian insurance companies would not insure asbestos workers.

1924   Cooke first used the term asbestosis in clearly describing the clinical features of the condition.

1927   Oliver referred to the need for respiratory protection when working in asbestos dust.

1930   Merewether and Price clearly showed the dose relationship between risk of asbestosis and asbestos dust exposure and recommended primary dust suppression as the main preventive strategy, with use of respirators as a second-line defense only.

1931   The U.K. Asbestos Industry Regulations (1931) were gazetted on December 31, 1931 under S79 of the Factory and Workshop Act 1901, as a result of the Merewether report.

1934   Johns-Manville lawyer V. Brown forced Anthony Lanza to alter an industry-sponsored study to say that asbestosis is milder than silicosis and give the company "a break" (*letter 21 Dec 1934, cited by Bayer, 1988*) (4).

1938   Quantified dust levels in asbestos work were first reported in NSW Australia in 1938. Five million particles per cubic foot (Owens counter) were tentatively regarded as a threshold value for asbestosis risk. This level appears to have been adopted from the U.S. threshold value determined by Dreessen and others in 1938.This level was also incorporated in the Victorian 1945 Harmful Gases, Fumes, Mists, Smokes and Dusts Regulations under the Health Act. The grave weakness of the Dreessen study was that most of the workers who had worked more than 20 years were not included. They left, as the authors admitted, because of asbestosis, thus severely biasing the study in the direction of underestimating the dose-related asbestosis risk.

Lung Cancer

1935   In 1935, the association of asbestos and lung cancer (bronchial carcinoma) was recognized in both the U.S. and U.K.

1936   Johns-Manville lawyer V. Brown wrote to Dr. L. Gardner, Director of the Saranac Laboratory carrying out animal research funded by Johns-Manville, about the relationship between asbestos and lung cancer (4):

> It is our understanding that the results obtained will be considered the property of those who are advancing the required funds, who will determine whether, to what extent and in what manner they shall be made public (*Letter 20 Nov 1936, cited by Bayer, 1988*).

1942–43 Hueper described the association between asbestosis and lung cancer and called for appropriate control of dust exposure. Hueper attacked industry for covering up occupational cancer (5).

Lung cancer associated with asbestosis was recognized as an occupational disease in Germany and Czechoslovakia.

1949–52 Merewether demonstrated clearly the excess lung cancer risk with asbestosis. This work was known in Australia as Merewether attended and contributed to the 3rd ILO International Conference on Pneumoconiosis, held in Sydney in 1950. The outcomes of this conference were reported in the *Medical Journal of Australia* in 1951.

1955   The issue of asbestos exposure as a cause of lung cancer was put beyond doubt by Doll in 1955. Doll found greater than 13 times the risk of lung cancer death in male asbestos workers who had worked for more than 20 years between 1922 and 1953. There was a dose relationship with duration of employment. Lung cancer deaths included endothelioma (mesothelioma) of the pleura. Three cases of lung cancer did not have asbestosis.

Turner and Newall tried to force the editor of the *British Journal of Industrial Medicine* not to publish the paper (3).

1955–57 The Asbestos Textile Institute blocked funding for studies on asbestos carcinogenicity for fear of bad publicity and putting the industry under suspicion.

The Quebec Asbestos Mining Association forced Dr. D. Braun to omit a finding of a clear excess of lung cancer deaths in asbestosis from a paper for publication. The paper gave negative findings on lung cancer in relation to asbestos exposure, which were subsequently discredited for lack of follow-up and invalid control groups (*Bayer The Health and Safety of Workers, 1988*) (4).

Knowledge of Asbestos and Mesothelioma and Fiber Type Differences

1933–55 Scattered cases of asbestos-related mesothelioma were described from the 1930s.

1957 It is probably reasonable to regard the first definitive association of mesothelioma with asbestos as dating from reports by Wagner and others in 1959–60. These workers reported 33 cases of mesothelioma collected between 1956–59, all but one with a probable crocidolite exposure. Many had exposure from living near mines rather than working in them. Wagner, in a later paper, stated that he had visited the U.K. in 1957 and discussed the association between crocidolite and mesothelioma with the occupational health authorities and the directors of the main British asbestos companies.

1962 In 1962, the 3rd edition of Hunter's *The Diseases of Occupations* referred to the remarkable association of mesothelioma with asbestos, citing the Wagner 1960 study. No fiber type distinctions were made.

The first case of mesothelioma in Australia was reported by Dr. J. McNulty (diagnosed in 1960, from Wittenoom).

1963 By 1963, Wagner had collected 120 mesothelioma cases. In one case there was exposure only to chrysotile, and in two cases no history of exposure was obtained. More than half the cases from the Cape asbestos area were environmentally exposed.

In 1963, the association of mesothelioma with non-occupational or industrial exposure was pointed out and the importance of exposures in a wide user group emphasized, including users of insulation material for pipes and boilers, builders and builders' laborers, and handymen.

1964   In 1964 an editorial in the *British Medical Journal* drew attention to the occurrence of mesothelioma at low exposures and did not distinguish between the hazards of different fiber types. It concluded that "all exposure to asbestos dust should be considered as hazardous, and supervision should be extended to insulation workers in ships, factories, and domestic buildings who may be intermittently but nevertheless heavily exposed to asbestos dust."

1964   In the U.S. warnings were placed on asbestos products by Johns Manville (1964), Eagle Picher (1964), Owens Corning (1964), Ruberoid, Fibreboard (1966); Pittsburgh Corning (1968); Keene (1969); Celotex (Philip Carey) (1971); Amatex, H K Porter, Raybestos Manhattan (1972).

1965   In 1965, Newhouse and Thompson described 83 mesothelioma cases. Of 76 with history available, 40 gave a history of occupational or domestic exposure. Among those with no occupational or domestic exposure, 30 percent lived within half a mile of an asbestos factory. This study drew attention to the risk of mesothelioma from environmental levels of exposure and exposure incurred in jobs not scheduled under the 1931 U.K. regulations. Carpenters cutting asbestos cement products were identified as a high-risk group.

1968   It was recognized that laggers in dockyard work were still getting asbestosis, indicating that the Dreessen standard (5 mppcf or 177 particles/cc) was not sufficiently rigorous.

    The British Occupational Hygiene Society recommended an exposure standard of 2 fibers/ml for chrysotile, amosite, and anthophyllite and 0.2 fibres/ml for crocidolite. These controls were intended to prevent asbestosis. The Society recognized that it was not possible to set a safe level for lung cancer or mesothelioma.

1969   In 1969, the 4th edition of Hunter's *The Diseases of Occupations* stated the following, in relation to the then Draft U.K. Asbestos Regulations of 1968:

> The new regulations apply to factories, some warehouses, ships under construction or in the course of repair. But the Factories Act cannot protect private users. We know that inhalation of dust from such activities as sawing or sanding material containing asbestos presents the hazard of malignant mesothelioma outside as well as inside industrial situations. It seems not unreasonable, therefore, to insist that

materials containing asbestos should be clearly marked to show this, so that adequate precautions can be taken by the users. For instance, amateur handymen sawing materials containing asbestos could easily wear a lightweight dust mask, and either work out of doors or in a well ventilated room. Meanwhile many doctors have asked whether the properties of asbestos are as unique as the salesmanship of the asbestos companies appears to indicate. There are many other mineral fibres such as glass wool, rock wool or slag wool, which have useful inherent fire-proofing properties but not the fibrogenic or carcinogenic effects on the lungs. Is it certain that the properties of asbestos justify the risks of asbestosis, carcinoma of the lung and mesothelioma which are entailed by its use?

This was repeated in the 5th edition of Hunter (1975) when the 1968 Regulations became law.

1970 Certainly, by 1970, the dangers of asbestos in causing mesothelioma were well known. The Australian National Health and Medical Research Council (NH&MRC) published the document Atmospheric Contaminants, Hygiene Standards for Contaminants of the Air of the Workplace, stipulating an occupational standard for asbestos of 4 fibers/ml for chrysotile and amosite asbestos (crocidolite exposure was assumed to be prevented completely).

A series of case-control epidemiological studies in several countries between 1965–75 confirmed the strong association. Positive animal studies were also obtained for all fiber types for a variety of exposure methods in this period. Results of cohort studies began to appear from the early 1980s. In some cohorts, 20 percent of the workforce will die of mesothelioma.

1974 In 1974, the first major report of the U.K. Mesothelioma Register (relating to cases diagnosed in 1967–68) described several cases of mesothelioma in insulation workers, building workers, dockers, workers handling asbestos cement products, and following hobby exposure incurred when sawing asbestos sheets and drew attention to the possibility of mesothelioma occurring at low dose. No fiber type distinctions were made.

1976 In 1976, an authoritative review by Becklake appeared in *American Review of Respiratory Diseases*. This review showed that plumbers, laggers, fitters, and carpenters using asbestos cement products should be regarded as groups at risk of mesothelioma and other asbestos-related diseases and that this had been recognized in the mid 1960s. The review also showed that mesothelioma could be caused by low-level exposures. The fiber gradient theory was referred to as a consensus view.

The Report of the British Parliamentary Commission in 1975 pointed to an attitude of complacency toward asbestos in medical and official circles. The soft attitude of the Factory Inspectorate toward management prior to the 1969 Regulations was pointed out strongly (6).

1970–86 Strict exposure controls introduced in many countries including Australia. Outright bans introduced in some countries. In 1982, the NH&MRC published its report on the Health Hazards of Asbestos, fully detailing the hazards of asbestos and procedures for dealing with it. The report commented on the impossibility of determining a safe threshold below which no adverse effect of asbestos existed and recommended as a result that exposure to all forms of asbestos be kept as low as reasonably practical. The report also commented that inability to determine a threshold did not prove that one did not exist (pp. 7–10). The report stated that mesothelioma incidence increased with increasing exposure (p. 7). Between 1977 and 1985, all Australian jurisdictions introduced stringent regulations for dealing with asbestos. In 1984 the Ontario Royal Commission report was published, giving a detailed evaluation of health hazards of asbestos. In 1985, the U.K. Health and Safety Commission published its Doll Peto report on the Effects on Health of Exposure to Asbestos. In 1988, The Australian National Occupational Health and Safety Commission published its Asbestos Code of Practice, covering in detail health hazards and procedures for dealing with asbestos in place. The Australian Mesothelioma Program was established in 1979 and has continued since, documenting the still-rising epidemic of mesothelioma in Australia (annual reports from 1989 to present). There have been numerous attempts to close it down by the asbestos mining and manufacturing industry, and friction continues between the scientific establishments of Western Australia and Eastern Australia, with the former siding with the victims of Wittenoom and the latter siding with the asbestos cement industry. There was a tendency to dismiss cases with very short exposures as "background cases" not due to asbestos. Hygienists cataloguing histories taken by nurses or trained interviewers reclassify slight histories as "no exposure" sometimes suggesting bias in interview.

1978 A weakly worded label was placed on asbestos cement products in Australia. It did not specifically warn of a cancer risk, and minimized actual risk of exposure.

1986   ILO Convention 172 on safety in the use of asbestos was adopted. To date, this has only been ratified by 22 countries. This action occurred 86 years after attention was first drawn to the hazardous nature of asbestos.

1986–   In the period 1959–82 all types of asbestos were generally thought
present to cause mesothelioma, with (from about 1965) a theory commonly held by the majority of crocidolite being the most potent, followed by amosite and then chrysotile. However, there was a fairly strong minority that felt that all types should be regarded as equally potent in causing mesothelioma, based on animal inhalation and implantation studies showing roughly equal effects per unit dose. This was reflected in the IARC Evaluation (Vol. 14, 1976).

1995   Mesothelioma cases associated with environmental exposure as children in the mining areas of Wittenoom, Australia, and the Cape and Transvaal in South Africa became apparent in significant numbers as mesothelioma incidence continued to increase throughout the world and it was recognized that for each mesothelioma case there were at least two asbestos-related lung cancers. The categories of exposure are increased, and more tradesmen are using asbestos products, such as carpenters, electricians, fitters, and plumbers, rather than miners and asbestos manufacturing workers. Cases with low exposures, including non-occupational exposures, become more frequent (7–9).

Massive litigation worldwide put many companies, including insurers, into bankruptcy and threatens ultimate reinsurers like Lloyds of London.

It is estimated that ultimately 5 to 10 million people will have died from asbestos-related diseases (10).

1999–   All new use of all forms of asbestos banned in the E.U., Australia, and
2003   many other countries. Canada appealed to the World Trade Organization against the French ban. The E.U. and U.S. supported France. Canada's appeal was rejected.

The means of control of asbestos-related diseases were known in principle in the 19th century and specifically in the 1930s, and have been slowly applied to the point where over 40 countries have now totally banned asbestos. Strict controls on any remaining use must be applied and specific plans for phased total closure of the industry worldwide put in place.

Chrysotile is now generally considered to be less potent in causing mesothelioma than crocidolite or amosite, but quantitative estimates of the relative dose-related risk of the fiber types vary widely. For all fiber types, there is a dose-response relationship between the risk of asbestosis, lung cancer, and mesothelioma. However, larger doses are required to produce asbestosis and lung cancer than are required to produce mesothelioma. There is substantial recent evidence that asbestosis is not a necessary prerequisite for attributing lung cancer to asbestos exposure. Asbestos and smoking have a multiplicative effect in causing lung cancer (11). Mesothelioma risk is not related to smoking.

For those already exposed and those who may yet be exposed, a systematic information program worldwide must be established. By providing adequate information there is motivation to avoid further exposure and to quit smoking. The right to know outweighs the concern of inducing unnecessary anxiety. A major challenge is to provide balanced and accurate information.

There is a need for better early diagnostic tools and chemo-preventive agents. Research into new therapies is also required.

Uniform standards of compensation for asbestos-related diseases are an urgent priority. Mesothelioma is now compensated for in many countries on the basis of minimal exposure, and lung cancer is being increasingly compensated for on the basis of exposure history without the necessity of fibrosis. Apportionment of liability according to the etiological fractions of asbestos, smoking, and other lung carcinogens at the individual level is a justifiable solution (12). On the other hand, if the compensation system for occupational diseases is integrated into the general social security system, a dichotomous concept is reasonable. A system in which compensation comes from different sources may cause problems. For a dichotomous system, occupational exposure sufficient to give a relative risk of 2, corresponding generally (but not always) to a probability of causation of 50 percent, the civil standard of proof in common-law countries, is a common cut off point (13).

Asbestos diseases remain an undeniable social responsibility. Although minimization of future exposures is the most important task, the health of past asbestos workers is a great social challenge. Hazardous asbestos exposure is not a past problem in the developed world and certainly will not be in those areas where asbestos use is still continued. New chrysotile use continues in some developing countries, and chrysotile is still mined in and exported from Russia, Brazil, Canada, and Zimbabwe. Mining for domestic use occurs in Russia, Brazil, China, and Kazakhstan. The main export markets are India, Sri Lanka, Indonesia, Thailand, Nigeria, Angola, Uruguay, and Equador. In the developing world, control of exposure is still very poor. In the developed world, demolition and removal work is not always done well, and there have been disturbing reports of high exposure even with respirator use. These workers will require thorough surveillance and education programs.

Silica

Exposure to silica is associated with the development of silicosis in workers. This has been recognized since the 16th century and characterized medically as "grinders' asthma" in the late 18th century. Many epidemiological studies have addressed the relationship between occupational exposure to crystalline silica and silicosis. In the early studies, up to 80 percent of the exposed workforce would be severely affected and probably die from the disease or its complications. Silicosis is usually chronic and takes years to develop, but sub-acute (months) and acute (weeks) forms also occur with heavy exposure.

Concern about this risk in the South African gold mines was sufficient for there to be a Commission on Miners Phthisis, which was reported in 1912, at a time when reduced dust concentrations were just beginning to lead to marked reductions in disease in these miners. Sadly, the need for better control did not become widely recognized, or if it was, short-term economics meant that effective action was not taken. In the first decades of the 20th century, crushed flint (almost pure silica) was introduced into the ceramics industry in the U.K. to support ceramics during the firing process. A high proportion of those who worked with the material died from silicosis. At about the same time in the U.S., the Hawk's Nest disaster was taking place in which several hundred workers working on a tunnel for a hydro-electric scheme died from acute silicosis (14).

Silica has also now been classified as a human carcinogen by IARC (Vol. 68, 1997). Both silica exposure and silicosis are associated with increased lung cancer risk. Animal studies show that silica can cause lung cancers.

In many developed countries, silicosis has been reduced greatly or even eliminated by use of well-known dust control methods and enforcement of exposure standards. For example, in Australia, new cases per year in an exposed workforce of 136,000 are about 40. In Finland, in an exposed workforce of 100,000, only 13 new cases per year are reported. In Singapore granite quarry workers (about 1,200 workers), silicosis incidence has been reduced from 178 cases per year in 1971–75 to 24 per year in 1991–95 following implementation of dust-control measures. In Japan the incidence has dropped from 8,100 cases per year in an exposed workforce of 270,000 workers to 3,780 cases per year between 1983 and 1993 following dust-control measures.

However, silicosis prevalence worldwide is estimated to be about 3 million, with 1 million in China. Prevalence overall is 10 percent of the silica exposed workforce, estimated at 30 million. In some enterprises, prevalence can be as high as 50 percent. Worldwide incidence of new cases per year is about 150,000. Thailand, Vietnam, and Indonesia have high incidence. Lung cancer deaths due to silica have been estimated at 4,500 per year worldwide.

There now exist quantitative dose-response models for silicosis risk as a function of cumulative exposure to respirable silica. Three major epidemiological studies from South Africa, Canada, and the U.S. are available. By using these models with measured exposure and workforce age distributions, it is possible to provide quantitative estimates of absolute numbers of cases to be expected at given exposure levels. For example, the average lifetime risk of silicosis at 0.1 mg/m^3 is 12 percent, at 0.05 mg/m^3 1.4 percent. A further model exists for silica-related lung cancer, taking smoking into account. The average lifetime risk of silica-induced lung cancer is 0.83 percent at 0.1 mg/m^3 and 0.47 percent at 0.05mg/m^3 assuming an average smoking amount (15).

However, the response of Australian regulators to the risk of cancer from silica exposure has been very slow and well illustrates the political process of dealing with a long-latency disease. The National Occupational Health and Safety Commission (NOHSC) appointed a working party to review the evidence and make recommendations on a standard change in 1988. This group comprised employer, employee, government, and neutral experts. No agreement has been reached as of 2003. Delays due to changes in government, abolition of the research function of NOHSC, changes in personnel, delays due to reviews of reviews and peer reviews of consultants' reports on other reviews, coupled with continuing availability of new evidence has made the process very difficult.

Coal-Related Exposures

Much of the knowledge on coal and lung disease has emanated from research done in New South Wales, Australia. Coal workers' pneumoconiosis, bronchitis, and emphysema were recognized quite early in Australia, relative to other countries, but not without many difficulties.

Until the passing of the Workers' Compensation Act and related legislation in 1926, there was no provision for the compensation of workers disabled as a result of the effects of dust inhaled at their work in NSW coal mines. The 1926 Act provided for compulsory regulated insurance and compensation for industrial disease, and lump sums were awarded for permanent loss of body parts. A Workers Compensation Commission administered the scheme and resolved disputes. Mining diseases such as silicosis were covered by special Acts.

There was difficulty in claiming compensation for coal-dust exposure until 1942 as silica dust was thought to be the only harmful dust and was covered by a separate Act. Coal miners had difficulty proving that their disability was due to coal dust and not silica dust. In spite of the work of Charles Badham, who had maintained since 1927 that coal workers' lung disease was different than silicosis, medical experts for mine owners' insurance gave evidence that silica was the only possible cause of lung disease in coal workers because it was the only constituent of lung dust soluble in body fluids.

A series of legal challenges in this period culminated in Pye v. Metropolitan (WCR 1936:47), which reached the Privy Council and established that the onus of proof was on employers to show that lung disease was undeniably due to silica rather than to simply suggest that, because it was not due to coal dust, it must be due to silica.

A 1942 amendment corrected the legislation as a result of this decision by allowing workers covered by the Coal Mines Regulation Act to claim for coal-dust exposure.

About the year 1929, the Workers' Compensation Commission commenced referring claims for compensation for pulmonary disease in coal miners to a special Pneumoconiosis Medical Board whose certificates assisted in the settlement of claims.

In 1948, it was agreed that a special "dust" Medical Board would certify miners' condition and fitness for employment and whether, if the miner was suffering from pneumoconiosis, disease was due to the inhalation of dust in coal mines. If there were other conditions involving incapacity for work, the Medical Board was to express an opinion as to whether and to what extent these conditions were due to the mineworker's employment.

The agreement also specified that one of the two medical referees constituting the Special Medical Board be either the Chief Medical Officer of the Joint Coal Board or his deputy. The Joint Coal Board, created in 1946, operated until 2002 and had very wide powers over the coal industry until about the mid 1980s. It operated a comprehensive occupational health program, with periodic detailed monitoring of coal workers for occupational diseases.

Over the following 10 years, dissatisfaction with Special Medical Board decisions again emerged occasionally, although by then it mainly appears to have been from Joint Coal Board Medical Officers—although it is imagined that this must have been mitigated by knowledge of the constitution of the Special Medical Boards.

A more obvious form of friction arose as Coal Mines Insurance Pty, Limited increasingly relied on a specialist medical examination conducted prior to the Special Medical Board. Although the company hotly and repeatedly denied it, the Miners Federation believed that this report could be improperly used to influence the Medical Board.

Over time other disputes arose over whether other medical information becoming available should be withheld from the Medical Board. Cases of more complexity were coming forward. This probably means that intercurrent cardiac and respiratory pathology were becoming proportionately more common in claims. In any case, it gradually seems to have become accepted that the Medical Board was entitled to all relevant medical information. In later years, legislative amendments confirmed this by allowing a Medical Board (by then known as a Medical Panel) to make its own call for information.

The later 1960s and 1970s were marked by medical discussions on whether and to what extent respiratory conditions other than pneumoconiosis could be work-related and on the cause of work-related incapacity. Nevertheless, industrially, this period was associated with a lower degree of dissatisfaction from mineworkers with Medical Board decisions.

In particular, recognition of chronic bronchitis and emphysema as occupational conditions in coal workers was a slow process. In NSW, studies from the 1930s recognized the relationship of emphysema to coal dust, and this work was carried out in the Joint Coal Board's medical and pathology program, which became a world leader in this field. Some key papers were published in the 1980s and 1990s establishing a sound epidemiological basis for causation of bronchitis and emphysema in relation to coal dust (16). Possibly the culmination of this saga was the 1998 U.K. High Court decision of Mr. Justice Turner in *Griffiths and Others v. British Coal Corporation*, where British Coal was found negligent in failing to take reasonable steps to control dust causing chronic bronchitis and emphysema in coal workers. Key evidence consisted of Australian published research, and Justice Turner was trenchant in criticizing the failure of British Coal expert witnesses to support their assertions on a solid evidence base and in making ex-cathedra pronouncements (17).

Vinyl Chloride

When workers exposed to vinyl chloride monomer (VCM) (polymerized to make the widely used plastic PVC) were found to develop a rare and fatal liver cancer, action was immediately taken to reduce the risk. Experience with the risks of vinyl chloride and their control shaped subsequent national and international policies on the control of other chemicals.

1. Prior to the discovery of the link to cancer, VCM was known to be an anesthetic and to present a fire hazard. In 1966, finger abnormalities (Raynaud's phenomenon and acro-osteolysis) were seen in workers cleaning polymerization vessels.
2. Animal studies mounted to investigate this condition found an incidental increase in cancers. Producers then funded further animal studies to investigate carcinogenicity, which were reported in 1974, and these showed an excess of angiosarcoma of the liver.
3. Within a few days of these results being known, cases of angiosarcoma in exposed workers were identified in the company records of a large PVC producer.
4. Employers, trade unions, and government immediately recognized the importance of these findings. Employees producing a key product with many important applications were at serious risk. They worked in large,

high-profile companies with integrated production, where cessation of PVC manufacture would have widespread economic effects.

5. National preventive strategies were developed, and there was extensive international collaboration. Producers were readily committed to these because there were only a small number of plants in each country, and they were worried about both the risk and its effects on the industry. It was possible to meet control costs within the capital intensive chemical industry. Elements included exposure reduction by engineering control, ventilation and work practice changes, continuous monitoring of levels of exposure on plants, and health surveillance of those exposed; all were supported by epidemiological, toxicological, and technical studies on the risks and their control.

6. Subsequently, the structure of the industry changed as old plants with high exposures or producing PVC with high residual monomer levels were phased out and new ones built with tight control and automated cleaning methods.

7. The effects of this are now being seen in a reduction in the number of new cases of angiosarcoma and their restriction to those who worked in the industry before stringent controls were adopted.

8. Many lessons were learned from the study of vinyl chloride:
   • It showed that animal studies could predict human occupational cancer risk, and this thus led to extensive studies of other industrial chemicals.
   • It showed that control measures could be rapidly agreed upon and introduced with involvement of government and both sides of industry.
   • It also greatly refined scientific thinking about studies of occupational disease, technical control measures, and surveillance of those at risk.

PROBLEMS IN THE FUTURE

In the developed and developing world, new structures of business enterprises and the new patterns of employment, such as the growing informal sector, home work, mobile work, downsizing, and restructuring, make systematic monitoring of workers' health and relation of exposures to outcomes more difficult (see discussions in Chapter 4). Epidemiological studies will more often be carried out with smaller and more scattered groups with higher turnover rates. Such mobile groups may be exposed to similar or different types of hazards in their consecutive jobs, which have taken place in varying environments, including periods of no exposure due to long-term unemployment. This will result in a shortening of exposure times, and mixing of exposures from different environments. This could lead to dilution or aggravation of effects and has the effect of making epidemiological follow-up of both exposure and outcome more difficult. Systems of personal cumulative occupational history monitoring of workers as they move between jobs have been proposed by some countries (e.g., Finland) but have met with considerable resistance in other countries (e.g., radiation workers in Australia). This is largely because of concern for subsequent legal liability. There will be fewer and fewer opportunities to detect cause and effect relationships by studying large groups of workers continuously exposed over long periods. New technologies, such as biotechnology, new chemicals, and information and communications systems may also cause previously unknown and unpredictable health and safety outcomes.

A vital role for disease surveillance systems will be sentinel-event monitoring to detect new adverse outcomes. Changes in economic structures and new developments in production systems have significantly changed the types of occupations in the last two decades of the 20th century and the early years of the 21st century. In developed nations, the number of white-collar and expert occupations has increased while the number in manual occupations, particularly agriculture, forestry, and manufacturing, has decreased. This has radically altered the distribution of exposures for many employees. Office-type jobs have exposures orders of magnitude less than those found in manufacturing environments. Development of psychosocial and psychological work-related conditions will have a much wider inter-subject variability and a much larger subjective component than classical conditions caused by frank injury or toxic exposure.

In developing countries, likely problems are combinations of exposures to well-established infectious and parasitic agents, climatic conditions, and chemical hazards new to the developing country. A worrying trend in recent years is the transfer of exposure to hazardous substances that are well regulated and controlled in established market economies to developing countries. Asbestos, some pesticides, and cigarettes are good examples. However, there are many difficulties in detecting adverse outcomes and cause-effect relationships in developing countries. Some of these are lack of exposure data, lack of confounder information, insufficient latency, difficulties in follow-up, fluctuating workforces, lack of industry cooperation, and lack of independent research funds.

While the average exposure levels have decreased with time in the developed world, the relative exposures between the developed and developing world have increased, and many more workers are exposed in the developing world. Thus, we will almost certainly see a repeat of the developed-world occupational epidemics of disease related to, for example, asbestos, silica, other carcinogens, sensitizers, and noise.

Exposures and outcomes in the informal sector are very difficult to monitor due to lack of personnel records and any systematically collected occupational safety and health data, but it is these very workplaces which are likely to have the worst outcomes. Even in the formal sector, recent personal data protection legislation has the potential to make it very difficult if not impossible to carry out longitudinal epidemiological studies or even case-referent studies. While protection against abuse of personal data by state and commercial database managers is a perfectly justifiable social good, it must be balanced against the likelihood of less satisfactory detection of occupationally-related conditions and the associated harm.

There will be a need to maintain good registers of morbidity and mortality of occupational disease. The recent WHO study on estimating the global burden of occupational disease found that only about 20 percent of nations had adequate systematic reporting systems on outcomes and only very few on exposures (18). Exposure registers are more useful for known outcomes than for new outcomes, although they may also play a role here.

A general finding is a severe under-reporting of disease in many nations. There is a need for systematic sample surveying to compare registered cases and compensated cases with real incidence. Very large biases can occur in registrations and compensation due to policy decisions on compensation, reluctance to recognize conditions as work-related for economic reasons, and difficulties of detection in certain regions. This is not restricted to developing countries and can be quite marked in developed countries.

Preventive Strategies

In principle, hazard surveillance represents one of the most effective means of preventing occupational injury and disease. For diseases of long latency, this approach offers an effective means of preventing the future burden of disease from what are known hazardous exposures to substances such as carcinogens. Because the surveillance of hazards does not rely on detecting patterns of excess disease or death, it is—at least in theory—a particularly promising technique for identifying targets for intervention before the disease process has begun.

Ideally, a hazard surveillance program should be able to identify what hazardous exposures are present in a workplace, establish whether effective control measures are in place, identify which and how many workers are affected, and assess the potential health effects of the exposure(s).

CONCLUSION: LESSONS FROM THE PAST INFORMING FUTURE PROGRESS

Morbidity patterns and the nature of health outcomes from occupational factors have become much more complicated than they were 100 years ago, when specific conditions related to specific exposures were dominant. For example, the effects of lead, mercury, phosphorus, aromatic amines, silica, coal, and asbestos produced only a few characteristic health outcomes. We can now have one disease with multiple exposures, or multiple diseases with multiple exposures. For example, coronary artery disease has been claimed to have 250 different risk factors, some of which are work-related or are work-related modifiers of other non-work risk factors and some of which are proxies for each other. There is also a larger than recognized occupational component in many other common diseases, such as arthritis, asthma, infectious disease, and lung cancer.

Furthermore, exposure-response relationships now need to be based on more subtle measures of both exposure and outcome. In the early days of occupational medicine and epidemiology, large numbers of heavily exposed workers with florid clinical symptoms of obvious disease were available for study. Fortunately, advances in prevention and control practice have (sometimes too slowly, as shown above) resulted in disappearance of occupational disease of this type. The occupational health problems of the 21st century will require more sensitive and powerful techniques for their detection. Further, it will no longer be acceptable to wait until obvious disease is present in large numbers before recognition and action take place, as was the case with coal, silica, and, especially, asbestos. The case study of vinyl chloride provided above shows that it is possible to act quickly.

Adverse health effects will have to be recognized on the basis of biological markers of preclinical disease or even by analogy with animal or tissue studies. Indeed, regulatory action should not require the existence of definitive human epidemiological studies. The lessons of ionizing radiation, silica, coal, and particularly asbestos in the 20th century have taught us that so-called safe exposure levels, particularly when promulgated by parties with vested economic interests, can be terribly wrong and can result in literally millions of excess deaths. Regulatory action should always give the benefit of the doubt to the worker, and industry must be prepared to plan its activity to absorb this. By creating global standards, economic incentives to operate at more than the acceptable risk level will be removed. No longer will an asbestos company executive be able to state that (in relation to the proposed 5 fiber/ml standard in 1972) "Achieving a standard of 5 will cost millions of dollars and cause a significant number of American jobs to be shifted to foreign workers to whom in many cases no standards apply" (U.S. OSHA Hearings, 14–17 March 1972, p. 225). The acceptable risk itself needs to be much lower than the 1 in 1,000 lifetime risk tolerated in the 20th century, and some authorities now insist on a 1 in 100,000 or even 1 in 1,000,000 lifetime risk. Regulators cannot delay controlling harmful exposures until scientific consensus exists. Decision-making under conditions of uncertainty will be inevitable. Such conditions will require considerations of fairness and concern about who will suffer and who will benefit. Because standards of distributive justice are involved, there will inevitably be political features in standard setting to control risk of occupational disease.

A continuing theme will be the problem of allocating the burden of uncertainty and the role of science in resolving such controversies. This theme is not just methodological but is in fact a conflict over public philosophy, a conflict of prudence and social equity.

Scientists are taught not to make claims that overreach their evidence; except when generating new theories, scientists assert conservatism as a principal value in science, and those who too readily extrapolate their findings to widely varying circumstances risk being accused of exaggerating and of exceeding their scientific authority. Critics making such charges may simply be defending what they view as an important scientific value. However, at the same time such critics may knowingly or unwittingly be serving the interests of those who prefer to deny the existence of a relation between a social enterprise, such as the asbestos or hard-rock mining industry, and some profound social cost, such as occupational cancer. When public policy is at stake, the question of relevant scientific certainty becomes more than an academic debate, and the allocation of the burden of uncertainty will become a crucial social question.

REFERENCES

1. Leigh, J. Occupational disease and injury: Legal constructs [Editorial]. *J. Occup. Health Saf. (ANZ)* 18: 395–397, 2002.
2. Lilienfeld, D. The silence: The asbestos industry and early occupational cancer research—A case study. *Am. J. Public Health* 81: 791–800, 1991.
3. Tweedale, G. *Magic Mineral to Killer Dust. Turner and Newall and The Asbestos Hazard.* OUP, Oxford, 2000.
4. Bayer, R. (ed.). *The Health and Safety of Workers.* OUP, Oxford, 1988.
5. Lemen, R. Challenge for the 21st century: How to prevent the global asbestos epidemic from expanding. *People and Work. Research Report 19*, pp. 21–32. FIOH, Helsinki, 1998.
6. Atherley, G. *Occupational Health and Safety Concepts. Chemical and Processing Hazards.* Applied Science Publishers, London, 1978.
7. Leigh, J., and Robinson, B. The History of Mesothelioma in Australia 1945–2000. In *Mesothelioma,* edited by B. W. S. Robinson and P. Chahinian, pp. 55–86. Martin Dunitz (Taylor and Francis), London, 2002.
8. Leigh, J., Davidson, P., Hendrie, L., and Berry, D. Malignant mesothelioma in Australia, 1945–2000. *Am. J. Ind. Med.* 41: 188–201, 2002.
9. Leigh, J., and Driscoll, T. Malignant mesothelioma in Australia 1945–2002. *Int. J. Occup. Environ. Health* 9: 206–217, 2003.
10. Rantanen, J., and Henderson, D. Criteria for diagnosis and attribution of asbestos diseases. *People and Work. Research Report 19*, pp. 12–18. Helsinki, FIOH, 1998.
11. Henderson, D., de Klerk, N., Hammar, S., Hillerdal, G., Huuskonen, M., Leigh, J., Pott, F., Roggli, V., Shilkin, K., and Tossavainen, A. Asbestos and lung cancer: Is it attributable to asbestosis or to asbestos fibre burden? In *Pathology of Lung Tumors,* edited by B. Corrin, pp. 83–118. Churchill Livingston, London, 1997.
12. Leigh, J., Berry, G., de Klerk, N., and Henderson, D. Asbestos-related lung cancer. Apportionment of causation and damages to asbestos and tobacco smoke. In *Sourcebook on Asbestos Diseases,* Vol. 13, edited by G. A. Peters and B. J. Peters, pp. 141–166. Michie, Charlottesville, 1996.
13. Henderson, D., Jones, M., de Klerk, N., Leigh, J., Musk, A., Shilkin, K., and Williams, V. The diagnosis and attribution of asbestos-related diseases in an Australian

context: Report of the Adelaide Workshop on Asbestos-Related Diseases, October 6–7, 2000. *Int. J. Occup. Environ. Health,* 10: 40–46, 2004.

14. Cherniak, M. *The Hawk's Nest Incident: America's Worst Industrial Disaster.* Yale University Press, New Haven, CT, 1986.

15. Leigh, J., Macaskill, P., and Nurminen, M. Revised quantitative risk assessment for silicosis and silica related lung cancer in Australia. *Ann. Occup. Hyg.* 41(Supp 1): 480–484, 1997.

16. Leigh, J., Driscoll, T., Beck, R., Cole, B., Hull, B., and Yang. J. Quantitative relationship between emphysema and lung mineral content in coal workers. *Occup. Environ. Med.* 51: 400–407, 1994.

17. Niall, P., and Wiles, N. Special medical boards for the NSW coal industry. *J. Occup. Health Saf. (ANZ)* 18: 431–435, 2002.

18. Leigh, J., Macaskill, P., Kuosma, E., and Mandryk, J. Global burden of disease and injury due to occupational factors. *Epidemiology* 10: 626–631, 1999.

CHAPTER 6

Work-Related Injuries among Adolescent and Child Workers: The Non-Reported OHS Epidemic

Claire Mayhew

Adolescent labor is common across both developing and industrialized countries, with at least 60 percent working on a full-time, part-time, or casual basis. In contrast, *child* labor appears to be widespread only in developing countries, although small pockets remain in industrialized countries. These young workers are frequently reported to be at increased risk of work-related injury, illness, and death.

This chapter focuses on the occupational health and safety (OHS) risks associated with the employment of adolescents and children in industrialized countries. While evidence about their work-related injuries and illnesses—and fatalities—is fragmentary, there are clear indications of a significant level of negative OHS outcomes. It is argued that those young people working outside of the formal system are at high risk, particularly those in family businesses, on farms, and sometimes completing illegal and/or dangerous tasks. The Australian fast-food industry, garment manufacture, and "market garden" farming are used as case studies. The author concludes by arguing that the work-related injuries and illnesses experienced by working adolescents in industrialized countries are extensive, but these data are not fully reflected in the official databases. Thus, this epidemic remains largely non-reported and hidden.

INTRODUCTION/BACKGROUND

There are varying definitions about what constitutes "child" labor. The International Labour Organisation (ILO) and the World Health Organization (WHO) concur that child labor is work performed before the age of 15.

The international data on child and adolescent labor are quite inadequate. As a result, in January 2003 the first meeting of the ILO "Statistical Information and

97

Monitoring Programme on Child Labour" (SIMPOC) was scheduled to improve quantitative and qualitative data about child labor across the world. A decade ago, worldwide estimates of working *children* under the age of 14 ranged from 55 to 200 million children (1, 2). More extensive data are now available, with an estimated one child in eight in the world performing work that could cause physical or mental damage, and a series of national reports have now been produced, including for Portugal, South Africa, and Cambodia (3). In 2003, it was estimated that there were around 186 million child laborers below age 15 in the world, with about two-thirds living in Asia, where about one child in five aged 5 to 14 was reported to be in the labor force (4). Further, the ILO estimated that 246 million children were involved in "unacceptable" forms of child labor (3). Of these, 8.4 million were trapped in slavery, prostitution and pornography, trafficking, or forced participation in armed conflict, with a further 179 million working in hazardous jobs such as construction, fishing, and mining (3, 4). That is, not only is child labor increasing over time, a significant proportion are involved in very high-risk jobs. Unfortunately, however, high fatality ratios among child workers are most likely to be found in countries where under-reporting of work-related deaths is most likely to occur (1).

A core problem in a globalized economy is the enhanced capacity for the international migration of hazards and risks. Thus, more hazardous industry or production tasks can be exported from countries where there is stronger regulatory protection to those nation states with lax labor laws. Hence, arguably, child workers in southeast and southern Asia are now more at risk of exposure to asbestos during manufacturing processes or demolition tasks that have been banned in industrialized countries. Similarly, child sex tourism may be a "growth" industry as industrialized countries have tightened loopholes.

Recent Initiatives from the ILO

The International Labour Office (ILO) has produced a series of publications that are designed to reduce the risks associated with child labor, including *Combating Child Labour: A Handbook for Labour Inspectors* (2002); *Children at Work: Health and Safety Risks* (2002); *Action Against Child Labour* (2000); and *In the Twilight Zone: Child Workers in the Hotel, Tourism and Catering Industry* (1995). Included within the recent ILO strategy to protect child workers was enhanced efforts to encourage signature of ILO International Conventions and Recom- mendations, especially ratification of the seven core Conventions: numbers 29, 87, 98, 100, 105, 111, and particularly 138 (the Minimum Age Convention, 1973).

In 1999, the ILO introduced the Convention on the *Worst Forms of Child Labour* (no. 182), which focused on elimination of the employment of children in:

• Forms of slavery, including sale, trafficking, debt bondage, or serfdom;
• The procurement or use of children for pornography or prostitution;

- Employment of children in hazardous jobs such as construction, deep sea fishing, diving, or forced recruitment into the armed forces;
- The procuring or use of children in illicit activities (e.g., production and trafficking of drugs); and
- Tasks that by their nature could harm the health, safety, or morals of children.

Convention 182 has been rapidly ratified by many countries, all of which are subsequently required to take immediate and effective action to prohibit and eliminate involvement of children in these activities. The ILO has also produced guidance material to assist countries in this process (see, for example, *Eliminating Hazardous Child Labour Step by Step*). As of June 2003, 132 countries had ratified Convention 182, which makes this the fastest-ratified Convention in the ILO's 82-year history. One interpretation of the rapid acceptance of Convention 182 is that populations across developing and industrialized countries deeply resent abusive child labor. However, to the embarrassment of the editors of this book, Australia—along with some other leading industrialized economies—has failed to ratify this Convention (although Australia was a donor country in 2002) (4).

Determinants of Child and Adolescent Labor

There is widespread agreement that poverty is the major determinant of child and adolescent labor, with many families dependent on either the additional income or unpaid domestic work from children that frees parents to earn a living (5). Yet there are a number of long-term negative economic consequences on families. For example, income from child labor can be an incentive for increased fertility, the *cheapness* may be a powerful disincentive for technological innovations, younger children may have significantly reduced investment in their human capital (and hence restrict future earnings), downward pressure may be exerted on adult wages where tasks are substitutable, and female children may be required to complete extensive domestic chores (1, 5). This situation is unlikely to improve in countries with a declining number of full-time jobs, an increase in part-time, casual, temporary, and outsourced work, or where growth occurs in sectors which are relatively union-free, such as textiles and footwear (6).

The convergence of economic and social stresses which produced the increase in child labor at the time of the Industrial Revolution in the western world have had a similar consequence in developing countries over past decades: weak economies, unstable world conditions, widespread poverty, limited social supports, high unemployment, inadequate educational opportunities, and relaxed enforcement of child labor laws (2).

In *developing countries,* children have been reported to be employed as underground tin miners in South America, as rug weavers in the Middle East, in the fishing industry in Indonesia, in the Cambodian sex industry, and in the manufacture of fireworks, glass blowing, textile weaving, and agricultural activities across a number of nations (1, 2, 7–9). Their working conditions can be so abject that authors debate whether their conditions of servitude constitute a modern version of slavery (10). There can be significant gender-based differences in the industry sectors where boys and girls work. If substantial domestic labor is included, around three-quarters of all Mexican girls and boys aged 12 to 14 participated in home-based or paid work (5). Nevertheless, the official data can significantly under-state the extent, and indeed be quite misleading. For example, in the Indian census of 1991, more than a third of boys and 50 percent of girls aged 5 to 14 did not attend school but were not identified as child workers (5). There are also marked differences between the work experiences of children in developing and industrialized countries.

In *industrialized* nations, the widespread use of *child* labor has disappeared, although small pockets remain, such as on family farms. Historically, child labor was endemic during the Industrial Revolution and was associated with long hours of work, heavy labor, limited remuneration, abuse, dangerous tasks, and the mutilation and death of many (11–13). Over the 20th century (and first few years of the 21st), child labor is resurgent in many industrialized countries, particularly in small "pockets of poverty" (14). For example, in Denmark approximately 50 percent of those aged 13 to 17 have part-time jobs, typically involving newspaper delivery, distribution of advertising circulars, and retail, catering, and casual cleaning jobs (15). Similarly, babysitting is almost universally accepted as a casual adolescent job. The resurgence of child and adolescent labor in the United States over the past two decades has been associated with four pressures: many "working poor," increased poverty, a growing pool of illegal immigrants, and relaxed enforcement of child labor laws (16).

ADOLESCENT LABOR IN
INDUSTRIALIZED ECONOMIES

The *legal* employment of *adolescents* in industrialized countries is widespread, and is usually held to be a "good" thing—especially if the teenager is not studying full-time. Work experience may strengthen the "work ethic," provide additional income to allow education to continue beyond compulsory school years, enhance future employment options, give experience in the "real" world, enhance self-discipline, develop new skills, and provide direct economic benefits (17). In some cases, part-time employment provides the sole basis for the food and shelter needs of adolescents without family or social supports. Part-time employment of adolescent children has been almost universally praised by *parents* who rarely question their children's desire for employment in fast-food or delivery jobs, with many believing that the work experience is beneficial in providing income, teaching children money management skills, and instilling a greater sense of responsibility.

Negative consequences may include reduced time for homework and extra-curricular activities, interruption of the adolescent "moratorium" period when cognitive development activities normally occur, fatigue or exhaustion, and excessive student competition for jobs, which may restrict the work opportunities of non-student job seekers (14).

Adolescent workers in industrialized countries are most commonly employed in *precarious* jobs. Precarious labor includes work that is casual, part-time, on a short-term contract, offered by small-scale owner/operators, subcontracted, or provided on a day-hire basis through an agency (18). Casual precarious workers typically have no holiday leave, sick leave, severance pay entitlements, and only limited protection against summary dismissal. People generally accept precarious employment because they have few alternatives—such as young workers with few skills and little bargaining power.

In *Australia,* the labor market position of adolescents has changed markedly over the past two decades due to: (a) a dramatic increase in youth unemployment; (b) plummeting full-time job opportunities; (c) a rapid increase in conjoint part-time work and full-time study; and (d) a sharp increase in educational retention ratios. As a result, around 60 percent of 15 to 19 year olds hold casual jobs, compared with 29.8 percent in 1984 (19, 20). The casualized youth labor force has been increased by backpacker tourists holding working visas, as well as those with only visitor status working illegally while traveling around Australia. For example, in 1994, 217,000 international backpackers visited Australia, with many working in fruit-picking, tourism, or hospitality work (21).

The *United States* has the largest proportion of adolescent and child labor among affluent countries, with around four million children and adolescents *legally* employed (14, 22). Of these, around 2.1 million were aged 16 to 17, and over 1 million aged 14 to 15 (23). An estimate by the U.S. General Accounting Office was that *at least* 11 percent of 15 year olds worked in prohibited jobs, with a report from the *National Safe Workplace Institute* estimating 676,000 of 12 to 17 year olds worked in the largely unregulated "underground" economy (24). Similarly, Dunn and Runyan found that ". . . 86% of workers younger than 18 years were involved in activities that appeared to violate the Fair Labor Standards Act of 1938" (25). More recently, it has been estimated that around 301,000 minors are illegally employed each year in the U.S. (26).

Adolescent labor in the U.S. is characteristically part-time and seasonal, with working hours increasing substantially during summer and decreasing during school terms (14, 21, 27). A rule of thumb is that 16 to 17 year olds work half time for half of the year; thus full-time equivalents are approximately one-fourth of the actual number employed (28). There is an increased propensity to work with age: in addition to the normal 32.5 hours of school each week, the average 15 year old in the U.S. worked 17 hours per week, and 16 to 17 year olds normally worked 21 hours per week (16, 26). These adolescent workers were concentrated in particular industries: garment, agriculture, service, retail, and manufacturing (16).

The regulatory framework protecting adolescent U.S. workers has been described in detail elsewhere, and will not be re-visited here (29). It is, however, important to review some significant changes in the employment patterns of adolescents over the past two decades:

- More teenagers are working and they are working longer hours;
- Students who work long hours often achieve lower grades than their non-working peers;
- Many work in fast-food industries where productivity demands may be extremely high during peak hours;
- Many adolescents work late in the evening in fast-food, video stores, and other service outlets;
- Service businesses may be open from 5 am till late evening—in contrast to employment patterns in the 1970s when adolescents typically worked on weekends or late afternoon when stores had more limited opening hours; and
- White children are more likely to be exposed to hazards and risks in fast-food because these jobs are concentrated in middle-class neighborhoods (30).

Parents are usually unaware of these important differences between their own work experiences and those of their children, including variations in the hazards and risks adolescent workers are exposed to (28).

OCCUPATIONAL HEALTH AND SAFETY AMONG ADOLESCENT WORKERS IN INDUSTRIALIZED COUNTRIES

The OHS consequences from work vary from one job to another and from country to country. The risks are essentially dependent on the industry sub-sector of employment and extent of enforcement of minimal OHS protections (31). In industrialized countries, the formal employment of adolescent workers is generally covered by the OHS legislation that applies to all workers. Yet, the available evidence indicates that adolescent workers have poorer OHS indices.

Fatalities among Working Adolescents in
Industrialized Countries

There have been few substantive studies of adolescent fatalities at work. The U.S. has a comparatively high occupational fatality rate for both the under 15 and 15 to 24 age groups (1). Two significant studies reported that Caucasian males working in agriculture, forestry, or fishing were markedly over-represented (32, 33). Motor vehicles have been reported to account for a quarter of all 16- and 17-year-old work-related deaths (34). Fatalities have been reported to be far more common for males, in non-unionized firms, and while adolescents were driving forklifts or tractors (35). Farming has been reported to account for an average of 300 fatalities a year to those aged less than 19 (25). Construction work was also reported to be high risk. Among female adolescents, homicide is a leading cause of work-related fatalities, probably due to the concentration of adolescent girls in retail establishments (25).

Illegal employment is far more dangerous to U.S. working children than is legal work: ". . . almost 10 times greater among children employed under illegal conditions than among those working in compliance with the laws" (26, 36). For example, over 40 percent of all occupational fatalities occurred while the young person was involved in work prohibited by U.S. federal child labor laws (17, 31, 35). OSHA investigations into 104 fatalities of workers under age 18 resulted in 70 percent of employers receiving violation citations (34).

Nevertheless, under-reporting may be rife in the U.S. In a comparison of OSHA investigations with NIOSH death-certificate data for 16- and 17-year-old workers, it was estimated that only 35 percent to 50 percent of work-related fatalities were investigated by OSHA (33). OSHA investigations exclude homicides, transportation fatalities, deaths in industries regulated by other federal agencies, and federal employees (33).

In Australia, a study of coronial inquest records for all traumatic work-related deaths over a 4-year period reported that 5.8 percent occurred to persons less than 20 years (37). Of these, 15.5 percent were aged 15 or less, 10 percent were 16, 19 percent were 17, 23 percent were 18, and 32 percent were 19 (37). Fully 95 percent of the dead workers aged 16 to 19 were male, with most working in construction, agriculture or manufacturing, wholesale or retail trade, or other service industries respectively (37). Many were driving a vehicle of some sort when killed on the job. Among those aged under 15, the vast majority were male, two-thirds were working on family farms, and 50 percent involved vehicles of some type or other (38). Because a farm is usually a home and a recreation site for the family who lives there, non-working children are also exposed to a range of hazards and risks. Using the same coronial database, it was estimated that 63.5 percent occurred to workers, 24 percent were bystanders, and 12 percent were "other" farm fatalities (37). Many were non-working children and adolescents, with the age group 0 to less than 4 years most at risk (who constituted 12.3 percent of all fatalities on farms) (37). That is, the specific hazards at particular workplaces (e.g., a farm) present a risk to all those who are exposed, irrespective of employment status or age.

It is important to note that as the employment patterns of adolescents alter, the risk factors also change. For example, an emerging cause of fatalities among adolescents is exposure to nitrous oxide ("laughing gas"). One U.S. study involved analysis of 6,390 U.S. fatalities and comparisons against Consumer Product Safety Commission data and reported that recreational use of nitrous oxide at work resulted in a number of fatalities (39). Nitrous oxide is used in many dental surgeries, veterinary clinics, hospitals, and in the food industry as a foaming agent for whipped cream dispensers. Dead workers were typically found in storerooms after they had placed plastic bags over the nozzle of the N_2O tank to collect the gas, and held the bag over their heads—resulting in hypoxia, syncope, and death. These researchers advised employers to control access to N_2O cylinders, attach warning labels to cylinders, substitute large cylinders of N_2O with prepackaged whipped cream, and to issue public warnings as exposure may be increasing because it offers an inexpensive "high" (39).

Work-Related Injuries and Illnesses among Working Adolescents in Industrialized Countries

Most of the international data indicate that younger workers have a higher incidence of injury compared with adults (32). Inexperience or inadequate training have been identified as likely causative factors (40, 41). Workers' compensation claims data indicate that the *types* of injury reflect specific hazards exposures in particular industry sub-groups. For example, in *Western Australia* there was an over-representation of injuries among young workers in manufacturing, agriculture, construction, and mining (42). A study in Washington State reported that injuries were most frequent in food service, retail and wholesale trade, and agriculture (43). Brooks and Davis (28) reported that more than half of all injuries occurred in retail trade, followed by services (20.2 percent), and manufacturing (11 percent). A series of factors have been blamed, including

- Adolescents are often employed in retail outlets where hold-up related violence occurs (44);
- Equipment is usually designed for adult proportions;
- Physiological differences in metabolism may result in increased absorption of chemicals;
- Males are likely to be injured more frequently than are females (probably due to the gender division of labor with boys concentrated in higher-risk jobs); and
- Because of the concentration of adolescents in retail and service jobs, they experience increased exposure to occupational violence; the risks of which are heightened in hotels and bars, cafés and restaurants, chemist shops, video outlets, newsagents, "corner" stores, and health care (2, 25, 27, 28, 34, 45).

One landmark study compared the pattern of formally reported injuries against survey data from 3,312 high school students and reported:

- Strains, sprains, cuts, burns, bruises, and fractures accounted for 96 percent of all injuries;
- 15 percent of injuries resulted in a permanent impairment;
- The likelihood of back injuries was directly related to weights lifted;
- Smaller individuals tended to have more serious manual handling injuries than their larger peers;

- Lacerations most commonly affected the hand (16 percent) and fingers (61 percent);
- Burns accounted for only 13 percent of all injuries but 36 percent of hospitalizations;
- Most burns were caused by cooking oils, equipment, or hot water;
- Many adolescents missed school when injured or ill, but not their casual jobs; and yet
- *Two thirds* of adolescent work-related injuries *were not reported* (46).

The data about adolescent work-related injuries and illnesses are incomplete because of under-reporting, fear of potential consequences from reporting, ignorance of entitlements to workers' compensation, and inadequacies with recognition of work-related illnesses. Additional difficulties arise because the primary occupation of many adolescents is "student," with "worker" status a secondary part-time occupation. As a result, even in Sweden it was reported that 75 percent of youth injuries were not registered (47).

Illegal employment is associated with higher risk of injury (and fatality). U.S. government authorities investigated 1,475 serious injuries among workers under age 18 and identified that serious injuries were over-represented among those doing prohibited work. For example, cooking and baking by those aged 14 to 15 is specifically prohibited, although one-third of injuries occurred among those working as cooks (25, 26, 30).

Hospital data provide a rich source of information on adolescent worker injuries, with a series of studies reporting comparable findings. A Massachusetts emergency department study reported that 7 percent to 13 percent of all child/adolescent injuries were work-related (24, 25). Of concern, one study involving analysis of 10,047 workers' compensation claims from workers under 18 found 44 percent resulted in permanent disability (34). The use of case-cutters (Stanley knives) has caused many severe occupational injuries to 14 to 17 year olds treated in emergency departments: ". . . one third of all lacerations were caused by a single tool, a case cutter, which is a razor used to open boxes" (17, 43, 48).

The risks appear to vary by age and gender of adolescent. Layne et al. (22) used a stratified national U.S. sample of hospital emergency treatment data and estimated a work-related injury rate of 7.0 per 100 full-time equivalents for males aged 14 to 17, and 4.4 for females. Banco et al. (48) used emergency department data to calculate an annual injury rate among 16 and 17 year old employees at 8 percent for males and 3 percent for female workers. Miller and Kaufman estimated that 19.4 percent of 16 and 17 year olds were injured compared with 10.6 percent of adults (49). Similarly, MMS (23) estimated that 96 percent of adolescent injuries occurred to those aged 16 to 17. Knight et al. (24) also noted that 17 year olds had the highest rates of occupational injury among adolescents. Further, in Sweden workers aged 17 were identified as particularly vulnerable compared with those aged 18 to 20 (50). That is, age 17 appears to be very high risk.

The possible reasons for differences in incidence at different ages include:

- Older adolescents may be involved in more hazardous work and/or operate more dangerous machinery;
- Older adolescents may have less supervision;
- Older adolescents may work longer hours (i.e., be exposed more);
- Older adolescents may be more willing to *report* their work-related injuries (16);
- Older adolescents may have less relevant training; and
- There may be a "healthy worker" effect whereby injured adolescents are more likely to leave and the uninjured remain (51).

Work-related illness: Little is known about the magnitude and severity of occupational illness among working adolescents. Limited recognition and recording of work-related diseases occurs because of imperfect physician awareness of the link between work and specific diseases, the long latency periods between exposure and the development of symptoms, and difficulties in establishing causal links for multifactorial conditions (52). Particularly for longer-latency conditions, links with teenage workplace exposures may be obscured because of the length of time before manifestation of disease (26). Nevertheless (53),

> Children are potentially exposed to formaldehyde and dyes in the garment industry, solvents in paint shops, pesticides in agriculture and lawn service, and benzene in gasoline service stations.

Adolescent workers on farms may have increased exposure to hazardous substances. Richter and Jacobs (54) noted that U.S. regulations permitted the exposure of 10- and 11-year-old potato harvesters to 25 pesticides (some of which were neurotoxic, carcinogenic, mutagenic, or teratogenic).

A study of 258 baker's apprentices in Austria reported that 20.9 percent developed specific allergic indicators (16.7 percent against wheat, 14 percent against rye, and 15.9 percent against barley) (55). In a later study of bakers in Italy, allergic symptoms were reported by 13.2 percent, asthma by 6 percent, and 4.1 percent complained of respiratory symptoms when working with flours (56).

Many adolescent/child workers experience fatigue, which is likely to be exacerbated around exam times, or if late evening work is extensive: ". . . fatigue from balancing work and school may contribute to injuries among adolescent workers" (57). Kinney (30) identified a number of serious mental health problems associated with adolescent employment, including short-term problems (such as stress at peak times) and long-term developmental dysfunctions (which may be latent for some time) that adversely impact future career development (e.g., through falling asleep in class).

In sum, while the number of working adolescents is substantial in western industrialized countries, all the indicators suggest that the extent and severity of their work-related injuries and illnesses are likely to be seriously under-reported (14, 26). That is, the OHS of teenage workers is likely to be a substantial public health problem in most industrialized countries. The discussion now turns to some empirical data gathered in Australia.

OHS INDICES AMONG WORKING ADOLESCENTS IN AUSTRALIA

As has already been identified, the official data are limited. Extensive empirical studies are probably the only reliable mechanism to obtain valid estimates, particularly when the employment practices are illegal, *children* are working, and/or very vulnerable groups are being employed (such as non-English-speaking adolescents or illegal migrants). In the following sections, data gathered during three separate industry studies are discussed that are likely to be indicative of the OHS exposures of precariously employed adolescents in industrialized countries. The fast-food industry provides a typical example of a *formal* employment situation commonly encountered by adolescent workers. In contrast, garment manufacture and farming are typical instances where both adoles-cents and children are exposed to the hazards and risks experienced in *informal* home-based work.

Adolescent Workers in the Fast Food Industry

A substantive empirical study was commissioned to identify the OHS issues for workers aged between 16 and 21 who were *legally* employed in fast food. The study was carried out in a major multi-national fast-food chain. Face-to-face interviews were conducted with 304 young workers randomly selected from 132 outlets across three states of Australia (58). The names of the interviewees were not recorded, and specific store outlets where interviews took place and the name of the company remain confidential.

Work-related injury patterns: Minor burns and cuts were very common, particularly for those who worked in kitchen areas, but these rarely resulted in time off from work. In contrast, the types of injury that required time off from work usually followed falls/slips/trips during cleaning tasks in kitchen areas (e.g., mopping floors) or from manual handling. In addition, verbal abuse from cus-tomers was relatively common, although the incidence of threats (7.6 percent) and physical abuse (1 percent) was minimal. That is, while low-severity injuries were very common (such as cuts and burns), injuries that required time off work were relatively rare and were usually sprains/strains to the back or lower limbs. Using the loss of five or more days off work as the basis for calculations, the annual injury incidence was estimated to be 2.3 percent. The most recent workers' compensation claims data available in Australia are recorded in the National Data Set (NDS) which includes successful injury or illness claims that resulted in 5 or more days off work. The compensated injury incidence in the NDS was very similar to the 2.3 percent incidence found in this study *even though these were young casual workers* (29, 58).

Demographic characteristics: Lost-time injuries occurred most frequently at age 18 to 19 (26.3 percent), and less commonly at ages 16 to 17 (10.5 percent). New workers on the job did *not* have an increased incidence, and *gender* was found *not* to be associated with particular patterns of injury in this study, probably because the jobs performed by males and females were very similar (58).

Each of the 304 young workers interviewed was asked to respond to three hypothetical scenarios, which were designed to assess how they would react in the event of an OHS threat. Overall, the responses from these three hypothetical scenarios were extremely positive, with the young casual workers having a superior knowledge of "risk assessment and control" strategies and of OHS legislative responsibilities. The Chief Investigator (who is the author of this chapter) concluded that the improved OHS performance in this particular fast-food chain was the result of a stringent OHS management system whereby: (a) OHS was integrated into all production tasks and was *not* a stand-alone area; and (b) because this management system was enforced across both company-owned and franchised stores (29). Additional risk reduction strategies recommended for all fast food, café, and restaurant businesses included

- For *stores with franchised outlets*, a franchisee agreement which requires implementation of a rigorous OHS management system (58);
- Because major fast-food chains have considerable market power, larger fast-food stores were encouraged to lobby suppliers to deliver bulk stores in "rip top" boxes which do not require the use of Stanley knives (case cutters) to open. As noted earlier in this chapter, the use of Stanley knives has been reported to cause many serious adolescent injuries in the U.S. (28, 34, 43);
- Reduction of burn injuries in the food industry can also be achieved through hazard-reduction planning. For example, fryers should have exhaust vents in close proximity, built-in grease filters, improved grease disposal systems, and automatic food-lowering devices and vat covers, and floor surfaces should be regularly cleaned with grease-cutting solutions (59). In addition, prohibitions can be placed on: (a) standing on top of a fryer while cleaning ventilation components; (b) rolling fryers with hot grease; (c) lifting metal receptacles containing hot grease; and (d) working close to hot fryers when floors are wet (45). Further, detailed risk-control procedures need to be enforced during the cleaning, filtering, and removal of oil/grease in *deep fryers*; and
- Enhancement of occupational violence risk control measures (60).

In sum, the OHS risks associated with high-risk tasks in *formal* employment of adolescents can be readily reduced. In contrast, *informal* labor presents quite different challenges.

Adolescent Workers in Home-Based Garment Manufacturing

Outworking was long thought to be an anachronism from the early Industrial Revolution that had died out in industrialized countries. However, outworking is resurgent across the industrialized world, usually in pockets of poverty in major cities, involving predominantly non-English-speaking background (NESB) females, relatively powerless labor, piecework payment systems, complicated chains of subcontracting, and widespread degradation of working conditions (61).

A recent Australian study compared the OHS of 100 factory-based employees against 100 clothing outworkers doing the same job tasks. Detailed face-to-face interviews were conducted with the assistance of interpreters to gather both qualitative and quantitative data. While the *types* of injury remained the same for both factory-based and outworkers, those working from home self-reported around three times the acute and chronic injuries of employees doing the same type of tasks, and also experienced more occupational violence (62).

It was also clear that in *at least* 3 of the 100 households where the author of this chapter conducted interviews with clothing outworkers, children of the households were helping with clothing manufacture and/or extensive household duties such as care of younger siblings, for example:

Started sewing as an outworker when I was 13.

. . . I started in 1987 aged 7. . . .

Need to ask children for help.

Protection of the OHS status of children and adolescents in outworker homes presents significant difficulties for authorities. Much of this child and adolescent labor will involve "assistance" with housework, care of siblings, occasional machining, intermittent exposure to hazards such as dusts from material, and work in settings not primarily designed for production, for example: "Sister and mother working with her in kitchen." Further, protective labor law and environmental standards are extremely difficult (if not impossible) to enforce in family dwellings.

Dusty affects family health.

Acid smell in all working area; high temps and dusty.

Dust in garage gets too much; has affected my daughter—she has asthma.

That is, the process of outworking can have significant negative conse-quences for children who assist their parents with work tasks, as well as through depredation of the home environment. Yet, no formal record of any of these negative OHS consequences is likely to exist.

Adolescent Workers on "Market Garden" Farms

Market gardening is an industry sector characteristically employing large numbers of migrant workers. Hence, this is a useful industry sub-sector within which to identify the OHS of migrants and their working children. Parker (63) conducted a major empirical study among market gardeners from a range of NESB backgrounds including those speaking Arabic, Maltese, Italian, and Cambodian who supplied the Sydney fresh-produce markets. Adolescent family members frequently "helped out" on the farms. In addition, interviewees reported extensive exposure of children, including instances where infants and young children were brought on to the fields when child care was unavailable. Hence, exposure to physical and chemical hazards occurred to all family members (64).

> The kids suffer, having to help their mothers before and after school. It's very bad if it's straight after spraying. It's very traditional to pick harvest 3–4 days after spraying.

Agricultural chemical exposures also occurred to fetuses via their pregnant mothers (including organophosphate pesticides) (65):

> We took the children everywhere with us on the farm. . . . I sprayed until I was 6 months pregnant. . . . I started again immediately after the baby was born. We put the children in the car, and covered the car. When the babies were older we left them with the younger sister, who left school to look after them . . . had several miscarriages. . . .

When small farms did not make sufficient money to cover household bills, outside employment was frequently sought either by the adults in the family or adolescents (66):

> If a grower is not receiving enough money, then either he, or his wife, or the children have to go out to work, which is destroying the social fabric.

Hence, fatigue from unpaid labor is not the only negative consequences for children and adolescents assisting with work on family farms. These children can also be exposed to a wide range of hazards and risks from before birth. Yet, officially, there may be no record at all, except possibly at hospital emergency departments or in local general-practitioner medical records.

DISCUSSION AND CONCLUSION

While the incidence of *child* labor appears to be extensive in developing countries, it is rare in industrialized nations. In contrast, *adolescent* labor is widespread across both industrialized and developing countries. If substantial contributions to domestic work tasks are included in estimations, the data indicate that at least 60 percent of the world's minors are working on a full-time, part-time, or casual basis in most countries. In addition to the risks to their OHS status, there may be significant impacts on ability to access education, future career paths, and on capacity to concentrate energy on cognitive learning requirements. Most at risk of a fatality are those working illegally, on farms, in fishing, and in the "worst forms" of child labor (as defined by the ILO).

The fragmentary information that is available on *child* labor in industrialized countries indicates that the extent is limited, with most working *informally* in family businesses of various types, usually under the instruction of NESB parents. In such scenarios, many of the parents are themselves precariously employed and have a limited capacity for alternative employment. Legal protections for such informal employment situations are limited, particularly when the tasks are completed in the family home or on a parental farm.

The available data suggest that those *adolescents* employed in the *formal sector* are likely to have proportionately fewer negative OHS incidents than those working in the informal sector or in family businesses. Nevertheless, all working adolescents are exposed to the "normal" hazards of the industry sector within which they are employed, with the additional risks that inexperience and precarious labor status entail. Further, there may be additional negative consequences on capacity for educational achievement and for their accumulation of human capital.

While responsibility for prevention of injuries to working children/adolescents is likely to cross over many government departments in each industrialized country, evidence indicates that when the policies and strategies are comprehensive and coordinated, major improvements can occur. For example, a 50 percent decline in work-related injuries among European adolescents was achieved by a concerted national effort involving a number of different authorities. A fundamental step in this process was implementation of the E.U. Directive on the Protection of Young People at Work (children under 13 are not allowed to work and a number of bans apply to those aged 15 to 17, including a prohibition against work where the pace is set by a machine as well as payment-by-results schemes) (67).

From the available international research literature, it appears that the core hazard-reduction strategies to reduce the OHS risks to working adolescents in industrialized countries are:

- Ratification of the ILO Convention 182, which calls for immediate action to ban the worst forms of child labor;
- Systemic "whole of government" policy initiatives by government agencies, with detailed recommended strategies to support these;
- A prohibition on adolescent work in hazardous occupations (including in family businesses) with enforcement of sanctions;

- A prohibition on illegal employment;
- The implementation of comprehensive OHS management systems by the owners/managers of organizations that employ adolescent workers; and
- Development of major OHS initiatives directed to reach NESB family businesses (including outworkers and family-run farms) to assist with hazard identification, risk assessment, and effective (and affordable) control strategies.

In sum, the majority of adolescents in industrialized countries now work on a full- or part-time basis in the *formal* sector, often in conjunction with full-time education. Their employment is concentrated in particular industry sectors, such as fast-food and other service industries. Nevertheless, the available comparative studies have all indicated that the work-related injuries and illnesses of adolescents in the *formal* economy are significantly under-reported. Ignorance of entitlements and vulnerability through precarious employment appear to result in many work-related injuries and illnesses remaining hidden.

Those adolescents and children working in the *informal* sector (including on family farms) are most at risk—not least because they are largely outside of the protective mechanisms that have been developed to protect all workers in advanced economies. The economic needs of their families may be acute, the available protective measures may be inappropriate for domestic premises where they work, there may be ignorance of OHS risks for both acute and long-latency conditions (and control mechanisms), and the precarious nature of parental employment all conspire to increase the risks. Indeed, there are few appropriate mechanisms available to record any such incidents experienced by informal-sector workers apart from some emergency hospital treatments.

As a consequence, the official databases are likely to significantly under-state the work-related injuries and illnesses of both child and adolescent workers in industrialized countries. Thus, the work-related injuries and illnesses of adolescent workers in industrialized countries remain a largely hidden epidemic.

REFERENCES

1. Richter, E., and Jacobs, J. Work injuries and exposures in children and young adults: Review and recommendations for action. *Am. J. Indust. Med.* 19: 747–769, 1991.
2. Landrigan, P., Pollack, S., and Belville, R. Child labor. In *Environmental and Occupational Medicine,* Ed. 2, edited by W. Rom. Little Brown and Company, Boston, 1992.
3. International Labour Organisation (ILO). *A Future Without Child Labour.* ILO, Geneva, 2002.
4. International Labour Organisation (ILO). *IPEC Action Against Child Labour: Highlights 2002.* International Programme on the Elimination of Child Labour, ILO, Geneva, 2003.
5. Galli, R. *The Economic Impact of Child Labour.* Discussion paper for the International Institute for Labour Studies at the ILO, Decent Work Research programme. University of Lugano, Switzerland, 2001.

6. International Labour Organisation (ILO). ILO Director-General press release in Bangkok and Geneva. ILO/97/33, December 9, 1997.
7. Lyall, K. Foreign objects. *The Weekend Australian,* February 1–2, 2003, p. 22.
8. Murdoch, L. Alone in a sea of cruelty. *The Sydney Morning Herald,* June 5, 2001, p. 13.
9. Sancho-Liao, N. Child labour in the Philippines: Exploitation in the process of globalization of the economy. *Labour Cap. Soc.* 27: 270–281, 1994.
10. O'Loughlin, E. Descent into lives of silent servitude. *The Sydney Morning Herald,* June 6, 2001, p. 17.
11. Thompson, E. P. *The Making of the English Working Class.* Penguin, Harmondsworth, London, 1982.
12. Engles, F. *The Condition of the Working Class in England.* Panther, St. Albans, London, 1976.
13. Mayhew, H. *Mayhew's London: Being Selections from "London Labour and the London Poor."* Spring Books, London, 1851.
14. McKechnie, J., Lavalette, M., and Hobbs, S. Child employment research in Britain. *Work Employ. Soc.* 14: 573–580, 2000.
15. Nielsen, P. Fewer child and youth accidents in Denmark. *Euro Echo,* No. 1, February 1997, p. 9.
16. Belville, R., Pollack, S., Godbold, J., and Landrigan, P. Occupational injuries among working adolescents in New York State. *JAMA* 269: 2754–2759, 1993.
17. Cooper, S., and Rothstein, M. Health hazards among working children in Texas. *South. Med. J.* 88: 550–553, 1995.
18. Mayhew, C. *Barriers to Implementation of Known OHS Solutions in Small Business.* National Occupational Health and Safety Commission and Division of Workplace Health and Safety, AGPS, Canberra, Australia, 1997.
19. Burgess, J., and Campbell, I. The nature and dimensions of precarious employment in Australia. *Labour Indust.* 8: 5–21, 1998.
20. Campbell, I., and Burgess, J. *National patterns of temporary employment: The distinctive case of casual employment in Australia.* Working paper no. 53. National Key Centre in Industrial Relations, Monash University, Melbourne, 1997.
21. Joint Standing Committee on Immigration, 1996, cited Quinlan, M. The implications of labour market restructuring in industrialised societies for occupational health and safety. *Working Paper 116.* School of Industrial Relations and Organisational Behaviour, University of New South Wales, New South Wales, 1997.
22. Layne, L., Castillo, D., Stout, N., and Cutlip, P. Adolescent occupational injuries requiring hospital emergency department treatment: A nationally representative sample. *Am. J. Public Health* 84: 657–660, 1994.
23. Massachusetts Medical Society (MMS). Work-related injuries and illnesses associated with child labor—United States, 1993. *MMWR* 45: 464–469, 1996.
24. Knight, E., Castillo, D., and Layne, L. A detailed analysis of work-related injury among youth treated in emergency departments. *Am. J. Indust. Med.* 27: 793–805, 1995.
25. Dunn, K., and Runyan, C. Deaths at work among children and adolescents. *Am. J. Disabled Child* 147: 1044–1047, 1993.
26. Kruse, D., and Mahony, D. Illegal child labor in the United States: Prevalence and characteristics. *Indust. Labor Relat. Rev.* 54: 17–40, 2000.
27. Centers For Disease Control and Prevention (CDC). Work-related injuries and illnesses associated with child labor: United States, 1993. *JAMA* 276: 16–17, 1996.

28. Brooks, D., and Davis, L. Work-related injuries to Massachusetts teens, 1987-1990. *Am. J. Indust. Med.* 29: 153–160, 1996.
29. Mayhew, C. Adolescent worker OHS. *J. Occup. Health Saf. Aust. N.Z.* 16: 137–143, 2000.
30. Kinney, J. Health hazards to children in the service industries. *Am. J. Indust. Med.* 24: 291–300, 1993.
31. Mayhew, C., Quinlan, M., and Bennett, L. *The Effects of Subcontracting/Outsourcing on Occupational Health and Safety.* Industrial Relations Research Centre Monograph, University of New South Wales, Sydney, 1996.
32. NIOSH. NIOSH study finds work injuries, illnesses among young employees pervasive, preventable. *NIOSH Update,* Publication No. 96–119, U.S. Department of Health and Human Services, Washington D.C., 1996.
33. Castillo, D., Landen, D., and Layne, L. Occupational injury deaths of 16- and 17-year-olds in the United States. *Am. J. Public Health* 84: 646–649, 1994.
34. Centers for Disease Control and Prevention (CDC). *NIOSH ALERT: Preventing Deaths and Injuries of Adolescent Workers.* CDC, U.S. Department of Health and Human Services, Cincinnati, May 1995.
35. Suruda, A., and Halperin, W. Work-related deaths in children. *Am. J. Indust. Med.* 19: 739–745, 1991.
36. Landrigan, P., Pollack, S., Belville, R., and Godbold, J. Child labor: Risks and prospects for prevention. In *The Identification and Control of Environmental and Occupational Diseases: Hazards and Risks of Chemicals in the Oil Refining Industry, Advances in Modern Environmental Toxicology,* XXIII, edited by M. Mehlman and A. Upton, p. 567. Princeton Scientific Publishing Co. Princeton, 1994.
37. National Occupational Health and Safety Commission (NOHSC). *Work-Related Traumatic Fatalities in Australia, 1989 to 1992.* Ausinfo, Canberra, Australia, 1998.
38. Franklin, R., Mitchell, R., Driscoll, T., and Fragar, L. *Farm-Related Fatalities in Australia, 1989-1992,* pp. 25–27. Australian Centre for Agricultural Health and Safety, National Occupational Health and Safety Commission, and Rural Industries Research and Development Corporation, Canberra, Australia, 2000.
39. Suruda, A., and McGlothlin, J. Fatal abuse of nitrous oxide in the workplace. *J. Occup. Med.* 32: 682–684, 1990.
40. Salminen, S. Work-related accidents among young workers in Finland. *Int. J. Occup. Saf. Ergon.* 2: 305–314, 1996.
41. Salminen, S. Occupational Accidents of Young Workers in Finland. Paper presented at the Third World conference on Injury Prevention and Control, Melbourne, 1996.
42. Worksafe Western Australia. *Code of Practice: Safety and Health of Children and Young People in Workplaces.* Worksafe Western Australia Commission, Perth, 1998; and Worksafe Western Australia and WorkCover W.A. (WWA). *State of the Work Environment: Occupational Injuries and Diseases to Young Workers Western Australia 1994/95,* No. 26. Worksafe Western Australia and WorkCover W.A, Perth, 1996.
43. Miller, M., and Kaufman, J. Occupational injuries among adolescents in Washington State, 1988–1991. *Am. J. Indust. Med.* 34: 121–132, 1998.
44. Mayhew, C. Occupational violence in industrialized countries: Types, incidence patterns, and "at risk" groups of workers. In *Violence at Work: Causes, Patterns and Prevention,* edited by M. Gill, B. Fisher, and V. Bowie, pp. 21–40. Willan Publishing, London, 2002.

45. Heinzman, M., Thoreson, S., McKenzie, L., Cook, M., Hoffman, R., Parker, D., and Carl, W. Occupational burns among restaurant workers—Colorado and Minnesota. *Arch. Dermatol.* 130: 699–701, 1994.

46. Parker, D., Carl, W., French, L., and Martin, F. Characteristics of adolescent work injuries reported to the Minnesota Department of Labor and Industry. *Am. J. Public Health* 84: 606–611, 1994.

47. Jacobsson, B., and Schelp, L. One-year incidence of occupational injuries among teenagers in a Swedish rural municipality. *Scand. J. Soc. Med.* 16: 21–25, 1999.

48. Banco, L. Lapidus, G., and Braddock, M. Work-related injury among Connecticut Minors. *Pediatrics* 89: 957–960, 1992. Cited Knight et al., op cit 22, p. 803.

49. Miller and Kaufman. Op cit no. 44, p. 121.

50. Persson, I., and Larsson, T. Accident-related permanent disabilities of young workers in Sweden 1984–85. *Saf. Sci.* 14: 187–198, 1991.

51. LaFlamme, L. Age-related injuries among male and female assembly workers: A study in the Swedish automobile industry. *Relat. Indust.* 52: 608–619, 1997.

52. Kerr, C., Morrell, S., Salkeld, G., Corbett, S., Taylor, R., and Webster, F. *Best Estimate of the Magnitude of Health Effects of Occupational Exposure to Hazardous Substances.* WorkSafe Australia Development Grant final report. National Institute of Occupational Health and Safety, AGPS, Canberra, Australia, April 1996.

53. Cooper and Rothstein. Op cit no. 17, p. 554.

54. Richter, E., and Jacobs, J. Work injuries and exposures in children and young adults: Review and recommendations for action. *Am. J. Indust. Med.* 19: 747–769, 1991.

55. Popp, W., Wagner, C., Kiss, D., Zwick, H., and Sertl, K. Prediction of sensitization to flour allergens. *Allergy* 49: 376–379, 1994.

56. De Zotti, R., Molinari, S., Larese, F., and Bovenzi, M. Pre-employment screening among trainee bakers. *Occup. Environ. Med.* 52: 279–283, 1995.

57. CDC, 1995. Op cit no. 34, p. 6.

58. National Occupational Health and Safety Commission (NOHSC). *Occupational Health and Safety Issues For Young Workers in the Fast Food Industry.* Written and conducted by Mayhew, C., Johnstone, R., Nicholson, M., Cribb, M., and Murphy, R. NOHSC together with the Division of Workplace Health and Safety (Qld.) and the WorkCover Authority of New South Wales, AusInfo, Canberra, Australia, 2000.

59. Massachusetts Medical Society (MMS). Occupational burns among restaurant workers: Colorado and Minnesota. *MMWR* 42: 713–717, 1993.

60. Mayhew, C. Occupational violence and prevention strategies. *Master OHS and Environment Guide,* pp. 547–569. CCH Australia, North Ryde, 2003.

61. Mayhew, C., and Quinlan, M. *Outsourcing and Occupational Health and Safety: A Comparative Study of Factory-Based and Outworkers in the Australian TCF Industry.* Industrial Relations Research Centre monograph, University of New South Wales, Sydney, 1998.

62. Mayhew, C., and Quinlan, M. *Outsourcing and Occupational Health and Safety: A Comparative Study of Factory-Based and Outworkers in the Australian TCF Industry,* Table 25. Industrial Relations Research Centre monograph, University of New South Wales, Sydney, 1998.

63. Parker, F. *Developing an Understanding of the Occupational Health and Safety Practices of Market Gardeners and Cut Flower Growers of Non English Speaking Background in the Sydney Basin*, p. 249. Report to the National Occupational Health and Safety Commission, Canberra, Australia, 2000.
64. Ibid, Parker, 2000.
65. Parker, F. *Developing an Understanding of the Occupational Health and Safety Practices of Market Gardeners and Cut Flower Growers of Non English Speaking Background in the Sydney Basin*, p. 188. Report to the National Occupational Health and Safety Commission, Canberra, Australia, 2000.
66. Parker, F. *Developing an Understanding of the Occupational Health and Safety Practices of Market Gardeners and Cut Flower Growers of Non English Speaking Background in the Sydney Basin*, p. 248. Report to the National Occupational Health and Safety Commission, Canberra, Australia, 2000.
67. Mayhew, C., 2000. Op cit no. 29.

CHAPTER 7

The Epidemic of Stress

Chris L. Peterson

This chapter focuses on the epidemic nature of occupational stress and identifies some antecedents, including work intensification, electronic surveillance, and Global Best Practice production methods. It also identifies how the individual is often seen as the problem in work-related stress rather than workplaces or production methods. In addition, some "best practice" approaches to dealing with stress are discussed. The author argues that stress—and stress-induced illnesses— are one of the largest and most debilitating "epidemics" of the 21st century.

BACKGROUND TO THE CONTEXT OF WORK STRESS

In 1936, Hans Selye published a definitive article in *Nature* (1) arguing that stress was part of the etiology of disease. Stress has since become accepted in the biomedical, medical, behavioral, and social sciences literature as an important area of study. Selye's original arguments were based around stress being part of the disease process. He outlined three stages of stress as part of the General Adaptation Syndrome, and described the experience of stress as an initial shock, a stage of resistance, and then a stage of exhaustion where a person might even die. This understanding of the process has been pivotal in stress research for some 70 years.

There has been substantive biomedical research into the role of chemicals and hormones in the stress response (2–4), and the link through a depleted immune system to the onset of disease. Based on this evidence, stress research became more a part of medical and behavioral explanations of ill health linked with negative life experiences (5). Further, during the 1970s a growing amount of empirical stress research was conducted in workplaces, and the links between workplace stress and illness started to become firmly established. Given this extensive research over recent years, it is surprising that relatively little attention

117

has been directed to the development of "best practice" models for dealing with stress at work.

Stress at work has recently become a more contentious topic than in the 1970s and 1980s (6). This has been largely due to factors such as the emphasis on the growth of free-market economies in developed countries, neo-liberalist economic management principles and practices, and greater income and resource polarization among the population in many nations. According to Coburn (7), neoliberalism has created a greater divide between the power of business and the working population (who, according to Coburn have been stripped of some of their working-class attributes, such as strong and supportive union movements). With this divide has come an ideological change. The neo-liberalist management philosophy has pervaded through the working population to become part of mainstream explanations of the way the world of work operates. Working people are being placed under greater pressure through downsizing, a reduced union support base, continued work intensification involving longer hours of work, and generally less stability at work. Management continues to maintain that stress is not real, or does not exist to any great degree (6, 8). They maintain, however, that there are individuals unsuited to the demands of work today who need to be weeded out (note 5).

Research Evidence on Stress

The emphasis of stress research has changed over the past two or three decades. Understandings about this "epidemic" developed from the middle of the last century and paralleled what was occurring in the socio-political context of work in the later part of that century. During the 1960s, there was a strong focus on biophysiological research, and this produced important insights into the functioning and effects of hormonal systems involved in the stress response. Stress literature started to become prolific during the 1970s, with further advances made in biophysiology which demonstrated important health effects from poorly organized and managed work. Pivotal in socio-psychological research was the work of Karasek (9, 10) which proposed that a key to understanding stress at work was the relationship between job demands and the amount of control exercised by employees.

During the 1980s, there were numerous studies focussing on the effects of stressors at work. Yet the framework for explaining the emerging "epidemic" of stress at work had not been clearly defined. However, there were many pivotal studies (e.g., 11–15) which took up these issues of underlying causes of stress at work. The more challenging focused on the problems of control at work as explanations of why employees become stressed (note esp. 11, 14, 15) . At this stage, however, there were relatively few studies which identified management practice, management ethos, and the management prerogative as primary causes of stress at work (note 5).

Early in the last century there were hallmark work practices introduced which have had a profound effect on the way that work is managed. These were a significant cause of ill ease and stress for workers. As early as the late 1920s with the introduction of Taylorism (40), there was a move in business practice to use "scientific" management techniques. These were employed to exploit previously untapped reserves from workers through the use of time and motion studies and methods which resemble some of the work intensification principles and practices instituted since the late 1980s and early 1990s in most developed economies. The result of Taylorism was the suppression of a number of important needs of employees at work. Much of the earlier part of the 20th century saw organizational psychologists trying to design systems of management and work which enhanced management's need for increased productivity, together with the fulfilment of a range of workers' needs.

During the late 1980s to early 1990s, there were changes in workplace organization and management that can be tied in with philosophical changes in management approach and ethos. These changes included environmental concerns, increasing globalization, the recognition of scarcer economic resources, increases in unemployment, and changes in labor-market policy. Coburn (7) reported that these neo-liberal policy changes fundamentally changed the balance between labor and management, and were pursued by more conservative styles of government in most developed economies. Together with these there were increased trends toward privatization of the public sector, increased downsizing of organizations, and increasingly open-market economies.

In the 1990s and early 2000s, issues such as the effects of work stress on health, family life, gender, parenting (note 16), and even decisions about retirement (17) became more common. Work intensified in terms of increased hours of labor in many countries (note 8), which was seen to have a great impact on the structure and functioning of family life (e.g., 18–23). In addition, research focused on issues such as substance abuse (including alcohol consumption) and on voluntary and involuntary continuation in the workforce, particularly in developed economies (24, 25). Other emerging related issues including post-traumatic stress (26), the home and work interface (27), and caregivers and work stress (28) also developed. Occupational violence and bullying have also emerged as a focus of more recent research into occupational health and safety problems (Mayhew, see Chapter 3), and in countries such as the U.S. are seen as priority OSH issues (29).

Peterson (6) recently provided data to show the effects of work intensification and job changes on stress. He reported that the most significant predicators of stress were a lack of decision latitude and control, followed by increased pace and effort. This evidence indicates that in the late 1990s, in Australia at least, "best practice" models which focus on these two elements are likely to have the most significant effects.

RECENT WORKPLACE PRACTICES LEADING
TO INCREASED STRESS

There has been a number of more recent workplace practices instituted, which have created particular stress-related work problems. Newer forms of work regulation and organization that may increase levels of stress include electronic surveillance, tele-work, and Global Best Practice techniques that increase production. These have all been part of a "tightening up" by management in a globalized economy where firms are increasingly operating in a market that is open and very competitive. Some new practices are direct forms of coercion by management, and some bring greater management control by imposing competitiveness between workers. The effect of deregulation, greater control and surveillance, and more flexible approaches to organization have had a number of beneficial effects. However, these new forms of control have left many employees more reliant on management and more vulnerable. As a result of increasing levels of stress among the workforce, organizations also suffer increased absenteeism, turnover, and reduced long-term commitment from many employees.

Electronic Monitoring

One recent trend in some industries has been increased stress induced by electronic surveillance (31). Johnstone and Cheng argue that "in recent years, with an environment of affordable technology, the availability of less easily observable or detectable monitoring devices, and a lack of adequate regulation, there has been an explosion in the use of electronic monitoring and surveillance in the workplace'" (31, p. 1). They cite an American Management Association (AMA) report, which observes that almost 80 percent of the largest companies in the U.S. had used electronic monitoring of some form during the year preceding the study. Of the practices observed, monitoring employee phone calls, reviewing voicemail messages and e-mail, and monitoring computers were common practices. In addition, videotaping of employee performance has been reported, as has monitoring connections to the Internet and reviewing employees' files. According to the AMA study, there were four main reasons for surveillance: evaluating performance; legal compliance; legal liability; and the restriction of the cost of use of services such as phone calls.

Johnston and Cheng (31) argue there is a correlation between the introduction of performance monitoring and occupational safety and health (OSH) difficulties. An increasing pace of work and use of monitoring devices can lead to an increase in lower-back problems, headaches, stress, tension, depression, anxiety, fatigue, and anger. In addition, use of these kinds of devices can lead to turnover, absenteeism, and therefore decreased productivity (31). One Australian case they cite is the company Franklins in New South Wales, where 800 workers took strike action over proposals by the company to introduce engineering work standards. These changes incorporated a series of electronic monitoring methods which represented an important challenge to privacy legislation. This dispute alerted the union movement to become more vigorous in its campaign to oppose electronic surveillance.

Tele-Working

Working with computers has bought a significant growth in part-time and temporary work. In addition, the workplace can be virtually anywhere, with much computer work outsourced and done at home. For example, estimates reveal that nine million people work from home in the U.S. (32). Similarly in Australia in 1999, 4 percent of Australians worked as tele-workers, with predictions the figure would reach 15 percent by 2009. There are a number of benefits of tele-work, according to Haselhoff (32): productivity and motivation increases and absenteeism decreases; employees can be retained despite relocating for other reasons such as a partner's change of job; and workers may stay with the one employer longer. There are also reduced operating costs and overheads. IBM, for example, has reported saving $1.4 billion due to its tele-working program.

Allvin and Aronsson (33) refer to tele-working as a new type of flexible employment along with homeworking, tele-cottages, and mobile tele-work that appear to provide more employee flexibility. For example, employees can more easily determine when and where they will work. This kind of work often implies more specialized forms of employment agreement which may not always be beneficial to employees.

However, Haselhoff (32) identifies a number of potential causes of stress for tele-workers, not the least significant being working in isolation. Added to this are: high-volume workloads; balancing work with demands from children and partners and the domestic workload; work pressure resulting from deadlines; excessive overtime; working at night and shiftwork; uncertainty associated with unpredictable workloads; a lack of co-workers; and a lack of collegiate support. Combined with this are the hazards associated with poor OSH prevention strategies and some restrictions on application of regulations at home-based worksites.

Thus, the independence of tele-workers may come at a cost for those who have to endure greater hardships. Those with high workloads and deadlines are particularly susceptible. For many, however, tele-working may be the only available employment alternative. Thus, tele-working is an important area (as with other types of outworking) where legislation is required to ensure that companies provide sufficient support and OSH protection to workers.

Global Best Practice Production Methods

There has been an emphasis on developing Best Practice Production processes to increase productivity across the industrialized world, stemming from globalization and reduction in trade barriers. Most developed countries have made significant inroads in Best Practice management and production methods over the past two decades. Van liemt maintains that, around the world, companies are adopting Best Practice methods of organizing production that aim to simultaneously reach the highest levels of quality, production, and flexibility at a competitive cost (34, p. 1). Methods that are used include "Just in Time" production, subcontracting out of labor requirements, Total Quality management, and other methods of plant production that are deemed to be more efficient.

Davidsson and Wernstedt (35) present an overview of Just in Time (JIT) production. With changes to rates of production, JIT has been developed to deal with the problems of overproduction and shortages and an inability to effectively deal with levels of customer demand. A primary objective of JIT is to reduce wastage and delay production for as long as possible. As such, it focuses on the supply side of manufacture and production, and requires flexibility in production processes.

Van liemt overviewed Global Best Practice and mechanisms through which it could be instituted successfully. The automobile and textile industries have both adopted best practice, as well as many other industries.

There are organizations such as Best Manufacturing Practice (BMP) which survey organizations nationally and develop indices and examples of case studies of management best practice. BMP (36) identifies and produces an index of industry best practice in the U.S. and provides opportunities through information transfer to exchange approaches to best practice in manufacturing in the U.S. and Canada. Global Marketplace (37) collects information in the European Union of best practice in business and manufacture among member states and provides a mechanism through which the exchange of best-practice ideas can occur between states.

Nevertheless, questions remain about the extent to which the quest for increased productivity and efficiency leads directly to increased stress for workers and management. Van liemt (34) assessed the effect of Global Best Practice on employee stress and labor relations. He maintains that "in the case of the buyer-supplier relationship, GBP (Global Best Practice) industrial relations rely on trustful, participatory cooperation for flexible, high quality, high productivity production" (34, p. 6).

However, there are important drawbacks to the "cosy" relationship between management and workers. Van liemt cites workers who feel that increased efficiency resulting from close management-worker collaboration is not in their interests. For example, the constant striving for efficiency may lead to over effort and greater work demand, and may lead to redundancies. *Kaisen* campaigns refer to where work is reorganized among the members of a group to eliminate gaps and slowtimes in operation. Repeated success with these operations lead to reducing the size of the work team, with one or more team members being made redundant.

New flexible production arrangements require a deal of adjustment by both workers and management, yet these new forms of "supportive" management may, in practice, not be so easy to institute. When industrial relations are more conflictual, with a stronger, more united union movement, there may be a "credibility gap" that arouses suspicion among employees (note 34). Managers may also have to acknowledge that responsibility for production problems do not lie with the workers but with the rules, working environment, procedures, and nature of the production system that management had created.

With best practice production methods, changes to management attitudes may need to be considerable at every level of the organization, but especially among those who work directly with workers on the shop floor. Manufacturing specialists and production engineers need to act on the suggestions of workers for improvements to production practices, to join in *kaizen* meetings and quality circle discussions, and treat shopfloor workers as basically equal. In particular, first-line supervisors have a delicate job if workers are given more responsibility through *kaizen* or quality circles, for example, to stop the production line. The roles and responsibilities of first-line supervisors can become quite unclear, and in fact many oppose these new work practices. Therefore, instituting these changes can be a recipe for conflictual relations and a particularly strong source of stress for both workers and management.

Allvin and Aronsson (33) argue that the move toward more flexible work will increase the number of problems that employees have in coping with co-workers. In addition, as management is increasingly focused on results, earlier ideas brought in about the actual process of production are now often less of a concern. Therefore, individual employees need to deal directly with many of the problems related to their job as their own problem (rather than being a management problem).

Production Global Best Practice also requires worker flexibility, and functional flexibility requires the removal of things such as job demarcations (and other job classifications), and these have been quite difficult to implement. Wainwright and Calnan (38) have also argued that flexible production modes have been equated to reduced regulation over employment practices, leaving many employees with unsatisfactory working arrangements. Trade unions have been particularly vocal in their opposition to the removal of job demarcations as it fundamentally undermines the strength of a consolidated protection of particular types of jobs. It is also a potential point of contention for workers and managers as to whether more difficult tasks are financially rewarded, non-standard contracts are offered (such as self-employment), and whether large penalties are paid for excessive overtime.

One of the major problems in relation to the stress epidemic has been the reduction in union presence in many organizations during the last decade. The previous protection of a strong union movement representing sets of defined jobs across industry sectors has withered away along with the practice in many countries such as Australia of collective bargaining at the plant level. Peterson (6) shows how, in Australia in the 5-year period between 1990 and 1995 there were significant reductions in the number of workers represented by a union, and that most involuntary downsizing, the uptake of work intensification practices such as longer hours, less significant pay increases, and greater effort expended on the job occurred in organizations without a union presence (note 6).

THE RELATIONSHIP BETWEEN NEW WORKING PRACTICES AND THE EMERGENCE OF A STRESS "EPIDEMIC"

Chandler, Berg, and Barry (8) have cited evidence of an extensive stress impact from new flexible production processes in the U.K. They maintain that stress for managers has been increasing, caused by changes in their roles in organizations, the increased number of hours that U.K. managers have been working in recent years, and the more flexible modes of production.

Similarly in Australia, Peterson (6) draws on data collected from the Australian Workplace Industrial Relations Survey (1995) to show that work intensification has been associated with increased stress in the Australian workforce during the past decade. Managers and professionals have been particularly affected by these workplace changes, including increased hours, greater effort, and more flexible modes of production, leading to significant increases in stress (6). Increased participation has been one of the outcomes of Global Best Practice, and Peterson (6) found that support and participation increased during the middle of the last decade in the Australian workforce. Nonetheless, effects of work intensification, unpicking the award structure, diminishing demarcations between jobs, and new skills requirements had marked effects on employee stress.

Peterson (39) argues that the Australian manufacturing industry has been significantly reduced through plant closure and downsizing, with significant consequences for increased levels of stress among both those remaining and those displaced. Similarly, Ferrie (24) and Murphy and Pepper (25) highlight the significant stress consequences following episodes of downsizing in the public and private sectors, particularly when this occurs repeatedly in a relatively unplanned fashion. That is, structural shifts in manufacture and the development of flexible modes of production that overextend the capacities of workers have led to increased levels of stress among workers and managers in the manufacturing sector.

Consequently, a review of the implementation of Global Best Practice instituted to provide competitive advantage in neo-liberal economies identifies that the stress effects have been most severe among managers. Many have had a difficult position in that they must foster a spirit of participation and cooperation while still maintaining budgetary and fiscal accountability. Staying competitive is important, but if it is at the cost of employees losing important collective and individual goals and increasing levels of negative health impacts, critical questions need to be asked about this management approach and philosophy. In addition, the diminution of the collective trade-union movement has meant that, in individual enterprises, employees are under more pressure to accept and adopt the situation as defined by management. Further studies are needed of the impact of Global Best Practice on employee and management stress in order to accommodate adjustments to management and employee relations and to the newer range of demands by the production process.

Stress as an Epidemic

Stress at work has been long considered to be an epidemic or to have emerged in epidemic proportions over the last decade. Part of this stress epidemic has been more an *apparent* rather than a *real* growth as awareness of stress at work has increased (and obviously many other work conditions have improved during the last century). That is, " public awareness of work stress has never been greater than at the current time, not least because of the number of high-profile court cases, dating from the mid-1990s (in the U.K.), in which employers have sought compensation for health problems putatively caused by adverse experiences at work" (38, p. 1). Wainwright and Calnan (38) claim that developed societies have seen a virulent and new epidemic of work stress "contributing to the loss of between 5 and 6 million working days (in the U.K.) and costing the country more that 5 million Pounds a year" (38, p. 1).

The Extent of the Epidemic

The consequences of stress on the human body include: increased depression, anxiety, thyroid disorders, heart disease, high blood pressure, ulcers; lower levels of self-esteem, job satisfaction, and motivation; as well as higher cholesterol levels (30, p. 2). In addition, anxiety and depression are the greatest stress-related conditions seen by general practitioners in the U.K. affecting 20 percent of the working population in the U.K. and more than 15 percent of those in the U.S.

Comcare (the Australian OHS and rehabilitation agency for federal employees) reports that the causes of stress among federal government employees (41) were:

- Interpersonal conflict (24 percent)
- Pressure from deadlines (24 percent)
- Anxiety caused by organizational change (22 percent)
- Physical or verbal abuse (17 percent)
- Performance counseling and other management processes (7 percent)

- Forced relocation and organizational restructure (6 percent)
- The extensive downsizing in the Australian public service (civil service) has resulted in increased stress levels for middle managers, supervisors, paraprofessionals, and professionals.

Safetyline, a Western Australian government publication (45), outlines several causes of stress. These include: organizational change; excessive workloads; pervasive monitoring; poor work environments; meaningless work; changing work requirements; inadequate equipment; poor relationships with colleagues; lack of support; emotionally demanding work; and a lack of control and influence.

Incidence ratios refer to the number of cases out of 100 that received compensation. In Australia, incidence rates for stress over 8 years from 1994– 2001 demonstrate that there has been a consistently high level of stress in the Australian workforce. The National Occupational Health and Safety Online Statistics database was examined (note 42). Incidence rates are presented for each year for occupational groups and for each state, showing a recent rise in stress-compensation cases in the most recent 2 years. The compensation statistics confirm Peterson's (6) conclusion that stress is now highest among managerial groups and lowest for blue-collar groups, a significant change from a decade or two ago.

Together, the data presented in Tables 1, 2, and 3 represent an "epidemic" of stress. Commonwealth figures (C'wth) for 1994/5 (Table 3) are several times higher than for subsequent years, and it was only 12 months later that Comcare developed "best practice" guidelines and policy for federal employees. Even then, Commonwealth stress figures are higher in subsequent years than all states, except for the Northern Territory.

However, there have been differences in incidence rates between the states over the 7-year period (note 42). For example, in the earlier years New South Wales had higher rates except for Tasmania (1994/5). Since then, Northern Territory has had either equal or the highest rates. This may reflect state differences in providing support for compensation or making compensation more difficult. However, in the Northern Territory it may also be due to the occupational mix, with a spread across some more dangerous industries, work occuring in more isolated regions, a higher overall turnover rate in that geographical area, and particular local pressures. The slightly higher incidence rate for 1994–6 can be explained by a later tightening

Table 1

Incidence rate for stress among Australian public service workers, by year

Years	1994–5	1995–6	1996–7	1997–8	1998–9	1999–2000	2000–1
Incident rate	0.9	0.8	0.6	0.6	0.6	0.6	0.8

Table 2

Incidence rate for stress among Australian public service workers,
by occupational group, by year

Years	1994–5	1995–6	1996–7	1997–8	1998–9	1999–2000	2000–1
Managers	0.9	0.8	0.7	0.6	0.6	0.6	0.9
Professionals	1.4	1.1	0.9	0.8	0.7	0.8	1.0
Paraprofessionals	2.6	2.1	1.6	1.4	1.3	1.5	1.0
Trades	0.3	0.2	0.2	0.2	0.2	0.2	0.3
Clerks	1.4	1.0	0.8	0.7	0.6	0.5	0.5
Personal service	0.5	0.5	0.5	0.5	0.5	0.5	0.8
Plant and machine	0.8	0.7	0.6	0.6	0.5	0.7	0.6
Laborer	0.5	0.5	0.4	0.4	0.4	0.4	0.8

Table 3

Incidence rate for stress among Australian public service workers, by state, by year

Years	1994–5	1995–6	1996–7	1997–8	1998–9	1999–2000	2000–1
NSW	1.2	1.4	1.0	1.0	0.7	0.7	0.9
Vic	0.0	0.6	0.0	0.0	0.5	0.4	0.7
Qld	1.1	0.5	0.5	0.3	0.4	0.6	0.8
WA	0.4	0.5	0.5	0.6	0.5	0.5	0.4
SA	1.0	0.5	0.9	0.8	0.8	0.7	0.9
Tas	1.8	0.1	0.9	0.6	0.8	0.7	0.5
NT	0.8	0.3	1.4	1.1	1.1	0.9	0.9
C'wth	3.8	0.8	1.4	1.3	0.9	0.6	1.3

up of regulations surrounding awarding compensation payments for stress, for example in Queensland (Table 1). Rates of paraprofessional stress claims are higher across all years, followed by professionals, managers, and clerks (Table 2). This confirmed self-reported data found by Peterson (6).

It was in the context of the social and political types of changes in work identified above that the "epidemic" of stress emerged. However, it was not the social and economic changes alone, marked by increased work intensification (longer hours, more effort on the job and decreased job security), that explain the causes of an epidemic. Coupled with this was the acceptance that stress was part of OSH and that it was legitimate to compensate workers for severe stress from work.

There are lessons from the legitimation of RSI as documented by Willis (43). Willis demonstrated that a contributing factor in the development of an epidemic was the medical and legal acceptance of the condition for compensation. After the legitimating process occurred (as with RSI), a large number of stress cases were submitted for compensation and accepted. There are difficulties, however, with this argument because it may draw some attention away from the fact that decades of research have gone into building the case for compensation and that medico-legal and political factors have historically acted as stumbling blocks to acceptance for compensation (i.e., they supported a management perspective). Willis (43) strongly acknowledges this point and in fact it is at the basis of his analysis. While compensation is a difficult process and there are a number of barriers to acknowledging that stress is a real condition, nonetheless, stress had become part of OSH due to the results of intensive research and efforts of significant interest and pressure groups.

BEST PRACTICE APPROACHES FOR
DEALING WITH STRESS

Ways of dealing with stress have been elaborated in the scientific literature over the past decade. Many of these approaches were based on stress management, and while they provided some palliative relief from symptoms of stress through short-term solutions, the *causes of stress* were rarely addressed. Jordan and coworkers (30) report that these largely ineffective programs tend to focus on the individual and ignore workplace conditions and pressures such as job design and workflow factors.

Truly preventive programs require addressing aspects of organizational and management change and changes in regulation. The following section outlines a range of approaches to reducing stress and dealing with the consequences of stress. In Britain, the Health and Safety Executive (HSE) commissioned a report on prevention and management of stress at work (30). They maintain that there are three ways of dealing with stress:

• Primary interventions focus on changing physical environments and socio-political factors to match workers needs.
• Secondary interventions help workers manage stress without modifying stressors in the workplace.
• Tertiary prevention focuses on employees experiencing difficulty and trying to adapt behavior without changing work practices.

Jordan and coworkers (30) argue that most interventions are secondary and tertiary rather than primary strategies that focus on the causes, such as organizational change. This is because: (a) senior managements usually do not take responsibility; (b) psychologists generally focus on individual factors; (c) there are difficulties involved in conducting intervention and evaluation studies; and

(d) there is a lack of empirical cost-benefit financial evidence. More detailed analysis of these approaches is provided below.

Best Practice Approaches—A Review

Jordan and coworkers (30) reviewed different types of approaches to dealing with stress in organizations. They reported three types of interventions that focused on different organizational and individual factors (30, p. 7). These were

- Programs focusing on the organization—training and selection; education and training; environmental and physical characteristics; communication; job restructure and redesign; or other organizational interventions.
- Programs focusing on individuals and organizations—support groups for co-workers; person-environment fit; roles; or autonomy and participation.
- Programs focused at the individual—relaxation; biofeedback; meditation; exercise; cognitive behavior therapy; employee-assistance programs; or time management.

In the review by Jordan and colleagues (30), only 40 percent of intervention strategies focused on organizational factors, 55 percent on the organizational/individual level, and 70 percent on the individual level. However, they maintain that programs should focus on organizational factors and involve senior and middle management.

The model developed in the review indicated several components of good practice stress intervention. These were:

- Involvement of top management
- Interventions focusing on individuals, teams, and the whole organization
- An appraisal of activities at work to assess OSH risks, and collection of baseline data for later comparison
- Comprehensive stress program prevention requirements, with improved communication channels
- A participative approach with middle managers, representatives of unions, and employees involved in the process
- A plan focusing on aims, resources, and responsibilities.

Out of 74 studies reviewed, only 9 used a work-focused approach. Features of these programs included:

- Specific interventions based on risk assessment
- A multi-dimensional approach
- The development of effective communication channels
- A participative approach.

One Netherlands intervention in a hospital reported an absenteeism rate of 9 percent. A survey was administered to collect data on risk factors and groups.

As a result of the findings, a series of interventions were introduced. These included a computer system introduced to control bed occupancy rates; employees provided with a departmental secretary; additional lifting equipment purchased and height adjustment tables introduced in the pharmacy; job rotation provided to give employees varied work; supervisors provided with training in performance reviews and managing absenteeism; courses in stress management and dealing with violence provided; and guidance manuals provided to those caring for sick employees. One of the important outcomes of the interventions was the recognition that stress can affect anyone in the organization.

Jordan and coworkers (30) report that there is an over reliance on stress-management programs in scientific studies, and an increasing importance placed on developing support structures and allowing managers and employees to participate in programs. They suggest that the most effective approach is to focus on both individual and organizational factors. Major factors in the success of interventions have been allowing employees to participate in planning programs, implementing changes, evaluating their effects, and support from management.

Best Practice—An Australian Government Experience

As early as 1996, Comcare mobilized a "best practice" response to stress at work for those employed in the federal government. The following have been reported as best practice responses to stress (41):

At *State* government level:

• Health and wellness programs funded
• Running of courses in leadership skills
• Provision of counsellors and psychological services
• Institution of health-promotion programs, including teaching of coping skills
• Critical incident stress counseling
• A focus by managers on needs analysis
• Structured rehabilitation programs provided to enhance employment in other agencies prior to return to work
• Development of employee-assistance programs.

At *Commonwealth (Federal)* government level:

• Identifying stressors such as organizational change; workload; hours of work; the environment; ergonomics; individual employee emotional health; knowledge, skill, and needs for training and support
• Access and priority given to the level of risk exposure, severity, and the adequacy of controls
• Prevention and management programs instituted, including planning; new programs; allocating resources; assigning responsibility; utilizing management information systems; implementing training; and coordinating approaches

- In addition, a risk management approach and a consultative approach in line with OHS philosophy incorporated line management into the OSH plan.

Recommendations from the Victorian Trades Hall Council (an Australian union body) (44):

- Governments support the call from the Australian Council of Trade Unions for reasonable limits to working hours
- The National Occupational Health and Safety Commission recognize work-related stress as an important issue
- That employers accept that stress is an important OSH issue
- That employers ensure adequate levels of staff, supervisory training, and consultation with workers and OSH representatives
- That unions continue to pursue stress as an important issue
- That unions ensure that Enterprise Bargaining Agreements include working conditions and not just wages
- That OSH representatives continue to be trained in the use of incident reports and Provisional Improvement Notices, and to address and attempt to resolve stress-related issues in the workplace.

Safetyline (45) recommends the following organizational procedures to reduce stress in the workplace:

- Jointly develop with staff organizational policy and grievance procedures covering preventative approaches
- Develop and implement policy among management in the first instance to demonstrate organizational commitment
- Ensure that people work according to their skill levels
- Provide genuine opportunities for participation in decisions about workload, roles, OSH, responsibilities, and career
- Create a culture where employees have a sense of ownership and control over their work
- Account for employees' out-of-work responsibilities.

In Australia, generally, the federal government agency ComCare has been more proactive in providing comprehensive "best practice" guidelines than state government agencies.

Changes to Working Hours

O'Neill (46) maintains that Australian workers have been requesting shorter hours to relieve the stress of work and to provide a better home/work interface. The Australian Workplace Industrial Relations Survey (1995) reported on by Peterson (6) demonstrated that hours of work had continued to increase through the decade.

He demonstrated in his analysis of a national database that increased working hours were a significant predictor of stress.

Chandler, Berg, and Barry (8) also maintain that, in the European Union, the U.K. has the longest working hours. Nonetheless, the public perception is that British workers are lazy. Restrictions to number of hours worked per week have already been introduced in Europe, but in the U.K. and in Australia the number of hours per week continues to increase. Some countries have demonstrated that a ceiling of a certain number of work hours per week can be established, concurrently reducing the stress associated with longer hours and possibly creating more jobs. However, as has been demonstrated by Global Best Practice in manufacture, employers are willing to offer less-regulated employment contracts to reduce expenditure and diminish the coverage of regulations. Therefore, effective national policy on working hours is required to reduce the incidence of stress, and this needs to be enforced.

Training Programs

One of the ways by which policy can reduce stress (and related issues such as bullying) in the workplace is through the delivery of training programs to managers to improve their awareness. The Australian New South Wales Department of Industrial Relations in 2000/2001 (47) adopted this policy. The advantage of training programs aimed at management are that they overcome the problems of some health-promotion programs, which encourage people to change their behaviors without necessarily having adequate resources (such as control and influence at work) at their disposal. The focus of training programs on management directs attention to those with some influence and control of work, who may be in a position to change the quality of supervision and the way that work is done.

Preventing Traumatic Stress

Many workers are vulnerable to the stressful effects following traumatic events. These may include police and fire service personnel, emergency workers, and even health care employees. Kelly (48) provides a best practice approach for dealing with exposure to traumatic events by multi-disciplinary rural health practitioners. She argues that these practitioners are susceptible to adverse events due to the multiplicity of their roles and to the limited rest time that they have to recover from stressful events at work. Kelly (48) maintains there are a number of sources of traumatic stress for these workers, including: moral conflicts associated with inadequate time to prepare for some of their roles in healthcare; the lack of anonymity; inter-relationships between perpetrators, victims, and families with problems such as domestic violence and crime; and the public nature of the practitioner's role. Added to this can be emotional trauma from dealing with death.

There are many additional factors which can exacerbate traumatic responses, including: inappropriate management attitudes; the community wide effect; living in a small community; legal issues; difficulties in communicating with the community; and the likely impact of increased stress on the family.

Based on a review of the Australian experience, Kelly (48) recommends that the following practices be engaged to reduce the impact of post-traumatic stress among rural health workers. Some of these may be relevant to other employees who are likely to experience posttraumatic stress:

- Where possible, prevent traumatic events.

If this is not possible,

- Provide skills training to management for more predictable events
- Provide an emotionally supportive organization, which might include training managers in appropriate support techniques. The supportive environment needs to have personnel trained to understand the nature of emotionally draining events on practitioners
- Make support services available for health care organizations and government departments to
  - Provide help lines
  - Offer employee assistance programs
  - Provide on-site interventions for communities, employees, and managers.

Kelly (48) details specific risk-assessment and action processes that can be adopted for those dealing with traumatic event-induced stress. Similar recommendations can be adopted by organizations where the environment has a number of stressors. This chapter, however, seeks to extend the principles upon which organizations should provide supports for those who experience stress.

Best Practice Principles for Dealing with Stress:
The Organization and Management Response

One of the major problems when an employee is stressed at work is the lack of a "safety net" at the outset of stress for the employee. Even in many of the more OSH "enlightened" workplaces, the usual passage for an employee who is stressed is into an employer-sponsored counseling program. At that point (even though the counseling program may provide some support for the individual), much has been lost. Without any mechanism to confront the *cause* of stress, the employee quickly becomes the victim, capable usually only of a passive response and recovery, not just from the event but from the organizational process in dealing with the event. In most cases, what is missing is a "safety net" that is policy for managers and OHS committees to adopt and enact. Stressful experiences often involve a line manager or an area of line-management responsibility, and may be related to an interpersonal conflict between employees, or with management, an unworkable work schedule, or the like. There needs to be a mechanism so that the employee can be protected from the effects of the stressful situation and stay within the organization to be helped to negotiate a new approach to the situation rather than being removed, with the problem which created the stress still remaining.

One system for dealing with employee stress has received a best practice award from Comcare (Australia). The system is based around training mediators, whose role is to intervene when stress is first reported and to provide negotiated support for the employee before their stress becomes a management issue or a potential threat to the employee's job. Peterson (49) presented a case study of an Australian national air services organization which showed how a system of trained mediators in the organization can provide a "safety net" for stressed employees and reduce absenteeism, sick leave, and turnover. A person who reports stress works to a trained negotiator may resolve the problem before it becomes a management issue. If there is a need to meet and negotiate with management, the mediator would be the third party providing support until the problem is resolved. At the same time the stressed employee is offered counseling support, but stays supported within the organization by their mediator to try and resolve the causes of stress.

CONCLUSION

The epidemic nature of stress has meant that it has become a firmly established part of the OSH debate. Management, however, does not always concede that stress is a problem and often tends to blame the individual employee for being susceptible to the condition.

Stress has developed into an epidemic over the past decade or so. With the development of neo-liberalism (7) there has been a greater emphasis in fostering managerial perspectives at work. Bray and Bray (50) argue for a re-evaluation of the practices of neo-liberalism. They focus on neo-liberalism's effects on emerging labor movements and emerging citizenship issues. King (51) also reports on the experience of changing European economies and the effects that mass privatization has had in making restructuring difficult. Part of the effect of neo-liberalism has been the development of Global Best Practice production methods (34) as a way of meeting the need for competitiveness. Flecker and Krenn (52) have examined the spread and effects that GBP has bought through new forms of human resources and skill levels in countries such as Austria, Sweden, and the U.K. Newer work practices such as outworking, electronic surveillance, tele-working and the like, and practices such as Global Best Practice for production signal a set of work principles and practices and management philosophy that require more attention in stress research. It is a pervading argument that in a global economy organizations must be competitive to survive, but some of this has come at a cost that is important to individual and collective needs. Without putting GBP into the context of the development of neo-liberal economies and increasing deregulation and open market economies, it can be difficult to develop a strong perspective and critique of these practices.

These types of social, political, and work-practice changes have created a much greater need for the development of "best practice" models for stress prevention that managers who are keen to address the epidemic of stress can adopt. "Best practice" models for dealing with stress are available in the literature, but it can be difficult for organizations to identify and adopt effective models as relatively few comprehensive approaches exist. Governments have produced effective guidelines, and the ILO has been involved in critical evaluation of the causes and outcomes of stress and ways of dealing with it. A number of other agencies have developed guidelines appropriate to their industry. Nonetheless, one area where substantial work is needed is on policies and practices to protect employees once they have developed stress. Not only management but OSH committees need to become more proactive in finding suitable solutions that lead to changes in work practices beyond simply providing counseling.

Effecting "best practice" stress prevention guidelines are a government responsibility. There are extensive costs for taxpayers from stress-induced ill health in all industrialized countries, through compensation, diminished productivity, and hidden costs borne by the community, families, and individuals. Stress prevention is also a trade union responsibility, and their role is particularly important as they can provide resistance to corporate encroachment into workers' entitlement on quality-of-life issues, and support workers tasks which are susceptible to stress. Consequently, a number of parties need to be involved in the development and implementation of policy guidelines and of strategies to reduce stress. These guidelines need to be initially directed at management and adopted by them in order to demonstrate organizational commitment to stress "best practice." Without significant and immediate effort, the "epidemic" of stress at work is likely to result in extensive loss of productivity, diminished profits for firms, and extensive costs externalized more widely on taxpayers across the industrialized world.

REFERENCES

1. Selye, H. A. A syndrome produced by diverse nocuous agents. *Nature* 138: 32, 1936.
2. Mason, J. W. The scope of psychoendocrine research. *Psychosom. Med.* 30: 565–575, 1968.
3. Mason, J. W. A review of psychoendocrine research on the pituitary-adrenal corticol system. *Psychosom. Med.* 30: 576–607, 1968.
4. Bush, I. E. Chemical and biological factors in the activity of adrenocortical steroids. *Pharmacol. Rev.* 14: 317–445, 1962.
5. Peterson, C. L. *Stress at Work: A Sociological Perspective.* Baywood, Amityville, NY, 1999.
6. Peterson, C. L. Changes at work in Australia and stress. In *Work Stress: Studies in the Context and Content of Stress at Work: Selected Readings,* pp. 11–32. Baywood, Amityville, NY, 2003.

7. Coburn, D. Globalisation, neo-liberalism, inequities and health: Beyond the income inequalities hypothesis. Paper delivered to the International Sociological Association, Brisbane, June 2002, 2003.

8. Chandler, D., Berg, E., and Barry, J. Stress in the UK. In *Work Stress: Studies in the Context and Content of Stress at Work: Selected Readings*, edited by C. L. Peterson, pp. 33–52. Baywood, Amityville, NY, 2003.

9. Karasek, R. A. Job demands, job decision latitude and mental strain: Implications for job re-design. *Admin. Sci. Q.* 24: 285–308. 1979.

10. Karasek, R. A. Job socialisation and job strain: The implications of two related psychosocial mechanisms for job design. In *Working Life: A Social Science Contribution to Work Reform*, edited by B. Gardell, and G. Johansson, pp. 75–94. Wiley, New York, 1981.

11. Frankenhaeuser, M., and Johansson, G. Stress at work: Psychological and psychosocial aspects. Special issue: Occupational and life stress and the family. *Int. Rev. Appl. Psychol.* 35: 287–299, 1986.

12. Gardell, B. Autonomy and participation at work. In *Society, Stress and Disease: Working Life*, edited by L. Levi, pp. 279–289. Oxford University Press, Oxford, 1981.

13. Levi, L. *Society, Stress and Disease: Working Life*. Oxford University Press, Oxford, 1984.

14. Aronsson, G. Dimensions of control as related to work organisation, stress, and health. *Int. J. Health Serv.* 19: 459–486, 1989.

15. Jackson, S. E. Participation and decision making as a strategy for reducing job-related strain. *J. Appl. Psychol.* 68: 3–19, 1983.

16. Brumpus, M. F., Crouter, A. C., and McHale, S. M. Work demands and dual-earner couples: Implications for parents' knowledge about children's daily lives in middle childhood *J. Marriage Fam.* 61: 465–475, 1999.

17. De Vaus, D., and Wells, Y. Stress among older workers and retirees. In *Work Stress: Studies in the Context and Content of Stress at Work: Selected Readings*, edited by C. L. Peterson, pp. 245–269. Baywood, Amityville, NY, 2003.

18. Obradovic, M., and Obradovik, J. Conflict of family and work roles: Causes, effects and unresolved research problems. *Drustvena Istrasivanja* 10: 709–730, 2000.

19. Lai, G. Work and family roles and psychological well-being in urban China. *J. Health Soc. Behav.* 36: 11–37, 1995.

20. Rwamporono, R. K. Social support: Its mediation of gendered patterns in work-family stress and health for dual-earner couples. *Dissert. Abstr. Int. Hum. Soc. Sci.* 61: 3792-A–3793-A, 2001.

21. Luecken, L. J., Suarez, E. C., Kuhn, C. M., Barefoot, J. C., Blumenthal, J. A., Siegler, I. C., and Williams, R. B. Stress in employed women: Impact of marital status and children at home on neurohormone output and home strain. *Psychosom. Med.* 59: 352–359, 1997.

22. Jones, F., and Fletcher, B. Taking work home: A study of daily fluctuations in work stressors, effects on moods and impacts on marital partners. *J. Occup. Organ. Psychol.* 69: 89–106, 1996.

23. Avison, W. R. Roles and resources: The effects of family structure and employment on women's psychosocial resources and psychological distress. *Res. Commun. Ment. Health* 8: 233–256, 1995.

24. Ferrie, J. Privatisation and downsizing in the UK public sector: Labour market change, job insecurity, and health. In *Work Stress: Studies in the Context and Content of Stress at Work: Selected Readings*, edited by C. L. Peterson, pp. 73–109. Baywood, Amityville, NY, 2003.
25. Murphy, L., and Pepper, L. Effects of organisational downsizing on worker stress and health in the United States. In *Work Stress: Studies in the Context and Content of Stress at Work: Selected Readings*, edited by C. L. Peterson, pp. 53–71. Baywood, Amityville, NY, 2003.
26. Freedman, S. A., Gluck, N., Tuval-Mashiach, R., Brandes, D., Peri, T., and Shalev, A. Y. Gender differences in responses to traumatic events: A prospective study. *J. Traumat. Stress* 15: 407–413, 2002.
27. Crouter, A. C., and Manke, B. The changing American workplace: Implications for individuals and families. *Fam. Relat.* 43: 117–124, 1994.
28. Wells, Y., and De Vaus, D. Work stress and caregiver stress. In *Work Stress: Studies in the Context and Content of Stress at Work: Selected Readings*, edited by C. L. Peterson, pp. 223–243. Baywood, Amityville, NY, 2003.
29. Johns Hopkins. Personal communication, April 2001.
30. Jordan, J., Gurr, E., Tinline, G., Giga, S., Faragher, B., and Cooper, C. *Beacons of Excellence in Stress Prevention Research,* Report 133. Health and Safety Executive, London, 2003.
31. Johnston, A., and Cheng, M. Electronic surveillance in the workplace: Concerns for employees and challenges for privacy advocates. Paper presented at the International Conference on Personal Data Protection, Personal Information Dispute Mediation Committee, Korea Information Security Agency, 2002.
32. Haselhoff, I. Teleworking: OH&S issues for employers. *Saf. Sci. Mon.,* Special Issue, 3: 1–8, 1999.
33. Allvin, M., and Aronsson, G. The future of work environment reforms: Does the concept of work environment apply within the new economy? *Int. J. Health Serv.* 33: 99–111, 2003.
34. Cited in Van liemt, G. Applying global best practice: Workers and the "new" methods of production organisation. Employment and Training Papers 15. Employment and Training Department, International Labour Office, Geneva, 1998.
35. Davidsson, B., and Wernstedt, F. Characterisation of Just-In-Time 2003. www.ide.bth.se/~pdv/Papers/AAMAS2002-WS.pdf.
36. Best Manufacturing Practice (BMP) 2003. www.bmpcoe.org/index.html.
37. Enterprise Europe, Global Marketplace, 2001. europa.eu.int/comm/enterprise/library/enterprise-europe/issue4/articles/en/enterprise 17_en.htm.
38. Wainwright, D., and Calnan, C. *Work Stress: The Making of a Modern Epidemic.* Open University Press, Buckingham, U.K., 1998.
39. Peterson, C. L. Stress amongst blue-collar workers. In *Work Stress: Studies in the Context and Content of Stress at Work: Selected Readings*, edited by C. L. Peterson, pp. 181–201. Baywood, Amityville, NY, 2003.
40. Taylor, F. *Scientific Management.* Harper, New York, 1947.
41. Office of the Commissioner for Public Employment Work Place Stress. A global disease of the 90's affecting all professions and all categories of workers. *Information Series*, No. 1. OCPE, Canberra, Australia, 1996.

42. Peterson, C. L. Stress among health care workers. *J. Occup. Health Saf. Aust. N.Z.* 19: 49–58, 2003.
43. Willis, E. RSI as a social process. *Commun. Health Stud.* 10: 209–210, 1986.
44. Victorian Trades Hall Council (VTHC). Stress, workload and job control. VTHC OHS Representatives Conference, June 19, 2002.
45. Safetyline essentials; Work related stress: Different meanings to different people. safetyline.wa.gov.au/pagebin/pg004998.htm, 2003.
46. O'Neill, S. Redistributing work: Methods and possibilities. Research Paper 26. Department of the Parliamentary Library, Parliament of Australia, Canberra, Australia, 1995–1996.
47. NSW Department of Commerce. Office of Industrial Relations Annual Report. www.dir.nsw.gov.au/about/annual/ar01/review.html, 2000/2001.
48. Kelly, K. Preventing job related posttraumatic stress disorder among remote health practitioners: Best practice guidelines. CRANA Occasional Paper No. 3. Council of Remote Area Nurses of Australia, Northern Territory, 1999.
49. Peterson, C. L. Dealing with stress-related disorders in the public sector. In *Occupational Health and Safety in Australia: Industry, Public Sector and Small Business* edited by C. Mayhew and C. Peterson, pp. 174–186. Allen and Unwin, St. Leonards, Australia, 1999.
50. Bray, D. W., and Bray, M. W. Beyond neoliberal globalisation: Another world. *Latin Am. Perspect.* 29: 117–126, 2002.
51. King, L. Shock privatisation: The effects of rapid large-scale privatisation on enterprise restructuring. *Polit. Soc.* 31: 3–30, 2003.
52. Flecker, J., and Krenn, M. Wandel der industrearbeit swischen nationalen traditionen und globalem "best practice." *Oster. Z. Soziol.* 21: 3–24, 1996.

CHAPTER 8

Pain Associated with Prolonged Constrained Standing: The Invisible Epidemic

Karen Messing, Katherine Lippel, Ève Laperrière,
Marie-Christine Thibault

The discussions in this chapter are focused on a widespread epidemic that remains largely invisible. There are a range of reasons for this "invisible epidemic," including the relative powerlessness of the workers who experience pain from prolonged standing, diagnosis difficulties, and inadequacies with the regulatory framework.

INTRODUCTION

In occupational health research, dangerous agents and conditions are identified so that they can be eliminated from the workplace and the affected workers can be compensated. Demonstrating a link between an exposure and a disease can cost employers money for prevention and compensation. Inability to make such links can slow prevention, interfere with compensation, and thus cost workers and their families their health, economic security, and even their lives. In addition, occupational accidents and diagnosed diseases are only part of the cost to the worker exacted by failure to identify harmful working conditions. Damage is made visible when the workers miss work or bear evidence of their condition: bandages, slings, or hearing aids. But a number of workplace conditions produce effects on health and well-being that are silent, since they usually do not lead to missed work, visible injury, or compensation. These mental and physical aggressors may still give rise to a great deal of pain and suffering. This chapter examines such a situation: the chronic, often intense pain associated with work in a prolonged constrained standing position.

It is our argument that the silent pain may contribute to the current epidemic of musculoskeletal disorders (1) as well indicating a possibility of future epidemics of cardiovascular problems (2, 3). Occupational health and safety strategies predicated on waiting for epidemiological data before undertaking prevention measures will inevitably lead to emergence of such new epidemics. The late 20th century saw an enormous movement toward deregulation as well as more restrictive interpretation of existing regulations. In some countries, tribunals are now expecting workers and their unions to demonstrate the need for prevention scientifically. This approach means that many North American jurisdictions ignore workers' reports of pain and discomfort, reports that could lead to earlier detection of risks. In this chapter, we describe one example of a situation in which relatively simple solutions that are available to reduce workers' discomfort and pain are being ignored because prevention strategies are focused essentially on those working conditions that have been demonstrated to be dangerous. By definition, the full consequences of ignoring these early warning signs are yet unknown.

Among workers of all ages, back pain associated with work is about twice as common among those who stand as compared to those who usually work sitting, even after controlling for lifting weights (4). Standing at work has also been associated with pain in the lower limbs (5–7). Recently, effects on the circulatory system have been identified: varicose veins (2); chronic venous insufficiency (8); and a poorer prognosis after diagnosis of coronary artery disease (3). Standing at work has also been associated with problem pregnancies (9).

In Quebec (Canada), 59 percent of the labor force report that they usually work in a standing position (4), and only one in six of these can sit down at will. The proportion of standing workers rises to 81 percent among youth (15–24). In Canada, North America, England, and Australia, supermarket checkout clerks, bank tellers, and sales personnel usually stand without walking very much. The reasons for prolonged standing in a relatively fixed position are not obvious. In principle, someone who is able to work standing in the same place for a long time should be able to do the job sitting, with minimum rearrangement of the work station. This is shown by the fact that in many countries in Europe, as well as in Thailand, Brazil, Costa Rica, and Morocco (to name just a few that the authors have observed), these jobs are usually performed in a sitting position. For example, in the MUSIC I study of a Swedish working population aged 20–64, only 19 percent of men and 15 percent of women worked standing during more than one-tenth of the day (10). By contrast, among French workers, 58 percent of men and 49 percent of women report that their work requires them to spend a long time standing (11). There also, younger workers and those in personal services are more likely to work standing.

Our research team became interested in this problem when a supermarket employees' union[1] brought a case before the Occupational Health and Safety Commission of Quebec in 1989. A supermarket checkout clerk who suffered from

---

[1] The Syndicat des travailleuses et travailleurs des magasins Provigo de Port-Cartier, affiliated with the Confederation of National Trade Unions.

back pain asked for a seat. The union was interested in obtaining seats for all checkout clerks and supported the clerk's request. During the hearing, a professor of ergonomics, Nicole Vézina, succeeded in demonstrating that the work could be done in a seated position or, even better, with a sit-stand stool that allows a worker to pass rapidly between sitting and standing postures. The worker's case was therefore accepted by the appeals commission in 1991.[2] Because article 11.7.1 of the *Regulation respecting industrial and commercial establishments* required that a seat should be supplied where the work requirements allowed it, the appeal tribunal's decision should have led to the clerks being allowed to sit.

However, at the time of writing, 14 years later, supermarket checkout clerks in Quebec still work standing, as do many bank tellers and most salespeople. A study of 23 restaurant and sales workers observed for a typical 8-hour day in 2001 (12) showed that food servers spent, on the average, 70 percent of their time in static standing, and 30 percent walking; shoe sales personnel spent 63 percent and 35 percent respectively; store and restaurant cashiers spent 90 percent and 9 percent (Figure 1). When they walked, 45 percent of the walking sequences were composed of only one or two steps, showing that it would be relatively easy to arrange the work site to allow for sitting. However, sitting time ranged from 0 percent to 2 percent and seats were not readily available. Many of these workers had back pain, more often among those who walked the least. Many also suffered from foot pain (Figure 2). A control group who spent most of the work time sitting had no pain at the end of the work day (data not shown).

We will examine obstacles to improving this situation, which fall roughly into three categories: (1) scientific approaches to working postures; (2) difficulties stemming from the regulatory framework on prevention and compensation; and (3) a lack of worker mobilization on this issue.

SCIENTIFIC RESEARCH ON PROLONGED STATIC STANDING

Rules of evidence in public health place the burden of proof on the workers. To avoid unnecessary effort and expenditure, public health authorities will not usually act on a condition until a link between exposures and a well-defined disease or condition is established with a very low probability of error. In scientific journals, the usual probability of error allowed is 5 percent (13). In civil litigation and workers' compensation cases, the link should theoretically be accepted when the probability of error is less than 50 percent (14), but in practice, compensation of injured workers does not in general begin until the link has been established to a greater degree of scientific certainty (15, 16) even though higher courts still

---

[2] *Provigo distribution inc. and Girard Syndicat des travailleuses et travailleurs des magasins Provigo de Port-Cartier (C.S.N.) and CSST. C.A.L.P. 539, 1991.*

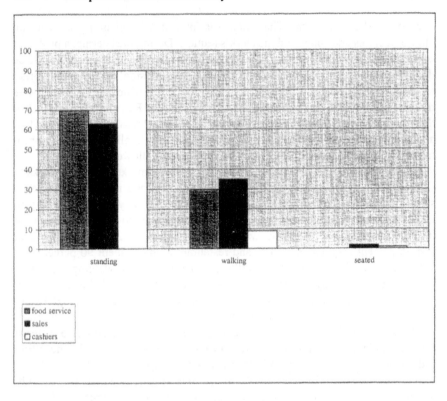

Figure 1. Percent standing and walking time among 21 restaurant and sales workers, during and 8-hour shift.

maintain that the relationship between work and disease or injury need only be shown to be more probable than not (17). In order to file a complaint against an employer for violation of health and safety regulations, evidence of the violation must be shown beyond a reasonable doubt, and the courts exact a quality of evidence as to the detrimental effect of a working condition that is tantamount to scientific certainty (14).

Establishing a relationship between a workplace exposure and a health effect comes primarily from epidemiological studies. Such studies collect data from very large groups of workers and seek associations between well-defined exposures and diagnosed conditions or responses to validated instruments (e.g., symptom inventories or questionnaire scales). Biological experiments can also help in establishing cause-effect links. In such experiments a group of subjects is exposed to a well-defined agent or condition and its responses are compared with those of a non-exposed group. Our argument here is that neither technique has been very efficient at determining the relationship between prolonged constrained

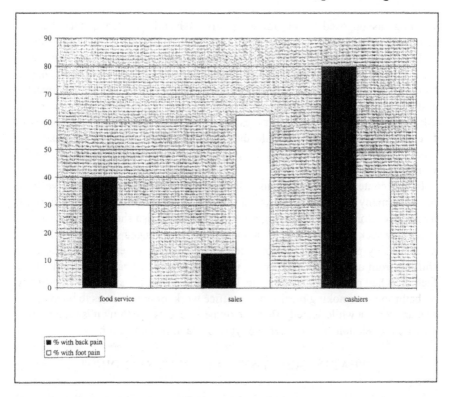

Figure 2. Leg and back pain among 21 standing workers.

standing and workers' health. We argue further that, since the scientific method does not take as its point of departure the questions asked by workers, it is ill adapted to obtaining results that will contribute to protecting their health.

Definition of the Exposure Variable

People who report that they usually stand at work may adopt a great variety of postures (18). Their *mobility* can vary from complete immobility (sewing-machine operators who must keep one foot on a pedal) to short steps (assembly line work involving one or two steps per operation) to longer walks (bank tellers who must often go to the vault) to sustained slow walking (security guards) to fast constant walking (railroad train cleaners). Their *trunk postures* can be straight, inclined (work with hospital patients), or bent over (nursery school teachers). They can have *access to seating or support for leaning* of varying duration and at intervals of different lengths, or have no access at all. Although some studies have associated standing (as opposed to sitting) with various health problems, none has yet distinguished adequately between more and less constrained standing postures, and confusion about a possible relationship between standing and health remains (19). This is an important point for workers because lack of evidence makes it harder to argue for a chair. No existing study makes it obvious that supermarket cashiers need a chair. In addition, it is hard to know exactly what workers should ask for. What kind of chair? Is it best to spend most of the time standing, with freedom to move around? Should the work station be arranged for maximum mobility, allowing for frequent sitting breaks, or for minimum mobility, so the worker can usually sit?

In the context of our work in collaboration with unions (20–22), we have talked to many workers who have told us that standing without moving is much more uncomfortable than moving around. They have also showed us the various ways they seek to relieve the pain associated with prolonged standing: by leaning on tables; by putting one foot on a telephone book or other raised surface; by shifting from one foot to another; by installing corrugated cardboard under their feet; or, when pain becomes extreme, by seeking excuses to sit for a while (going on bathroom or smoking breaks, doing office work, or hiding so as to be invisible to management while seated). Because of these reports, we think it is important to explore the relationship between the types of standing and health.

WHAT DO SCIENTISTS SAY ABOUT STANDING?

We present here a summary overview of a literature search done in the principal databases.[3] Our overall conclusion was that the few studies that attempted to document the effects of standing posture did not do it in a way that reflected

[3] The initial searches were done in 1998. For these searches, we retained only articles in scientific journals which had an English-language abstract or which were in English, French, Spanish, Italian, or German. For the MEDLINE search, since abstracts were not usually available for articles published before 1985, they were only examined if the title was not general and indicated a strong possibility that the article would be relevant; articles published more recently were examined if the title and abstract indicated they would be relevant. For the CISILO searches, only titles were available on the initial search, which resulted in 287 titles. All titles appearing relevant were pursued further. We searched the MEDLINE database in four ways. Search 1: ("Cardiovascular/epidemiology" or "musculoskeletal/ epidemiology" or "phlebitis" or "fibromyalgia" or "venous insufficiency" or "edema" or "hypertension" or "blood pressure") in keywords and ("standing" and "occupation" or "posture" and "occupation") and anywhere in the text. Search 2: ("Physiology" and "standing") anywhere in the text. Search 3: ("Prolonged standing") anywhere in the text. Search 4: ("standing" and "posture" and "occupation") anywhere in the text. We also searched MEDLINE for anything on "hairdressers" or "dentists" since these professions require standing for prolonged periods in a confined area. We searched the Arbline database for ("standing" or "posture" and "occupation") and for ("standing" and "cardiovascular" or "musculskeletal"). We searched the NIOSHTIC and CISILO databases for ("standing" or "posture") and ("cardiovascular" or "musculo-skeletal") in the abstract or title. During 1998–2003, we followed the major journals likely to report studies of the effects of standing. In 2003, we repeated the search in the PubMed medical database, using "standing" and "occupation."

questions asked by supermarket checkout clerks, bank tellers, kitchen help, or sales workers. Also, the studies concerning the effects of standing were not usually published by authors working in the English-speaking North America/Europe/ Australia/New Zealand community which is considered to constitute mainstream science, and very few were published in journals with high impact factors.[4] A review of the existing papers concluded that no evidence existed on a relation of standing/walking with back pain "because of the contradictory findings . . . and [in at least one case] a badly defined measure of exposure, namely, a yes-no question about frequent prolonged standing" (19, p. 398).

A number of studies did associate standing/walking (taken as a single exposure) with low back pain, venous insufficiency/varicose veins, and problems with pregnancy (2, 3, 5, 8, 23, 24). However, none of the epidemiological studies attempted to separate static standing from walking. This was at least in part because some researchers had found that workers and observers did not agree when asked to assess the proportion of time spent walking as opposed to standing at work. Workers' ability to estimate time spent according to body posture corresponded with observers' estimates for standing and walking taken together but not when the two were separated. Workers reported more walking time and less standing time than observers (25).

No definitions were given for standing versus walking in this very influential study (25). No attempt was made to understand why workers appeared to underestimate their standing time, or observers to overestimate it. It would seem a simple matter to separate standing from walking, but a short observation period will reveal that, since true immobility cannot be sustained for more than a few minutes, workers almost always move their feet to some extent. Only two research groups (one of them ours) have tried to define walking for these purposes (18, 26, 27). Neither has yet been able to invest the funds necessary to observe large groups of workers in the necessary degree of detail.

Thus, results of epidemiological studies have not been helpful for redefining work stations or specifying conditions for prevention of pain due to static standing, and this situation has not yet given rise to much scientific interest.

With experimental studies the problem is different, in that the journals where the work is published are better accepted and the exposure variables are usually well defined, but the results still do not reflect workplace conditions. In these studies, prolonged standing was associated with discomfort, spinal shrinkage, swelling of the lower legs, and changes in cardiovascular parameters (28–31). However, most studies required subjects to remain standing without moving their feet for long periods in a laboratory setting, a situation rarely found in real work

---

[4] Impact factors are calculated for a scientific journal based on the number of times journal articles are cited in succeeding studies. When health scientists in Canada apply for funds, reviewers are asked to check the impact factors of their publications in order to rate the candidates' productivity.

situations where workers commonly shift from foot to foot, take short steps, or lean on anything handy (18, 26).

The Effect

Discomfort is the most commonly reported effect of prolonged standing and that which figures most prominently in conversations with workers. However, only the worker can report pain. Therefore "evidence" of pain is not considered *a priori* to be objective, and its ascertainment gives rise to extensive discussion in the epidemiological literature (32–34). Over the last 15 years, political battles have raged in Australia, North America, and Europe over the recognition and prevention of pain in the upper limbs, at the expense of affected workers (35–37). Some conservative scientists dispute the use of symptom reports in these studies (38), and even some more progressive scientists do not consider pain reports to have high validity (39). Almost no research has been done on factors linked to pain in the lower extremities. Research on lower back pain yields inconsistent results, possibly because prolonged sitting is also associated with lower back pain, and standing and walking are not distinguished in most studies.

There is therefore no convincing study that establishes a relation between prolonged static standing and any pathology. Despite some physiological reasons for expecting an association, there has been no long-term study of any potential effects of constrained standing, such as the probability of cardiovascular disease or stroke.

WHAT SCIENTISTS THINK ABOUT STANDING

Based on these studies, scientists conclude that there is no evidence to link static standing with health effects. In informal conversations with researchers, we have found it very difficult to excite interest in the effects of constrained standing. Very many of those interested in human posture and movement are professors of kinesiology, ardent exercisers, or joggers who are most concerned lest workers become too sedentary. At the Swedish National Institute for Working Life, researchers are so convinced of the positive effects of standing that some have arranged their computer work stations so as to type standing (40), although they do not spend all day in a constrained standing position. One of these researchers was only persuaded to become interested in constrained static standing by a reminder of sensations he had experienced in museums. We have now dubbed this type of occupational exposure "museum walking" in order to interest researchers whose own occupational exposures may not have included prolonged static standing.

In a recent seminar in the Université du Québec à Montréal biology department, a physiologist concluded his review of studies on fatigue by saying to our research group, "You should not concentrate so much on subjective sensations, but get objective data." When asked how he explained the fatigue felt by workers exposed to static standing, unexplained by his presentation on muscular fatigue, he replied: "These are emotional questions." One of the students, a part-time sales clerk, described to him how she worked in two positions, one more constrained than the other. She said she felt much more discomfort in the more constrained task. The researcher replied that this might be due to "nervous fatigue."

Since feminist science is traditionally open to experience (41), we expected that a feminist audience would be more sensitive to workers' reports of pain. However, an experience at a scientific meeting on women's health disabused us of this idea. We began our presentation with the story of an encounter with a saleswoman who worked all day standing and had severe back and leg pain but had never asked her employer for a chair. She had explained to us: "I don't think my boss cares whether or not I smile at work." The reaction of the researchers in the room was unexpected: almost all responded that salespeople *should* work standing and that they would expect salespeople to stand at all times so as to appear available. No one appeared to find it strange to require that a saleswoman should experience pain so as to put clients at ease.

We wonder whether the fact that researchers come from a social class where they are rarely exposed to the pain associated with prolonged constrained standing, and the fact they have little contact with those exposed, makes them less likely to investigate the problem thoroughly.

WORKERS' RESPONSES

Workers themselves do not often question their employers' choice to have them stand. We recently interviewed 30 workers in the service sector (average age 28, body mass index 22.7 or slightly below the ideal weight for their height) who usually stand at work in relatively static positions (42). Only two could sit whenever they wanted to. All but one reported pain in the back and/or lower limbs, and most detailed changes in their lifestyle related to this pain (effects on recreation and sports activities, taking medication, seeing health care specialists, etc.). None of these workers had made any kind of claim for compensation or official intervention and only two had attempted to change their working posture. Reasons for not taking positive action for change included: not attributing much importance to their own comfort; fearing negative reactions from the employer if they asked for changes; having found some ways to deal with the pain on an individual basis (medication, leaning on counters, buying expensive shoes); and feeling that other aspects of the job were more problematic (getting to work enough hours for economic security, getting time off for meals, not being required to work unpaid overtime). The workers appeared to find it difficult to ask to be made comfortable at work, expressing fear that clients and supervisors would think they were lazy (42). Given the reactions of scientists described above, the workers' fears appear justified.

ERGONOMIC SOLUTIONS

As mentioned, workers have developed ways to alleviate pain associated with static standing. Whistance et al. (43) reviewed the literature and report that individuals who stand for a long time preferentially adopt asymmetrical postures, presumably to diminish lordosis (spinal curvature that puts weight on the joints in the lower back). Hansen et al. (44) showed that standing workers in a simulated postal sorting task slowly moved their center of gravity forward in order to relieve their backs. Salesclerks and restaurant workers who stand during 96 percent of their work day, walking during a third of that time, lean against supporting surfaces to alleviate pain (18).

These worker strategies could be facilitated by appropriate equipment. Adjustable chairs (45) and tables (40) can be used to allow workers to alternate quickly between sitting and standing positions. More complete approaches can be taken to re-engineering work to make it more comfortable. In a boot factory where workers stood all day, many with one foot on the pedal of a sewing machine, 77 percent of workers experienced pain. In this workplace, the Occupational Health and Safety Commission enforced action, and Vézina et al. (46) completely re-engineered the working environment, resulting in a drastic reduction in leg and foot pain. Ergonomists have also identified several aspects of the checkout clerk's worksite that should be changed to facilitate a comfortable working posture, in addition to providing a seat (20, 45, 47). Bank tellers' standing posture was rendered necessary by the arrangement of their computers and calculators, as well as certain details of anti-theft precautions. Due to a campaign by inspectors at the Québec Occupational Health and Safety Commission, and to union pressure, these arrangements were changed in some banks, and tellers now work seated. However, the will to make these changes is not yet present in most workplaces.

THE REGULATORY FRAMEWORK GOVERNING
PROLONGED STANDING

In Quebec, as in many other jurisdictions in OECD countries, promotion of healthy working conditions is addressed by the regulatory framework through a two-pronged strategy: occupational health and safety legislation prescribes rules obliging employers to provide safe working conditions under penalty of a fine if they fail to do so; and experience-rated workers' compensation premiums allow compensation boards to charge higher levies if working conditions lead to more costly compensable injury. Occupational health and safety legislation may be based on a more prescriptive approach, where specific rules apply to a vast array of working conditions, or it may adopt a more process-based approach, whereby employers and unions are called upon to work together to promote healthier workplaces (49, 50). While many European countries have opted for a more process-based approach in recent years, Quebec is still clearly applying a regulatory framework that specifies a myriad of specific rules. A general duty clause[5] dictates in fairly general terms employers' obligations to provide safe workplaces. Although it suffices to invoke the general duty clause to obtain a court order for a remedy,[6] in practice it is far more common to see the specific regulations applied by the courts. Prevention may be promoted either by sanction or by experience-rated incentives. In recent years, far more emphasis has been placed on experience rating than on occupational health and safety legislation (51, 52).

Prolonged standing is uncomfortable, even painful, but it is not usually disabling, and in cases where it may contribute to disability, it is difficult to prove causation. Workers' compensation legislation in Quebec, as elsewhere, only provides for compensation in the event of temporary or permanent disability arising out of employment. In a climate adverse to regulatory sanctions, where reliance for prevention incentives is primarily attained by experience rating, those working conditions that do not lead to compensable disability will not receive much attention when it comes to prevention.

For decades, Quebec health and safety regulations have obliged the employer to provide seats to workers when feasible,[7] and administrative tribunals ordered employers to do so, at least for supermarket cashiers, over a decade ago.[8] Yet cashiers still work standing up. How is this possible? In cases where legislators choose to identify specific risks to workers, the workers and their unions in principle no longer have to prove the working condition to be detrimental to their health; they only need prove that the protective provision has been violated. For example, it should not be necessary to prove that standing is detrimental to workers' health if the regulation specifically provides that a work station should allow a worker to sit when possible. Some employers have unsuccessfully tried to show that allowing them to sit could be detrimental to workers' health. As we shall see, employers have recently tried, with some success,[9] to confuse the administrative tribunals by relying on their previous argument (that a regulation should not apply if it leads to more dangerous working conditions) to now actually limit occupational health and safety legislation to *dangerous* working

---

[5] S. 51 of the *Occupational Health and Safety Act*, R.S.Q. c. S-2.1.

[6] *Domtar Inc.* c. *C.A.L.P.*, [1990] R.J.Q. 2190 (C.A.Q.)

[7] *Regulation respecting industrial and commercial establishments*, R.R.Q., c. S-2.1, r.9, s. 11.7.1, now in the *Regulation respecting occupational health and safety*, R.R.Q., c. S-2.1, r.19.01, s. 170.

[8] *Provigo distribution inc. and Girard Syndicat des travailleuses et travailleurs des magasins Provigo de Port-Cartier (C.S.N.) and CSST*, [1991] C.A.L.P. 539.

[9] The employer succeeded in preventing the application of the regulation in *Démo Pop* and *CSST Montreal 4*, CLP79635-71-9605-R, 31st of March 1999, confirming the reversal of a review board decision: *Démo Pop* and *CSST Montreal 4*, [1996] B.R.P. 112. The same employer was nevertheless convicted of violating the same regulation by the Labour court in *CSST* v. *Demo Pop*, T.T. Montréal 500-63-003805-998, February 14, 2000 (D.T.E. 2000T-372).

conditions, thus putting into question the legitimacy of all regulations designed to protect worker well-being when security is not at risk. It is ironic that in an age where, inspired by the WHO definition of health (53), many national jurisdictions are updating their occupational health and safety legislation to govern worker well-being explicitly (54), while in Quebec it is becoming actually less clear that regulatory provisions designed to protect worker well-being will be consistently applied.

Negotiation of more comfortable working postures is theoretically possible, since almost half of Quebec workers are in unions (55). However, those exposed to prolonged static standing tend to be young workers in non-standard, non-unionized, short-term employment. In the service occupations such as sales and cashier work, they tend to be women (13, Chapter 1). These workers' individual power is not sufficient to allow them to negotiate comfortable working postures, especially since they need to use all their negotiating power to gain minimal conditions such as sufficient hours, pay for all hours worked, and lunch breaks. Although, in major retail organizations, their jobs are increasingly unionized in Quebec, the unions tend to be in an unequal rapport with management, and job security and salary issues are a higher priority.

When working conditions are detrimental to worker health, even if they are simply uncomfortable and not disabling, it is time to question the legitimacy of a *status quo* that accepts that uncomfortable working conditions can be imposed on workers.

While one might think that it is up to the state, if not to guarantee safe and comfortable work at least to guarantee that employers provide working conditions that are not detrimental to the worker's health and well-being, this assumption may not be taken for granted in the beginning of the 21st century. To its credit, the CSST, the inspectorate authority in Quebec, has taken initiatives before the courts to order employers to provide chairs to some non-unionized employees, but during 5 years of litigation, the courts and administrative tribunals have sent out contradictory messages. Regulatory provisions obliging employers to provide chairs or benches when feasible have existed for decades, but are very rarely subject to litigation. Although the administrative tribunal ordered the employer of a large food chain to provide seating to cashiers in 1991, little was done about it other than the creation of a joint committee mandated to debate modalities of implementation of the court order. Twelve years later, the committee is still meeting and the debate goes on.

In 1995, the CSST inspectorate tried to apply the regulatory provisions, ordering that the opportunity to sit be provided to non-unionized women whose job was to invite supermarket customers to taste new products. Relying on the clearly worded health and safety regulation that provides that "Workers shall have chairs or benches put at their disposal when the nature of their work so permits," the CSST inspector gave the employer 30 days to correct the violation and provide a chair to the workers. The employer contested the correction order, and the review board confirmed the order,[10] which was subsequently struck down by the administrative appeal tribunal for reasons, which we will examine, invoked by the employer.

Parallel to the administrative process, the CSST undertook penal action before the Labour Court, and the Labour Court convicted the employer for having failed to provide seating, despite the employer's arguments that failure to provide seating did not endanger the worker.[11] This was a particularly significant decision given that the administrative tribunal had, in the interim, held that the regulation obliging the employer to provide seating, first adopted over 30 years before, was incompatible with the objectives of the *Occupational Health and Safety Act*. That *Act*, according to the administrative tribunal, provided protection only against dangerous working conditions and could not be invoked only to promote comfort and well-being.[12] The employer had questioned the legitimacy of the inspector's order, despite the clear wording in the regulation, by suggesting that to make the worker stand was not dangerous to the worker and therefore not a violation of any regulation validly adopted under the *Occupational Health and Safety Act*. This line of argument, set aside by the Labour Court, could have been relegated to the file of legal oddities were it not for the fact that it was held to be correct in the administrative tribunal decision regarding the same order of the inspectorate. Even more preoccupying is the fact that this Byzantine decision of the administrative tribunal was confirmed in review.[13] In 2003, the law was still nebulous given these contradictions in judgments by the different tribunals.

The interest of this case is that it illustrates the dominant discourse of both employers and some administrative tribunal decision-makers to the effect that working conditions that aren't "dangerous" are not only acceptable, they are subtracted from the regulatory authority. In 2001, the regulatory authority revamped the occupational health and safety regulations. Although the actual content of the provisions governing prolonged standing was not changed, the reaffirmation of the legislative will regarding the provision of chairs allows us to conclude that the new regulation clearly aims to do more than simply protect workers against danger. Section 3 of the *Regulation respecting Occupational Health and Safety*[14] provides that "The purpose of this Regulation is to establish standards pertaining in particular to the quality of air, temperature, humidity, heat stress, lighting, noise and other contaminants, sanitary facilities, ventilation,

---

[10]*Démo Pop* and *CSST Montreal 4*. B.R.P. 112, 1996.

[11]*CSST* v. *Demo Pop*, T.T. Montréal 500-63-003805-998, February 14, 2000 (D.T.E. 2000T-372).

[12]"La Commission des lésions professionnelles retient que la CSST ne peut invoquer la seule notion de confort et de bien-être pour l'application de l'article 11.7.1 du règlement S-2.1 r.9 et ainsi, ignorer l'objet même de la loi et ainsi, la notion de danger pour la santé et la sécurité et l'intégrité physique des travailleurs et travailleuses qui est la base même de la Loi sur la santé et la sécurité du travail." *Démo Pop* and *CSST Montreal 4*, p. 13. CLP, 79635-60-9605, May 7, 1998.

[13]*Démo Pop* et *CSST Montreal 4*. CLP 79635-71-9605-R, March 31, 1999.

[14]R.R.Q., c. S-2.1, r.19.01

hygiene, sanitation and cleanliness in establishments, area conditions, storage and handling of dangerous substances, machine and tool safety, certain high risk tasks, individual protective equipment and the transportation of workers to ensure the quality of the work environment, to safeguard the health of workers and to ensure their safety and physical well-being." As of September 2003, we could find no case law concerning charges brought against employers under this new regulation, so it remains to be seen whether the new regulation will dissipate the ambiguity created by previous case law.

CONCLUSION

In Canada, Australia, and many other countries, a relatively powerless group, young workers in non-standard jobs, experiences pain every day. This situation is tolerated and even encouraged by supervisors, employers, scientists, and the public. The North American occupational health and safety system is not well adapted to identification and prevention of conditions that do not produce recognized pathology, especially those that don't involve visible, easily defined causes (16, 56). In order to prevent the pain from prolonged standing and other unacceptable working conditions, clear messages must be sent by unions, occupational health institutions, and the legislature that occupational health is not simply about danger. Unions have been explicitly granted the right to lay charges against employers[15] who are in violation of their obligations, yet we found no evidence of such charges having been laid in any cases involving musculoskeletal disorders or prolonged standing.

An occupational health and safety strategy that seeks to promote comfortable and healthy working conditions can only come about when evolution of public discourse makes it unacceptable for workers to suffer in order to convince supervisors and customers that they are available and working hard. As Sennett and Cobb (57) said years ago, "Society injures human dignity in order to weaken people's ability to fight against the limits class imposes on their freedom." At present, the class position and gender composition of service work do not facilitate any struggles for dignity and respect.

The idea that workers may be made to do degrading, demeaning. or painful work on an on-going basis simply because it is not dangerous is outrageous and contributes to the growth of this widespread epidemic. Yet the current climate, as illustrated by some of the arguments brought forward by some employers in recent years, clearly allows usual working conditions to inflict pain and even degradation. In Quebec, the *Charter of Human Rights and Freedoms* guarantees "Every person who works has a right, in accordance with the law, to fair and reasonable conditions of employment which have proper regard for his health,

[15]An *Act respecting Occupational Health and Safety*, R.S.Q. c. S-2.1, s. 242.

safety and physical well-being."[16] This argument is never raised before the specialized tribunals called upon to apply occupational health and safety law, yet those wishing to maintain the *status quo* do not hesitate to raise technical arguments in order to prevent application of regulatory provisions. Currently, if a working condition does not lead to a compensable injury, it escapes regulation in the eyes of some decision-makers, even when the cost of preventing the discomfort is negligible. Occupational health and safety should not be predicated on a simple cost-benefit analysis. Yet current prevention policies, relying mostly on experience rating, seem to allow employers to impose any working condition that is not associated with increased costs of compensation, regardless of the workers' rights to be treated with respect and dignity and to be ensured decent working conditions. As a result, there is an "invisible" epidemic of pain that accompanies jobs where prolonged standing is required. De facto deregulation may turn out to be an important contributor to the development of new epidemics in the 21st century.

ACKNOWLEDGMENTS

We thank France Tissot, Suzy Ngomo, and Maud Randoin who provided data used in this chapter. Sylvie Fortin, Ève Laperrière, Geneviève Rail, Susan Stock, France Tissot allowed us to use material from papers in preparation. We acknowledge useful conversations with Nicole Vézina. We have received support for work reported in this chapter from the Fonds FCAR and the Social Sciences and Humanities Research Council of Canada. The authors are members of the Invisible qui fait mal research team, in partnership with the Centrale des syndicats du Québec, the Confederation of National Trade Unions, and the Québec Federation of Labour, supported by the Fonds québécois de recherche sur la société et la culture. Karen Messing is the recipient of a Senior Investigator Award from the Canadian Institutes of Health Research.

REFERENCES

1. O'Neill, R. *Europe under Strain.* European Trade Union Technical Bureau for Health and Safety, Brussels, 1999.
2. Tüchsen, F., Krause, N., Hannerz, H., Burr, H., and Kristensen, T. S. Standing at work and varicose veins. *Scand. J. Work Environ. Health* 26: 414–420, 2000.
3. Krause, N., Lynch, J. W., Kaplan, G. A., Cohen, R. D., Salonen, R., and Salonen, J. T. Standing at work and progression of carotid atherosclerosis. *Scand. J. Work Environ. Health* 26: 227–236, 2000.

[16]*Charter of Human Rights and Freedoms.* R.S.Q. c. C-12.

4. Arcand, R., Labrèche, F., Stock, S., Messing, K., and Tissot, F. Environnement de Travail et santé. In *Enquête sociale et de santé 1998*, pp. 525–570. Institut de la statistique du Québec, Québec, 2000.

5. Ryan, G. A. The prevalence of musculo-skeletal symptoms in supermarket workers. *Ergonomics* 32:359–371, 1989.

6. Madeleine, P., Voigt, M., and Arendt-Nielsen, L. Subjective, physiological and biomechanical responses to prolonged manual work performed standing on hard and soft surfaces. *Eur. J. Appl. Physiol.* 77: 1–9, 1998.

7. Van Dieen, J., and Oude Vrielink, H. H. Evaluation of work-rest schedules with respect to the effects of postural workload in standing work. *Ergonomics* 41: 1832–1844, 1998.

8. Tomei, F., Baccolo, T. P., Tomao, E., Palmi, S., and Rosati, M. V. Chronic venous disorders and occupation. *Am. J. Ind. Med.* 36: 653–665, 1999.

9. Mozurkewich, E. L., Luke, B., Avni, M., and Wolf, F. M. Working conditions and adverse pregnancy outcome: A meta-analysis. Review. *Obstet. Gynecol.* 95: 623–635, 2000.

10. Wiktorin, C., Hjelm, E. W., Karlqvist, L. Nygård, C., and Winkel, J. Exponiering i arbete och under fritid enlight enkät och intervju i Stockholmsundersökningen 1. In *Stockholmsundersökningen 1*, edited by M. Hagberg, and C. Hogstedt, pp. 51–54. MUSIC Books, Stockholm, 1991.

11. DARES 2000. *Efforts, Risques et Charge Mentale au Travail: Résultats des Enquêtes Condition de Travail 1984, 1991 et 1998*. Les dossiers de la DARES, Hors-série/99. La Documentation Française, Paris, 2000.

12. Laperrière, E., and Thibault, M.-C. *La Posture Debout: Comparaison Entre 4 Situations de Travail*. Research report. Département des Sciences Biologiques. Université du Québec à Montréal, Montréal, 2001.

13. Messing, K. *One-Eyed Science: Occupational Health and Working Women*. Temple University Press, Philadephia, 1998.

14. Cranor, C. F. *Regulating Toxic Substances: A Philosophy of Science and the Law*. Oxford University Press, New York, 1993.

15. Lippel, K. L'incertitude des probabilités en droit et en médecine. *Rev. Droit Univ. Sherbrooke* 22: 445–472, 1992.

16. Lippel, K., Messing, K., Stock, S. R., and Vézina, N. La preuve de la causalité et l'indemnisation des lésions attribuables au travail répétitif: Rencontre des sciences de la santé et du droit. *Windsor Yearbook of Access to Justice* XVII, pp. 35–86. Windsor, Canada, 1999.

17. Lippel K., and Fabris, S. La fibromyalgie: Peut-elle donner lieu à une indemnisation? *Méd. Québec*, 38: 81–83, 2003.

18. Messing, K., and Kilbom, A. Standing and very slow walking: foot pain-pressure threshold, subjective pain experience and work activity. *Appl. Ergon.* 32: 81–90, 2001.

19. Hoogendoorn, W., van Poppel, M. N. M., Bongers, P. M., Koes, B. W., and Bouter, L. M. Physical load during work and leisure time as risk factors for back pain. *Scand. J. Work Environ. Health* 25: 387–403, 1999.

20. Vézina, N., Chatigny, C., and Messing, K. A manual materials handling job: Symptoms and working conditions among supermarket cashiers. *Chron. Dis. Canada* 15: 17–22, 1994.

21. Messing, K., and Seifert, A. M. Listening to women: Action-oriented research in ergonomics. *Arbete Hälso* 17: 93–104, 2001.

22. Lippel, K. Droit et statistiques: réflexions méthodologiques sur la discrimination systémique dans le domaine de l'indemnisation pour les lésions professionnelles. *Rev. Femmes Droit* 14: 362–288, 2002.

23. Fortier, I., Marcoux, S., and Brisson, J. Maternal work during pregnancy and the risks of delivering a small-for-gestational-age or preterm infant. *Scand. J. Work Environ. Health* 21: 412–418, 1995.

24. Ha, E., Cho, S. I., Park, H., Chen, D., Chen, C., Wang, L., Xu, X., and Christiani, D. C. Does standing at work during pregnancy result in reduced infant birth weight? *J. Occup. Environ. Med.* 44: 815–821, 2002.

25. Baty, D., Buckle, P. W., and Stubbs, D. A. Posture recording by direct observation, questionnaire assessment and instrumentation: A comparison based on a recent field study. In *The Ergonomics of Working Postures: Models, Methods and Cases*, edited by N. Corlett, J. Wilson, and I. Manenica, pp. 283–292. Taylor and Francis, London, 1986.

26. Selin, K., Winkel, J., and Stockholm-MUSIC I study group. Evaluation of two instruments for recording sitting and standing postures and number of foot steps. *Appl. Ergon.* 25: 41–46, 1994.

27. Laperrière, E., Ngomo, S., Couture, V., and Messing, K. Validation of questions on working posture in a sample of standing workers in Québec. *Int. J. Industr. Ergonomics* In press.

28. Eklund, J., and Corlett, N. Shrinkage as a measure of the effect of load on the spine. *Spine* 9: 189–194, 1984.

29. Seo, A., Kakehashi, M., Udu, S., Tsuru, S., and Yoshinaga, F. Bioelectrical impedance measuring method for standing load evaluation. *J. Occup. Health (Japan)* 37: 83–87, 1995.

30. Seo, A., Kakehashi, M., Tsuru, S., and Yoshinaga, F. Leg swelling during continuous standing and sitting work without restricting leg movement. *J. Occup. Health (Japan)* 38: 186–189, 1996.

31. Jacob, G., Ertl, A. C., Shannon, J. R., Furlan, R., Robertson, R. M., and Robertson, D. Effect of standing on neurohumoral responses and plasma volume in healthy subjects. *J. Appl. Physiol.* 84: 914–921, 1998.

32. Schierhout, G. H., and Myers, J. E. Is self-reported pain an appropriate outcome measure in ergonomic-epidemiologic studies of work-related musculoskeletal disorders? *Am. J. Ind. Med.* 30: 93–98, 1996.

33. Bjorksten, M., Boquist, B., Talback, M., and Edling, C. The validity of reported musculoskeletal problems. A study of questionnaire answers in relation to diagnosed disorders and perception of pain. *Appl. Ergon.* 30: 325–330, 1999.

34. Brauer, C., Thomsen, J. F., Loft, I. P., and Mikkelsen, S. Can we rely on retrospective pain assessments? *Am. J. Epidemiol.* 157: 552–557, 2003.

35. Reid, J., Ewan, C., and Lowy, E. Pilgrimage of pain: The illness experiences of women with repetition strain injury and the search for credibility. *Soc. Sci. Med.* 32: 601–612, 1991.

36. Leclerc, A., Touranchet, A., Rondeau du Noyer, C., et al. Le rôle des facteurs hormonaux dans le syndrome du canal carpien chez la femme. *Arch. Malad. Prof.* 59: 30–31, 1998.

37. Lippel, K. Compensation for musculo-skeletal disorders in Quebec: Systemic discrimination against women workers? *Int. J. Health Serv.* 33: 253–281, 2003.

38. Nathan, P. A., and Meadows, K. D. Neuromusculoskeletal conditions of the upper extremity: Are they due to repetitive occupational trauma? *Occup. Med.* 15: 677–693, iii, 2000.
39. Harber, P., Pena, L., Bland, G., and Beck, J. Upper extremity symptoms in supermarket workers. *Am. J. Ind. Med.* 22: 873–884, 1992.
40. Karlqvist, L. A process for the development, specification and evaluation of VDU work tables. *Appl. Ergon.* 29:423–432, 1998.
41. Reinharz, S. *Feminist Methods in Social Research.* Oxford University Press, Oxford, 1992.
42. Messing, K., Randoin, M., Tissot, F., Rail, G., and Fortin, S. La souffrance inutile: La posture debout statique dans les emplois de service. *Travail, Genre et Sociétés.* In press.
43. Whistance, R., Adams, L. P, van Geems, B. A., and Bridger, R. S. Postural adaptations to workbench modifications in standing workers. *Ergon.* 38: 2485–2503, 1995.
44. Hansen, L., Winkel, J., and Jørgenson, K. Significance of mat and shoe softness during prolonged work in upright position. *Appl. Ergon.* 29: 217–224, 1998.
45. Vézina, N., Geoffrion, L., Lajoie, A., Chatigny, C., Messing, K., and Courville, J. *Les Contraintes du Poste de Caissière de Supermarché et L'essai de Banc Assis-Debout.* Collection Études et Recherches. IRSST, Montréal, 1993.
46. Vézina, N., Stock, S. R., Simard, M., Saint-Jacques, Y., Boucher, M., Lemaire, J., and Trudel, C. *Problèmes Musculo-Squelettiques et Organisation Modulaire du Travail dans une Usine de Fabrication de Bottes Phase 2: Étude de L'implantation des Recommandations.* Collection Études et Recherches. IRSST, Montréal, 2003.
47. Johansson, A., Johansson, G., Lundqvist, P., Akesson, I., Odenrick, P., and Akselsson, R. Evaluation of a workplace redesign of a grocery checkout system. *Appl. Ergon.* 29: 261–266, 1998.
48. Seifert, A. M., Messing, K., and Dumais, L. Star wars and strategic defence initiatives: Work activity and health symptoms of unionized bank tellers during work reorganization. *Int. J. Health Serv.* 27: 455–477, 1997.
49. Frick, K., Langaa Jensen, P., Quinlan, M., and Wilthagen, T. *Systematic Occupational Health and Safety Management.* Pergamon, Oxford, 2000.
50. Walters, D. (ed.). *Regulating Health and Safety Management in the European Union.* Presses Interuniversitaires Européennes, Brussels, 2002.
51. Kralj, B. Experience rating of workers' compensation insurance premiums and the duration of workplace injuries. In *Research in Canadian Workers' Compensation,* edited by T. Thomason and R. P. Chaykowskipp, pp. 106–122. IRC Press, Kingston, 1995.
52. Law, D. Appeals litigation: Pricing the workplace injury. In *Workers' Compensation: Foundations for Reform,* edited by M. Gunderson and D. Hyatt, pp. 299–326. University of Toronto Press, Toronto, 2000.
53. WHO 2003. Preamble to the Constitution of the World Health Organization as adopted by the International Health Conference, New York, 19-22 June, 1946; signed on 22 July 1946 by the representatives of 61 States (Official Records of the World Health Organization, no. 2, p. 100) and entered into force on 7 April 1948. www.who.int/about/definition/en/ (September 20, 2003).
54. Schaufeli, W. B., and Kompier, M. A. J. Managing job stress in the Netherlands. *Int. J. Stress Manage.* 8: 15–34, 2001.

55. Parent, R. Les Québécois sont les plus syndiqués en Amérique du nord. *Le Devoir,* March 19, 2003, p. B3.
56. Messing, K., Lippel, K., Demers, D., and Mergler, D. Equality and difference in the workplace: Physical job demands, occupational illnesses, and sex differences. *Nat. Women Stud. Assoc. J.* 12: 21–49, 2000.
57. Sennett, R., and Cobb, J. *The Hidden Injuries of Class,* p. 153. Vintage Books, New York, 1972.

CHAPTER 9

The Discourse of Abuse in Return-to-Work: A Hidden Epidemic of Suffering

Joan M. Eakin

As we scan the horizon for hidden and emerging work-related risks and epidemics, we must not exempt from scrutiny the institutional systems, regulatory structures, and professional practices that exist to promote, protect, mend, and compensate the health of workers. That is, we must not overlook the possibility, however ironic, that the systems we have put in place to address occupational health could themselves be harmful. The concept of "iatrogenesis," used mostly in medical contexts, refers to the process whereby treatment itself induces adverse conditions in those it is intended to assist. The notion can be broadened to encompass adverse effects of system-level interventions and institutional arrangements. In the field of occupational health, for example, Lippell (1) identifies "anti-therapeutic" effects of compensation systems and related managerial practices such as private policing (2), and Shain (3) proposes that aspects of labor law can be injurious to health, particularly the employer-employee relationship and provisions that limit worker participation.

The possibility of system-level iatrogenic effects in occupational health emerged in the course of a recent study of return-to-work (RTW) (4, 5), the domain of occupational health policy and practice concerned with enabling individuals to resume employment after work-related injury or sickness. The research revealed the presence of an institutionalized mistrust, or "discourse of abuse," in the policy and practice of RTW and its pernicious effects on the experience of injured workers and on the process of RTW. In this chapter, drawing on data from this research, I demonstrate how, in the context of RTW, the discourse of abuse is constituted and operates, and how it creates suffering for injured workers by adding social injury to existing physical injury. The research suggests how such experience might augment disability, and impede successful rehabilitation and resumption of employment. Although the analysis was spawned by and con- structed upon findings from a study of a particular occupational health issue (RTW) in a particular place (Ontario, Canada), I attempt to make evident the

159

generic aspects of the phenomenon and I raise the possibility that the case of RTW is a proxy for a hidden epidemic of suffering that extends far beyond the field of occupational health.

RETURN TO WORK

Although most workers injured at work recover and get back to their original jobs successfully, others take a long time to get back to work, or make repeated unsuccessful attempts, or are unhappy in the jobs they return to, or never return to the labor market at all. Unsuccessful RTW has profound personal implications for workers and their families, is disruptive and costly for employers, and represents a major financial liability for compensation agencies and for society at large. Internationally, because so much is at stake, much effort is being devoted to finding ways to improve the success rate of re-employment after work-related injury (6). A whole "industry" has grown up around RTW, in both the public and private domain, including regulatory provisions, disability management specialists, rehabilitation programs, professional training, best practices, and assessment tool production, and so on. The literature on the subject is extensive, and focuses mainly on policy and practice matters, program evaluation, and epidemiological research on the determinants and predictors of successful RTW outcomes (5).

The challenges are considerable because RTW is a complex process that depends as much on social, psychological, and organizational factors as on the nature and severity of physical injury and disability (7, 8). One approach that is being widely adopted internationally is the strategy of "early return" and "modified work," whereby injured workers are returned to work as soon as possible, before full recovery, to jobs that have been altered in various ways to accommodate the worker's injuries and functional limitations and to avoid re-injury (e.g., alternative jobs, reduced hours, alterations to the equipment or work station, assistance from others). This approach is legitimated and encouraged by a convergence of studies demonstrating its cost-effectiveness (9) and a shift in scientific and professional opinion toward early activity and social re-engagement as being "good" for the injured worker's physical and psychological recovery (10–12).

Ontario's Model of "Early and Safe" RTW

In Ontario, the notions of early return and modified work have been incorporated into a set of regulatory and institutional policies called "Early and Safe Return to Work" (ESRTW) which have been in place since 1997. An important feature of Ontario's approach is that it is embedded within an overarching occupational health and safety framework that is based on principles of workplace "internal responsibility," and involves the shift of responsibility for the administration of

ESRTW away from centralized government management to the workplace itself. The policy of "self-reliance" places obligations regarding ESRTW squarely on the shoulders of the employer and the injured worker, with the role of government being reduced to setting the ground rules, monitoring and facilitating the process, and intervening in times of major conflict or breakdown in internal management (13).

THE RESEARCH PROJECT: FOCUS AND METHOD

The empirical research upon which this chapter draws was directed at the understanding of the *process* of an early return approach, particularly its *social* dimensions at the workplace level, and its manifestation in *small workplaces* where RTW appears to be especially difficult (14–16). The research aimed to describe and explain how employers and injured workers understood and responded to the ESRTW approach, and how their experiences were related to the socio-cultural organization of working life in small workplaces and to the policy and professional practices framing the approach.

The research design was qualitative, specifically integrating elements of "grounded theory" (17) and "structural-interactionist" (18, 19) analysis. This blend provided the means to link individual subjectivity, social interaction, and broader social and policy structures. The data included documentary materials, observations, and transcripts of in-depth interviews with injured workers, employers, and RTW professionals. The documentary data included legislation, regulatory and policy statements, educational and promotional material, Website content, and bureaucratic reporting forms.[1] The texts were analyzed for underlying intent, assumptions, and expectations of ESRTW, using "discursive" analytic techniques (20, 21) and other methods for exploring how everyday activities and relationships are governed both at and beyond the local setting (22).

The interviews were conducted using special methods for encouraging participants to recount their experiences in their own terms, with minimal prior framing of the issues by the researchers (23, 24). Worker interviews were mostly conducted by an assistant who was herself an injured worker, which appeared to promote trust and candor. Both employers and injured workers were asked to talk about the general nature of their work lives and about the experience

---

[1] Some examples include: WSIB Form 6 & 7 (Worker's and Employer's report of Injury/Disease), Timely Return to Work Form (Functional Abilities); "A Review of WSIB's NEER and CAD-7 Experience Rating Programs" (WSIB, March 2000); Ontario Ministry of Labour, "A Better Health and Safety System for Ontario Workplaces," January, 1988; Office of the Employer Advisor, "Return to Work: Strategies, Implementation & Measures of Success" (Spring 1999), "Managing Workplace Injuries: Answers for Small Businesses" (February 1998); Office of the Worker Advisor, "Information Sheets;" Canadian Injured Workers Alliance Newsletters (1997–98); The Industrial Accident Victim's Group of Ontario Reporting Service, "Return to Work Obligations and the Individual Worker" (Vol. 12, No. 2, August 1998).

of/management of injury, compensation, and RTW. Interviews were taped, transcribed verbatim (along with detailed observations), and analyzed by means of various comparative interpretive procedures for distilling, linking, and progressively conceptualizing and theorizing the data (17, 25, 26). The analysis was designed to reveal the meanings attributed to phenomena and the underlying logic of participants' understandings and practices (27).

Participants were recruited from a number of sources, including the Ontario agency responsible for compensation and prevention, the Workplace Safety and Insurance Board (WSIB), associated occupational health and safety agencies, labor and community organizations, medical and legal aid clinics, and personal referrals. Participants were chosen to ensure diversity in terms of types of industry, injury, and time off work, as well as to meet the "theoretical sampling" (28) needs of qualitative analysis.

The ensuing sample included 17 employers and 21 injured workers from independent small enterprises (<50 employees) in construction, service, health care, transportation and manufacturing. Seven employers and workers were *pairs* in the same workplaces. A sub-set of participants was re-interviewed on one or more occasions over a period of one year to provide longitudinal perspective on their experience. Of the injured workers interviewed, 16 were men and 5 were women. A little more than half of the workers had high school or less and/or trade apprenticeship level education. A range of injuries was sustained, including fractures, cuts, and crushes as well as back and neck strains or disc problems and soft tissue injuries in the extremities. Workers were away from work for different lengths of time before initial attempt to resume work: two workers were away for less than a week, seven for one or two months, three for almost six months, and three for one or two years (for three workers, time off work could not be determined). Of the 17 employers interviewed, 10 were men and 7 were women. More than half of the employers had high school or apprenticeship education. Four compensation board and rehabilitation professionals were also interviewed to gain perspective on their role in the RTW process and to permit fuller understanding of worker/employer experiences.

THE DISCOURSE OF ABUSE

The notion of "discourse" refers to a set of interrelated knowledge and ways of thinking that are embedded in language (words, texts), practices (behaviors, actions), and material objects and spaces (bureaucratic forms, physical arrangements). Discourse is produced and reproduced at multiple levels: it is simultaneously "out there" in public consciousness, the media, and organizational arrangements, and "inside" the subjectively lived experience of individual persons. In relation to RTW, the "discourse of abuse" refers to the pervasive, institutionally-embedded expectation that participants in the work injury compensation and support system will violate, misuse, fail to comply with, or otherwise "abuse" its requirements and entitlements. In particular, workers are thought likely to claim injuries they do not have, or exaggerate pain and disability for self advantage, or claim compensation benefits to which they are not entitled.

The first step in examining the discourse of abuse and its iatrogenic effects is to explore its geography—where it is manifested, its location in the landscape of RTW. Government authorities (via its bureaucracy, institutional arrangements, and professional practitioners), employers, and injured workers themselves all actively participate in producing and reproducing the discourse of abuse.

Institutional Participation: "Motivating" Compliance

From the standpoint of the system, the transfer of responsibility for the conduct of RTW from a centralized external authority to the workplace inevitably creates a problem of control: how to make the workplace parties fulfill their responsibilities on behalf of the system, in accordance with the administrative and therapeutic logic underlying the approach. In Ontario, a variety of measures, primarily economic, are used to control the process. For example, financial rebates and penalties constitute primary mechanisms for "motivating" (29) employers to play their proper role in ensuring workplace health. The compliance of injured workers with ESRTW, although much less explicitly articulated, is also fundamentally economic: if injured workers do not comply with the regulations or fulfill their duty to "cooperate," they risk being denied or losing claims to compensation and other benefits (30).

More explicit disciplinary mechanisms are also evident. For example, the WSIB has a specific administrative branch, charged with the management of fraud and non-compliance. Considerable visibility is given to problems of misuse of the system and the Board's "zero tolerance" policy is featured prominently in its Website along with a toll-free, anonymous hotline for reporting suspected abuses.

Control over the ESRTW process is also achieved through the day-to-day bureaucracy and administrative practices of the WSIB. For example, the requirement for physician validation of injury and readiness to return to work implies de facto that the condition of the injured worker is not self evident, that the worker's own estimation may be problematic, and that diagnosis and prognosis are contested arenas. The bureaucratic form that employers are required to use to report lost time injuries is another generative site of the discourse of abuse. A special box appears on the form, inviting employers to enter any concerns about the circumstances of the injury or the worker's claims, and advising them of their right to submit evidence of abuse. Textual cues such as these draw employers into the discourse of abuse by flagging the existence of concern and the need for vigilance, and by facilitating their role in surveillance.

The professionals executing the mandate and mission of the WSIB also participate in the discourse of abuse. In some cases, as with adjudicators whose very job it is to assemble and evaluate evidence regarding eligibility for compensation awards and access to services and benefits, the issue of the validity of claims and potential fraud is directly in their radar screens. Such professionals spoke of being highly attuned to "oddities going on" and of their ability to "sniff out secondary gain" and fraud, perhaps by calling the doctor's office to see if the injured worker was really there, or by listening for suspicious background noises in phone calls to injured workers.

In a less direct fashion, professional advice to workers and employers also functions to reproduce the discourse of abuse. Government advisory agencies designed to counsel employers and injured workers and facilitate self reliance, produce written guidelines that advise on "best practices" in RTW management, such as the need to document all communication and to gather evidence of compliance and cooperation. One rehabilitation professional said that he regularly advises injured workers on the importance of demonstrating their motivation to get back to work early, and even urges newly injured workers to make evident their "cooperation" by dropping by the workplace on the way home from the hospital.

Employer Participation: "The Free Ride"

The discourse of abuse is also actively participated in by employers. Two notions of abuse were discernable in almost all employer interviews. The first included reference to misrepresentation of injury to gain personal advantage, particularly by faking or malingering or exaggerating pain or disability. Brendon (all names are pseudonyms), an owner of an auto repair business, confided that "nothing adds up" in relation to his employee's injury claim. His interview is textured by expressions of suspicion and doubt:

> It was an injury that he (injured worker) has *already had* for some time, okay? So, *I don't know.* . . . And then it just got worse and worse and when he pushed the car, that was it, he couldn't walk anymore, *evidently.*

The italicized text in this segment of data suggests a sub-text: disbelief in the genuineness of the worker's injury. Such imputations are pervasive in the data, embedded in employers' language, phrasing, and bodily expression. A statement such as "There's no question he hurt himself" affirms the existence of the opposite possibility; trivializing language ("a sore thumb") serves to discount the seriousness of an injury; generalized accounts ("Operators doing the same procedure all day for 10 years and all of a sudden—they're tired of it, and their neck is sore") subtly discredit by constructing the event as a commonly used "story" that can be summoned at will.

In addition to misrepresentation of injury, employers refer to a second form of abuse: "taking advantage of the system." Employers are concerned with injured workers seeking a "free ride" on public institutional support. They question if workers are claiming compensation for injuries incurred outside of their workplaces, at home, or at other jobs. Misuse of the system is often associated with the additionally damning imputation of not wanting to work, typified in this employer's portrayal of an injured worker:

> He decided it (modified job) wasn't for his benefit to do any work. He could sit at home and watch TV, I assume.

Interestingly, "taking advantage of the system" was also applied to workers availing themselves of rights and privileges to which they are entitled, such as time off work for seeking medical care, or reimbursement for drug costs. Particularly where relationships between employer and injured worker were strained, employers often interpreted the worker's use of benefits—even merely an inquiry about benefits—as reason for concern.

The employer's perception of fraudulent representation of injury and "taking advantage" of the system prompted a range of responses which both fed on and fed into the discourse of abuse. Some employers indicated that they actively try to verify the injured worker's condition or claims and to report any irregularities or signs of deceit. Examples in the data include soliciting affidavits from co-workers regarding the circumstances of the injury, taking discrediting photographs of an injured employee taking out the garbage at his home, and hiring a private investigator for surveillance of the injured worker.

Small employers' engagement in the discourse of abuse is linked to the severe difficulties they can encounter with the loss of a key employee through injury, and the administrative demands of ESRTW. One manager in an automobile repair shop, for example, struggled with the problem of an injured mechanic off work for an indefinite period of time:

> I can't just phone an employment agency and say "send me a good mechanic but when the other guy gets back" . . . it's impossible in our trade. Basically I was forced to have an empty service bay (one out of five) for a year. Then you gotta sit at the meeting every month and say why your department didn't make any money!

Strain of the sort suggested in this quotation can make employers "ripe" for taking up the discourse of abuse.

Injured Worker Participation: "Faking It"

Injured workers feel the effects of the discourse of abuse conveyed through institutional and employer practices, and they themselves participate in its production. Most of the workers in our sample saw themselves as under continuous scrutiny regarding the validity of injuries and their entitlement to compensation and time off work. Interviews contained frequent reference to not being "believed," and to "proving" the validity of their injuries. The words of Duncan, a worker in a small foundry, are widely echoed in the data:

> The (employers) would dispute me, sayin' that I was fakin' the injury . . . what they would sit there and say is, "Oh he just doesn't want to work" . . . and then they'd send more papers they wanted the doctor to fill out, which is fine, I mean, but you know it was just a steady battle all the time.

Most workers acknowledged the disapprobation attached to the "free ride":

> If a person hasn't been injured and you tell him that you're collecting workers' comp, they think you're scamming the government. Right away, "Oh here's a lazy guy, collecting this" (John, printing).

Imputations of "milking the system," however, do not appear to correspond to any fixed boundary between what use of rights is acceptable and what is not. The term seemed to be more in evidence where relations between employers and injured workers were strained and hemorrhaging trust, or when the injured workers had not been working long at the company. In the latter case, it may be that injured workers may not have had time to build any moral capital that might make employers perceive their actions in a more favorable light, or give them the benefit of the doubt.

The ESRTW model creates possibilities for judgment regarding abuse that go beyond aspersions of faking and misusing public support. For example, the need to get back to work as quickly as possible after injury, and to "cooperate" with offers of modified work, can generate new problems of credibility and legitimacy for injured workers. How do you know (and show) that you are "ready" (or not) to resume work? What constitutes a bona fide reason for turning down an offer of modified work? How acceptable is fear of re-injury as a reason for delaying early return? A whole additional set of motivations and behaviors join "faking" under the lamplight of scrutiny. Yet, the complexities and subtleties of meaning associated with the requirements of ESRTW are substantial, as we see more in the next section.

In sum, the discourse of abuse is embedded in institutional structures, texts and material practices, and in the talk and actions of employers and injured workers. By participating in the discourse through talk and action, by acting as though it were real, organizations and individuals create the "fact" of abuse. For example, the belief that abuse is a problem in need of constant vigilance simultaneously creates, confirms, and perpetuates the existence of the problem and the actions to manage it. I turn now from the geography of the discourse to its implications, particularly for the experience of injured workers.

THE PERFORMANCE OF INTEGRITY

The discourse of abuse led many injured workers to experience an erosion of their moral reputation, put at risk their economic and social security, and disfigured their health-related behavior and their trajectory through ESRTW.

Moral Discredit

For many injured workers, the discourse of abuse constituted a profound threat to their moral identity, their sense of personal worth and integrity. Many spoke movingly of their suffering under constant imputations of dishonesty, and felt morally discredited and stigmatized by what they saw as characterization of the injured worker as "living off the system."

> It's not about, "Oh wow, I got a free ticket! Ooh, hoo, I got hurt and I got a ticket, I'm set for life" [sing song voice], which my wife runs into a lot of time with the welfare. That's, you know, that's a big dig right there, people livin' off the system. I hate that, that bothers me, that's a personal thing (Scott, welding).

Moral disgrace, and the emotional distress associated with it, are evident in the content and tone of many workers' narratives, compounding the suffering and vulnerability already affixed to the experience of bodily injury and uncertain futures, and propelling them into efforts of self defense.

Achieving Credibility

To prevent or mitigate moral discredit from the latent, ambient accusations associated with the discourse of abuse, injured workers need to constantly "perform,"[2] or publicly demonstrate, their personal credibility and integrity. Indeed, much of what they say and do, consciously and otherwise, is part of a performance to make their injury, disability, and compliance manifest and believable.

Examples of such performance were everywhere. One worker reported that he checked out of the hospital against medical advice to defend against the suspicion of self indulgence and to demonstrate eagerness to get back to work and loyalty to the employer. Another described taking pain medication unwillingly to prove the existence of continued pain. Almost all said that they have or would conceal previous work-related injuries so as not to convey a stigmatizing image of being "injury prone," or "that kind of worker." Some workers said they hesitated to inquire about retraining possibilities to avoid being perceived as "ungrateful" or "over eager" for entitlements, designations that could tarnish their reputations.

Injured workers also have to "perform" in terms of the cooperation required of participants in ESRTW. But since there is no clear delineation of what constitutes "cooperation," such a state must be negotiated on an ad hoc basis. Hami, a construction worker, struggled with the decision about how long to stay at home before attempting to return to work. To go back quickly would convey commitment to his job and his employer, but might undermine others' perceptions of

---

[2] "Perform": Goffman's sociological notion of communicating and achieving particular social identities, and of managing damaging imputations of social deviance (31).

the seriousness of his injury. To stay at home too long could inconvenience his employers and co-workers and prompt them to suspect him of "babying" himself. His ultimate decision was based not on how he actually felt (which was very poorly) but on the symbolic moral meaning or the act—what he believed his timing and actions might convey about him as a person and as a worker. Once back at work, he was unhappy with the modified work arrangements, as he was in constant pain and feared re-injury, but he hesitated to complain in case it jeopardized his self-presentation as honest (his moral claim) and as "cooperative" (his material claim).

The need for performance also overflows into non-work life. Tony, a trucker with an injured shoulder, recounted his fear of being seen by neighbors and judged (worse, being reported to the authorities) as too able-bodied to be legitimately off work:

> I just really can't paint the living room, you know what I mean? It hurts my shoulder, and God knows, if somebody came here and seen me painting the living room, what would happen? [people would say] "you can't work but you can come and paint the living room?"

The discourse of abuse, then, threatened injured workers' moral identities and their financial security. Many experienced great emotional distress, and got swept up in the constant need to perform their integrity and good intent, in the workplace and beyond. Such threats had consequences for injured workers' social relationships with employers and co-workers.

SOCIAL DISLOCATION

The discourse of abuse can lead to disruption in the moral relations of work, and contribute to a spiral of unproductive and self-defeating responses from injured workers.

Moral Rupture

I have shown elsewhere (18) how illness and injury in small workplaces can disrupt existing patterns of social relations between employers and workers and precipitate a breakdown in trust. Such damage has also been observed in relation to RTW (32) and in the present study. John, a printer, feels betrayed when he comes to believe his employer is concerned more with avoiding liability than with accommodating his disability from a hand crushed in a printing press. He was embittered by the absence of an offer of modified work and his ultimate lay off, expecting more for his 20 years of work and loyalty.

The discourse of abuse is often enmeshed in such breakdowns in trust, or compounds the strains generated in the course of RTW. During the process of returning to work, Hami, the injured construction worker mentioned earlier, experienced a major moral rupture with his employer who had given him his first job as an immigrant and who had formerly "always been like a father" to him. The rupture was rooted in several aspects of the ESRTW process, the most important of which was Hami's perception that his boss doubted his version of the accident and the extent of his subsequent disability—both of which signified to him symbolically that his employer cared more about the business than about him as a person.

The discourse of abuse was also implicated in the strains with co-workers in relation to ESRTW. Injured workers spoke often of the ways in which modified work and the privileges of injury bred resentment and accusations of employer favoritism from other workers ("When I was shifted to the dispatch, they (co-workers) says 'Why is this guy sitting in the back of the chair answering the phones and playing on the computer while we're out here sweatin' our ass off'"). The perception of inequality can drive wedges between workers, intensifying suspicions of "abuse" and the injured worker's quest for legitimation and acceptance.

Social Hardening

Moral disillusionment can set the context for the worker's understanding of the modified work offered and of the employer's "motivation," and prompt a more combative stance vis-à-vis the employer and the compensation system. Hami's dismay over the loss of his close relationship with this boss colored his subsequent interpretation of the latter's earnest efforts to accommodate his injury. Instead of appreciating the offers as generous and helpful, he began to see them as exploitative and unreasonable. Such a transformation, evident in the experience of several injured workers, contributed to what could be called "social hardening," the tendency progressively to "play it smart" or "play the game," typically through availing themselves more assertively of legal entitlements and benefits. John, a printer, grew increasingly angry about his boss's imputation that he "indirectly caused" his own injury. He declared, "I finally started to play it smart, and let the government retrain me," despite the fact that resorting to this option functioned merely to confirm his employer's suspicion that he was using the system for his own advantage, which then, of course, further eroded their moral confidence in each other.

CONCLUSION

Data from this project demonstrate the existence of a pervasive discourse of abuse surrounding the management of and experience of ESRTW in Ontario. The imputation of deceit and misuse embedded in public consciousness, institutional structures, professional practices, and in the responses of employers and co-workers can create the incessant need for injured workers to prove their innocence and proper motivation, can damage social relationships in the workplace, and can lead to resistance and hardening that further fuels conflict and mistrust. Although these findings cannot be generalized in any statistical sense on the basis of this type of ethnographic investigation, they are suggestive of the potential for suffering and perverse outcomes that lie within such institutionalized mistrust.

Psychosocial Harm

ESRTW is envisaged as an improved approach to the prevention of chronic disability. It is believed that early return decreases social isolation and loss of socially supportive aspects of work such as relationships with co-workers, and that "safe" modified work can avoid problems of re-injury. The findings of this research, particularly those related to the discourse of abuse, cast some doubt on these expectations, and even raise the possibility that ESRTW may harm those it is intended to help and impede successful RTW.

In the literature (33) and in ESRTW policy, safety is largely conceived in *physical* terms: "safe" modified work does not risk the physical re-injury of the recovering worker, and core concepts such as "light work" refers to the intensity and duration of physiological output. Without in any way diminishing the relevance of physical considerations in RTW, findings regarding the discourse of abuse suggest that "safety" needs to be conceived more broadly to encompass social security, including both social *sources* of harm and social *consequences* of harm. The discourse of abuse is itself a social phenomenon (it is produced through interaction) and it has social effects (stigma, distress, moral degradation, interpersonal conflict).

The discourse of abuse, through effects such as these, can be considered iatrogenic in so far as it induces suffering beyond what injured workers would otherwise experience in relation to their damaged bodies and lives. Moreover, there is evidence in the literature that such negative social experience may have implications for physical healing and rehabilitation. The issue of legitimacy in health-related behavior is widely recognized in the sociology of health (34, 35), and has also been linked to work injury-related pain, disability, and rehabilitation outcomes (36–39). In the case of RTW and the discourse of abuse, and in addition to the obvious issue of emotional distress, it is plausible that the repeated necessity to prove the veracity of one's pain and disability, to defend one's moral integrity, and to remain ever vigilant to the discrediting meanings that might be attributed to one's behavior, might become so engrained in injured workers' day-to-day practices that the resumption of alternative postures becomes progressively more difficult, and recovery and resumption of normal lives ever more elusive.

Prevention and Change

How, then, might it be possible to break the damaging effects and the recursive cycle of mistrust associated with the discourse of abuse? Several considerations are important in assessing the possibilities for prevention and change, including the structural implications of workplace size, RTW policy, and the broader social policy environment.

A first consideration regards the issue of workplace size. Since the discourse of abuse is produced and reproduced through social interaction, and since small workplaces have distinctive social and cultural formation (40), it is likely that the discourse might operate differently in such milieux than it does in larger organizations. Specifically, the discourse of abuse may be particularly corrosive in environments marked by highly personal social relations of work, relationships based heavily on trust (18, 41), and few organizational means to resolve conflict beyond the arbitrary exercise of power by the employer. At a system level, the discourse of abuse and its damaging sequelae can be expected to be particularly hard to combat because of the inherent difficulties associated with inducing health-related change in such settings (40, 42).

A second consideration is the policy environment within which the discourse of abuse is located. The policy of self reliance governing Ontario's ESRTW strategy has broad implications for RTW (4), some of which intersect with the effects of the discourse of abuse. Most importantly, the transfer of administrative responsibility for ESRTW from a centralized governmental agency (the WSIB) to individual workplaces shifted attention off of service provision onto compliance and converted employers into unwilling disciplinary agents on behalf of the state (43). Both in turn helped spawn and perpetuate the discourse of abuse. Addressing the problems associated with the discourse will be difficult within a policy structure that depends on it.

A third issue in addressing the discourse of abuse is that it extends far beyond its particular manifestations in Ontario's ESRTW strategy and its concrete expression in human experience and behavior. Its presence and effects are also found in other arenas within the field of occupational health and safety, particularly those related to regulatory and compensation systems (1). Beyond occupational health, institutionalized suspicion is a core feature of insurance organizations (44), and of social welfare agencies (45, 46). A discursive concern with abuse is endemic in situations involving the control of access to public resources, and is thus undoubtedly accentuated by neo-liberal economic and political rationalities.

A final consideration arises from the fact that the discourse of abuse resides in many places—in the social spaces between interacting individuals, in organizational structures and processes, in regulatory and policy arrangements, in general public awareness. There is no one port of entry into a dialectic problem such as this. At the micro, interactional level it is possible that its iatrogenic effects could be mitigated by greater professional sensitivity to the role of trust in the management of disability. At the meso level, organizations might play their part in reducing the bureaucratic practices that support the discourse. At the macro level, policymakers might consider if different regulatory and institutional arrangements might generate differing levels of systemic mistrust. A multi-layered approach is needed to counter the hidden, systemically embedded nature of the discourse of abuse and its subsequent "epidemic" of suffering.

ACKNOWLEDGMENTS

This chapter draws on research conducted with Ellen MacEachen and Judy Clarke, of the Institute for Work & Health in Toronto. The project was generously funded by the Ontario Workplace Safety and Insurance Board.

REFERENCES

1. Lippel, K. Therapeutic and anti-therapeutic consequences of workers' compensation systems. *Int. J. Law Psychiatry* 22: 521–546, 1999.
2. Lippel, K. Private policing of injured workers: Legitimate management practices or human rights violations? *Policy and Pract. Health Saf.* In press.
3. Shain, M. *Labour Law is a Hazard to Your Health: Implications for Reform.* Centre for Health Promotion, Toronto, 1992.
4. Eakin, J., MacEachen, E., and Clarke, J. "Playing it Smart" with return-to-work: Small workplace experience under Ontario's policy of self reliance and early return. *Policy Pract. Health Saf.* Forthcoming.
5. Eakin, J., Clarke, J., and MacEachen, E. *Return to Work in Small Workplaces: Sociological Perspective on Employers' and Workers' Experiences with Ontario's Strategy of Self Reliance and Early Return,* Working paper #206. Institute for Work and Health, Toronto, April 2003.
6. Thornton, P. *International Research Project on Job Retention and Return to Work Strategies for Disabled Workers.* International Labour Office, Geneva, 1998.
7. Hogg-Johnson, S., and Cole, D. Early prognostic factors for duration on temporary total benefits in the first year among workers with compensated occupational soft tissue injuries. *Occup. Environ. Med.* 60: 244–253, 2003.
8. Friesen, M. N., Yassi, A., and Cooper, J. Return-to-work: The importance of human interactions and organizational structures. *Work* 17: 11–22, 2001.
9. Krause, N., Dasinger, L., and Neuhauser, F. Modified work and return to work: A review of the literature. *J. Occup. Rehabil.* 8: 113–139, 1998.
10. AHCPR AfHCPaR. *Acute Low Back Problems in Adults.* Clinical Practice Guideline Number 14. U.S. Department of Health and Human Services, Public Health Service, Washington D.C., 1994.
11. Waddell, G., and Main, C. J. A new clinical model of low back pain and disability. In *The Back Pain Revolution,* edited by G. Waddell, pp. 223–240. Churchill Livingstone, London, 1998.
12. Waddell, G., Feder, G., and Lewis, M. Review: Advice to stay active is effective for acute low back pain but bed rest is not. *Evid. Based Med.* 3: 109, 1998.
13. Nichols, T., and Tucker, E. Occupational health and safety management systems in the United Kingdom and Ontario, Canada: A political economy perspective. In *Systematic Occupational Health and Safety Management,* edited by K. Frick, P. L. Jensen, M. Quinlan, and T. Wilthagen, pp. 285–310. Elsevier Science Ltd, Oxford, 2000.

14. Cheadle, A., Franklin, G., Wolfhagen, C., Savarino, J., Liu, P. Y., Salley, C., et al. Factors influencing the duration of work-related disability: A population-based study of Washington State workers' compensation. *Am. J. Public Health* 84: 190–196, 1994.
15. Clarke, J. *Work-Ready 1: Report of Qualitative Component from Ontario.* Institute for Work and Health, Toronto, 1999.
16. Oleinick, A., Gluck, J., and Guire, K. Establishment size and risk of occupational injury. *Am. J. Indust. Med.* 28: 1–21, 1995.
17. Glaser, B., and Strauss, A. *The Discovery of Grounded Theory.* Aldine, Chicago, 1967.
18. Eakin, J., and MacEachen, E. Health and the social relations of work: A study of the health-related experiences of employees in small workplaces. *Sociol. Health Illn.* 20: 896–914, 1998.
19. Porter, S. Critical realist ethnography. In *Qualitative Research in Action,* edited by T. May. Sage Publishing, Thousand Oaks, CA, 2002.
20. Hammersley, M., and Atkinson, P. *Ethnography: Principles in Practice.* Tavistock, London, 1983.
21. Wetherell, M., Taylor, S., and Yates, S. *Discourse as Data.* Sage Publications, London, 2001.
22. Smith, D. *The Everyday World As Problematic: A Feminist Sociology.* University of Toronto Press, Toronto, 1987.
23. Kvale, S. *Interviews: An Introduction to Qualitative Research Interviewing.* Sage Publications, Thousand Oaks, CA, 1996.
24. Gubrium, J., and Holstein, J. *Handbook of Interview Research.* Sage Publications, Thousand Oaks, CA, 2001.
25. Silverman, D. *Interpreting Qualitative Data: Methods for Analyzing Talk, Text and Interaction.* Sage Publications, Thousand Oaks, CA, 1993.
26. Coffey, A., and Atkinson, P. *Making Sense of Qualitative Data.* Sage Publications, Thousand Oaks, CA, 1996.
27. Bourdieu, P., and Wacquant, L. *An Invitation to Reflexive Sociology.* University of Chicago Press, Chicago, 1992.
28. Strauss, A., and Corbin, J. *Basics of Qualitative Research.* Sage Publications, Newbury Park, CA, 1991.
29. Ontario MoL. *A Better Health and Safety System for Ontario Workplaces.* Government of Ontario, Toronto, 1998.
30. *Ontario Workplace Safety and Insurance Act.* 1997.
31. Goffman, I. *The Presentation of Self in Everyday Life.* Doubleday Anchor, Garden City, NY, 1959.
32. Williams J. Employee experiences with early return to work programs. *Am. Assoc. Occup. Health Nurses* 39: 64–69, 1991.
33. Staal, J., Hlobil, H., VanTulder, M., Koke, A., Smid, T., and VanMechelen, W. Return-to-work interventions for low back pain: A descriptive review of contents and concepts of working mechanisms. *Sports Med.* 32: 251–267, 2002.
34. Werner, A., and Malterud, K. It is hard work behaving as a credible patient: Encounters between women with chronic patin and their doctors. *Soc. Sci. Med.* 57: 1409–1419, 2003.
35. Lillrank, A. Back pain and the resolution of diagnostic uncertainty in illness narratives. *Soc. Sci. Med.* 57: 1045–1054, 2003.

36. Smith, J., Tarasuk, V., Shannon, H., and Ferrier, S. *Prognosis of Musculoskeletal Disorders: Effects of Legitimacy and Job Vulnerability.* IWH working paper #67. Institute for Work and Health, Toronto, 1998.
37. Tarasuk, V., and Eakin, J. The problem of legitimacy in the experience of work-related back injury. *Qual. Health Res.* 5: 204–221, 1994.
38. Niemeyer, L. Social labeling, stereotyping, and observer bias in Workers' Compensation: The impact of provider-patient interaction in outcome. *J. Occup. Rehabil.* 1: 251–269, 1991.
39. Reid, J., Ewan, C., and Lowy, E. Pilgrimage of pain: The illness experiences of women with repetitive strain injury and the search for credibility. *Soc. Sci. Med.* 32: 601–612, 1991.
40. Eakin, J., Lamm, F., and Limborg, H. International perspective on the promotion of health and safety in small workplaces. In *Systematic Occupational Health and Safety Management: Perspectives on an International Development,* edited by T. Wilthagen, pp. 227–247. Elsevier, Oxford, 2000.
41. Eakin, J. "Leaving it up to the workers": Sociological perspective on the management of health and safety in small workplaces. *Int. J. Health Serv.* 22: 689–704, 1992.
42. Walters, D. *Health and Safety in Small Enterprises.* P.I.E.-Peter Lang, Bruxelles, 2001.
43. Eakin, J., MacEachen, E., and Clarke, J. "Playing it Smart" with return-to-work: Small workplace experience under Ontario's policy of self reliance and early return. *Policy Pract. Health Saf.* 2003. In press.
44. Ericson, R., Doyle, A., and Barry, D. *Insurance as Governance.* University of Toronto, Toronto, 2003.
45. Moffatt, K. Surveillance and Government of the Welfare Recipient. In *Reading Foucault for Social Work,* edited by L. Epstein, pp. 219–245. Columbia University Press, New York, 1999.
46. Tarasuk, V., and Eakin, J. Charitable food distribution as symbolic gesture: An ethnographic study of food bank work in Ontario. *Soc. Sci. Med.* 56: 1505–1515, 2003.

CHAPTER 10

Occupational Health and Safety, and Occupational Rehabilitation: The Nature of the Prevention–Rehabilitation Continuum

Gregory C. Murphy

It is the thesis of this book that investment in research into the new epidemics is urgently required if we are to have an adequate understanding of preventive strategies that can be introduced. While this understanding is being developed, it is apparent that current systems of occupational rehabilitation will be increasingly called upon to deliver services to those with chronic illness or serious injury.

To adequately respond to work-related illness or injury, a soundly based occupational rehabilitation system is required. This chapter examines the building blocks of effective occupational rehabilitation, particularly as occupational rehabilitation services involve the attitudes and behaviors of those employees living with chronic illness and permanent impairment.

OCCUPATIONAL REHABILITATION AND WORKERS' COMPENSATION SYSTEMS

From their inception, the development of effective and efficient workers' compensation rehabilitation schemes has proved difficult to achieve, both in Australia and in similar overseas nations such as the United States. Considine's (1, p. 2) description of the situation that occurred in Australia prior to the reforms of the 1980s could well have been applied to other nations with similar workers' compensation laws based on identifying employer negligence and avoidable risk-taking by the employer, alongside possible once-and-for-all, lump-sum payments to injured workers: "For more than 100 years Australian governments had grappled unsuccessfully with the consequences of inequality and inefficiencies in the workers' compensation area. Industrial accidents and diseases were rising so rapidly (that they cost more than) double the more widely-published road accidents." The situation in the United States was equally unsatisfactory, and Niemeyer (2) reported that at one period in the two decades of the 1980s–1990s there were eight consecutive years of unprofitability for workers' compensation insurers, during which costs exceeded premium income by as much as 23 percent.

In an attempt to overcome some of the deficiencies in the original Australian workers' compensation schemes, including major difficulties caused by workers delaying return to work, a series of reforms to workers' compensation occurred in most Australian states and territories in the 1980s. These were led notably by the Victorian government's introduction of "WorkCare"—a no-fault workers' compensation scheme which, inter alia, guaranteed weekly payments to workers for all work-related ill-health conditions. It was the hope of the legislators that guaranteed financial compensation would minimize legal disputes about entitlements and thus lead to quicker and more durable returns to work. As part of the WorkCare scheme, substantial resources were put into the provision of rehabilitation services by Approved Rehabilitation Providers (ARPs), organizations approved by the Victorian Accident Rehabilitation Council to deliver occupational rehabilitation services. Unfortunately, these ARPs were often staffed by rehabilitation and health professionals not sufficiently skilled and knowledgeable about the vocational aspects of their role (3).

Following the introduction of WorkCare in the state of Victoria in 1985, other Australian governments followed suit with essentially similar schemes, although the Commonwealth government's no-fault Comcare scheme for federal government employees introduced in 1988 had a number of distinct features such as the creation of workplace-based (non-professional) Case Managers within each organizational unit. The Comcare scheme has consistently outperformed all Australian state-government schemes in terms of its return-to-work achievements, although the federal government's workforce characteristics (with a generally higher level of transferable skill) undoubtedly contributes to this superior return to work rate.

All the Australian no-fault workers' compensation schemes have struggled to achieve the return-to-work rates that would have assured their long-term financial viability. Although the financial analysis of the efficiency and effectiveness of workers' compensation schemes is complex, it is apparent that the major threat to the successful operation of any workers' compensation scheme is the failure to achieve expected return-to-work rates, or more specifically, the failure to contain (for the overwhelming majority of claimants) work absences to relatively brief periods of time away from the workplace. Early on in its life, the viability of the WorkCare system was threatened by the fact that a not insignificant minority of claimants accounted for the majority of weekly compensation payments. Thus, when the Victorian WorkCare scheme in its early years reported unexpectedly high rates of long-term claimants (over 10 percent of claimants were off work for over a year, see AAC (4) the scheme's unfunded liabilities quickly rose to more than $2 billion. Even after the Victorian government's original WorkCare scheme was revised into the current WorkCover scheme, the scheme continued to suffer from persistently high rates of claimants who, once injured, were away from work for more than six months (5). The wage-replacement costs for these long-term claimants are the main item that threatens the financial viability of all no-fault workers' compensation schemes.

A full analysis of the reasons for the financial difficulties of many of the no-fault workers' compensation schemes (3, 6) is beyond the scope of this chapter, which is more focused on the workplace issues relevant to the prevention of ill-health conditions and the effective maintenance at work or return to work by those with ill-health conditions. It is these more workplace-related matters that are the focus of the remainder of this chapter.

SOME RECENT ADVANCES IN OCCUPATIONAL REHABILITATION

From the workplace perspective, a fundamental change occurred in the way that most large organizations approached occupational rehabilitation with the emergence of the Workplace Disability Management (WDM) movement (7). The key elements of the approach have been described elsewhere (8) but a fundamental premise of the approach was that too much decision-making regarding rehabilitation goals and the content of service plans had been taken out of the hands of employers and other work-based groups, and resided in the hands of parties external to the workplace, such as local doctors, providers of rehabilitation services, and administrators of various insurance companies or within government regulatory authorities. While the WDM approach (which was mainly adopted by large enterprises) had some major successes, particularly in achieving high return-to-work rates and in lessening the proportion of claimants who spent extended periods (e.g., more than six months) away from the workplace, the approach, after capitalizing on its original successes, was, perhaps not surprisingly, limited by the fact that it was essentially driven by improved communication and enhanced trust within the employer organization not by any proper appreciation of the three main bodies of knowledge relevant to the achievement of high rates of workplace safe practice and employee retention at work or of return to work following the onset of ill-health conditions. These three key knowledge areas are briefly discussed below, as they pertain to the individual worker.

WORKPLACE SAFE PRACTICE

The provision of a safe working environment is an expected initial building block for all occupational health, safety, and rehabilitation programs. The achievement of high rates of safe practice within any workplace is dependent (assuming optimal equipment being in place) on workers' knowledge of correct procedures, their capacity to enact correct procedures, and the work environment supporting workers' enactment of correct procedure, particularly through techniques such as safe practice goal setting, information feedback, and positive reinforcement (9). In the overwhelming majority of workplaces (and particularly in manufacturing settings), high levels of safe practice can be achieved. Problems are inevitable in situations where a harmful action or agent is not known or fully appreciated, as is the case in situations involving some chronic diseases, the slowly developing overuse injuries, or continual distressing interactions between organizational members.

In human-service organizations (or other work settings where the work tasks essentially involve exchanges between individuals) the difficulties in creating and maintaining a "safe" work environment are well recognized, largely because of the practical impossibility of standardizing the work environment (10). Thus, while safe practice can be relatively easily described and prescribed in a manufacturing environment, it is far from clear how one can standardize interactions between work colleagues or between service providers and customers, and thereby "assure" employee well-being in service organizations.

THE MENTAL HEALTH BENEFITS
OF WORK

It has now been established that moving "in" and "out" of employment has predictable effects on employee health and well-being (11). For the overwhelming majority of individuals, moving from unemployment to employment has a significant positive effect on these individuals' health and well-being (about half a standard deviation on General Health Questionnaire (GHQ) scores). Similarly, the movement away from employment is linked with a decrease in health and well-being (about a third of a standard deviation on GHQ scores). The demonstration of the nexus between absence from the workplace and decreased mental and physical health supports the validity of the "occupational bond" construct proposed by Shrey (7, 12) as part of the WDM approach (7, 12) central to the development of effective management of workers who become injured or who live with chronic ill-health conditions. Shrey's (7, 12) approach involves: (i) maintaining close, open communication between the organization's management representatives and the employee with the injury or chronic ill-health condition; and (ii) communicating, in a non-aggressive way, that a return to work is the normal expectation.

While there is evidence that for some individuals some workplaces do not yield the expected benefits (13, 14), the findings for the overall benefit of work are quite robust across different groups of workers, as well as across nations whose cultural values are similar to Australia's (11). The exact mechanisms of these general effects are not fully understood although major theoretical models of the mental health benefits of work have been advanced by prominent occupational psychologists such as Jahoda (15) and Warr (16). Using the concepts contained in their theoretical models, employers and employees, working together, could identify employee-job matches or job re-design targets which would prevent many of the more psychologically based worker distress claims.

HEALTH AND REHABILITATION PSYCHOLOGY

Living Successfully with Chronic Ill-Health Conditions and/or Re-Establishing One's Self following Serious Injury

Scientific knowledge about living successfully with a chronic condition or re-establishing oneself in the community following serious injury is limited. One problem has been that, for a variety of reasons, the literature on psychosocial correlates of chronic disease has for many decades been separate from the literature on psychosocial aspects of successful rehabilitation following serious injury (17). One clear example of this is the role of Bandura's (18) construct of "self-efficacy." While self-efficacy has long been a key study variable within the program of research developed by the Stanford Chronic Disease Self-Management Group (19), the construct has received little attention by rehabilitation psychologists investigating rehabilitation outcomes following such disabling injuries as spinal cord injury (20). Recently, Murphy and Reid (21) outlined a framework for integrating the two fields. This framework identified two major sets of variables (those to do with personal control; those to do with social support) which were proposed to be common to: (a) successful living with chronic illness; and (b) successful community re-establishment following serious injury. Until the validity of models such as those of Murphy and Reid (21) or of Devins (22) have been adequately tested, we will have an inadequate base from which to launch any effective secondary prevention or rehabilitation initiatives that might help improve on current suboptimal levels of occupational rehabilitation success. Summarized below is current knowledge about the key factors relevant to maintenance at work, or return to work, following disease onset or injury occurrence.

REHABILITATION PERSPECTIVES ON THE "NEW" THREATS TO THE HEALTH AND WELL-BEING OF EMPLOYEES

From a rehabilitation psychology perspective, with the exception of health issues having to do with precarious employment, there is no reason to expect that previously developed understanding will not apply to the emergent epidemics. Based on previous experience with chronic illness and work injury, it can be predicted that there will be a need for professional services in four main areas: pain behavior, attribution style, exercise enhancement, and social support.

Described below are key issues to be addressed when any of these four areas are involved in the situation of any workers with health problems, whether work-related or not.

Pain Behavior Management

Many chronic diseases and work injuries involve pain. If workers' pain is not handled effectively by medical and allied health personnel, then there is a high risk of health problems being complicated by the development of chronic pain syndrome, which is extremely debilitating to the individual (especially in terms of withdrawal from expected social roles), and extremely expensive to the workers' compensation system in terms of payment for medication, for visits to GPs and specialists, and for time away from work. The key processes underlying effective rehabilitation programs for chronic pain patients are well established (23, 24), but achieving a coordinated implementation of the correct approach is extremely difficult, especially when such diverse parties as family members, co-workers, private practitioners in psychology, and medical specialists need to contribute in a complementary manner for any rehabilitation plan to succeed. An additional problem exists in the case of pain problems associated with chronic ill-health conditions. Because of the long time periods involved in the full development of the diagnosed conditions, the learning history of those who develop chronic pain syndrome is such that effecting any change to key pain behaviors can be even more difficult than is the case with pain behaviors learned after traumatic injury.

Explanatory Style

The revolution in psychology that saw cognitive behavior therapy become the dominant treatment approach in clinical psychology (25–27) has not been fully appreciated by health and rehabilitation professionals dealing with injured or unwell employees. While academic psychologists for almost two decades have written generally about the health benefits of certain cognitive styles (see early landmark papers by Kamen and Seligman, 28; and Taylor and Brown, 29), there has been relatively little research using cognitive styles constructs to describe or predict the behaviors and attitudes of employees living with chronic disease or adjusting following traumatic injury. For example, even though Roberta Trieschmann (30), in her influential 1988 monograph on the psychology of spinal cord injury, wrote that "it would be interesting to determine if optimists do better in response to spinal cord injury than do pessimists" (p. 92), not one research article on this topic was identified by Murphy (20) in his review of the literature in this field. In the field of chronic disease, more work involving an explanatory style has appeared. Two notable examples (although based on different theoretical models) are the research programs of Affleck and colleagues (31) and of Devins and colleagues (32). Both of these research programs have produced some interesting findings pertaining to the explanatory style of those living with chronic diseases. For example, Affleck et al. (31) reported that pessimism correlated significantly with pain catastrophizing and pain-related activity limitations among a sample of individuals suffering from rheumatoid arthritis. The practical implications of such findings about optimism-pessimism and explanatory style (or related individual differences in attributional style) are largely dependent on the development of effective interventions that can foster optimism and other cognitive styles that are related to more positive experiences or achievements among those living with chronic conditions or adjusting to serious injuries. Unfortunately, the evidence for the effectiveness of group programs designed to foster optimism, resilience, or similar attributes is extremely limited (33). Further, although it is not a priority, given the lack of research in a wide range of areas to do with the nature and role of explanatory style for those living with chronic illness, the study of explanatory style and related attributional style constructs among *employees* living with chronic conditions has never, to the present author's knowledge, been reported.

Exercise Enhancement

Many chronic disease sufferers report low levels of regular exercise. The general and specific health benefits of exercise are well established (34, 35). For chronic diseases such as various cancers and diabetes, there have been extensive health benefits identified as proceeding from regular exercise (36, 37). Thus, employers interested in the minimization of the rates and extent of chronic illness among organizational members have often invested in the promotion of employee exercise, even though well-controlled evaluations of the effectiveness of such workplace-based health programs is minimal (38).

One major deficit in our knowledge in this area relates to the "mechanisms" by which exercise has its beneficial effects, either in protecting against disease development or by contributing to the better management of those living with diagnosed conditions such as multiple scelerosis (39). It could be held that much of the claimed benefit of exercise for those living with chronic conditions or disabling injury is due to improvement in mediating psychological processes pertaining to the assessment of one's achievements and of one's relationships with significant others. These last two areas are, of course, central to any employee's decisions about continuing to work or returning to work following ill health or injury.

Social Support

The literature concerning social support and its behavioral consequences (including health and employment consequences) has undergone substantial change in the last decade (40). Whereas in the 1970s and 1980s there were frequent reports of expected and observed positive effects of social support on individuals' health and related behaviors (41, 42), by the start of the 1990s researchers were far more restrained in their claims about the expected "benefits" of social support. Thus, Schwarzer and Leppin (43), in their review of the social-support literature, concluded that "social relationships might have rather inconsistent effects" (p. 435) on health or related dependent variables. Of particular interest to those in the occupational health and rehabilitation field is the role of social support in ameliorating the impact of chronic disease and injury and in facilitating employment-related achievements.

Over the last decade or so, the theoretical understanding of the nature of social support and its expected emotional and behavioral consequences has improved so that we now much better understand the role of social "support" in enhancing employee self esteem and in facilitating employment-related behaviors. Two key researchers (i.e.,Vinokur, and Wanberg, see below) and one major theory (the Theory of Reasoned Action developed by Ajzen and Fishbein, (44)) have led the way to improved knowledge in this area. Thus, for occupational health and rehabilitation personnel, it is important to understand that social relations will be "supportive" only to the extent that the *content* of the messages received from "supporters" is consistent with valued outcomes, such as increased personal control by the individual or strengthened motivation to return to work by those employees who may be away from work because of illness or injury. Consistent with this thesis are the series of studies which have shown, inter alia, that social support will lead to enhanced employment-related achievements only when the social "supporters" positively evaluate and communicate support for such behaviors as job-seeking or return to work (45, 46).

CONCLUSION

Occupational rehabilitation systems have two major aims: the achievement of high rates of return to work; and the achievement of durable and satisfying return-to-work situations. Assuming medical treatment and physical rehabilitation to be optimal, the key to achieving high rates of return to work and the maintenance of people at work after suffering a chronic condition involves the prevention of the development of unnecessary "complications" within the individual and the removal of unnecessary environmental barriers to return to stable, satisfying work.

Regardless of whether employees' health problems involve chronic disease or serious injury, a relatively small number of variables need to be monitored to achieve the best work rates. These are the key questions: (a) Are pain behaviors being appropriately managed? (b) Are programs available to teach employees how to move away from unhelpful "explanatory styles" that are linked to poor health and related outcomes? (c) Are exercise levels adequate to promote general health and well-being? (d) Is social support appropriately focussed on behaviors and attitudes relevant to a safe return to work or safe maintenance at work?

It is hoped that management within work organizations will have identified and attempted to remove all unnecessary environmental barriers, including barriers associated with the (negative) attitudes of some staff and management representatives. The importance of communicating positive attitudes regarding return to work is suggested by the advice of Levi in his extremely thorough population study of the sequelae of spinal cord injury, an injury with the most devastating of impairments and related disabilities: "Return to work is to be communicated as the normal scenario for those suffering a spinal cord injury" (47, p. 36). If high post-injury employment rates can be observed among certain groups of those living with spinal cord injury, and they have been (48–50), why is it that those with disabilities are (increasingly) non-participants in the labor force (51)?

The preceding chapters of this book have described in detail certain occupational diseases, stressful work conditions, and behavioral problems at work. This chapter has described key concepts relevant to keeping individuals working safely and to achieving high return-to-work rates following work absence associated with illness or injury. Avoidable problems have been identified (such as preventing the development of chronic pain syndrome), the importance of exercise promotion has been emphasized, as has the role of explanatory style for influencing employment achievements following the return from any ill-health condition. Lastly, the conditions under which social support can be expected to yield positive work-related outcomes have been described.

Effective occupational rehabilitation has a clear preventative perspective, quite complementary to the primary prevention efforts of those interested in workplace health and safety. Knowledge from both areas is required if Australian workplaces are to be maximally safe, and to ensure that the sustainability of our workers' compensations systems are soundly based on maintaining at work the increasing numbers of people living with chronic illness and on achieving high return-to-work rates among those suffering workplace-based injury.

REFERENCES

1. Considine, M. *The Politics of Reform: Workers' Compensation from Woodhouse to WorkCare*. Deakin University, Centre for Applied Social Research, Geelong, Australia, 1991.
2. Niemeyer, L. Health care reform. In *Sourcebook of Occupational Rehabilitation*, edited by P. King, pp. 68–82. Plenum, New York, 1998.
3. Rowe, B. *Final report of the WorkCare Committee*. Government Printer, Melbourne, 1988.
4. Accident Compensation Commission. *Annual Report 1989-1990*. Government Printer, Melbourne, 1990.

5. McGlade, M. Return to Work Performance within Occupational Rehabilitation. Paper presented at the Australian Society of Rehabilitation Counsellors' Meeting, Melbourne, August 2003.
6. Thomason, T., Scmidle, T., and Burton, J. *Workers' Compensation.* Upjohn Institute, Kalamazoo, MI, 2001.
7. Shrey, D. Worksite disability management and industrial rehabilitation. An overview. In *Principles and Practices of Disability Management in Industry,* edited by D. Shrey and M. Lacerte, pp. 3–54. GR Press, Winter Park, FL, 1995.
8. Murphy, G., Foreman, P., and Young, A. Differences in the organisational behaviour beliefs held by Australian employer representatives and health professionals involved in occupational rehabilitation: Implications for workplace disability management. *Int. J. Hum. Resour. Manage.* 8: 18–28, 1997.
9. Komaki, J., Heinzmann, A., and Lawson, L. Effects of training and feedback: Components of a behavioural safety program. *J. Appl. Psychol.* 65: 261–270, 1980.
10. Hasenfeld, Y. *Human Service Organisations.* Prentice Hall, Englewood Cliffs, NJ, 1983.
11. Murphy, G., and Athanason, J. The effect of unemployment on mental health. *J. Occup. Organ. Psychol.* 72: 83–99, 1999.
12. Shrey, D. Effective workplace-based disability management programs. In *Sourcebook of Occupational Rehabilitation,* edited by P. King, pp. 389–409. Plenum, New York, 1998.
13. Graetz, B. Health consequences of employment and unemployment. *Soc. Sci. Med.* 36: 715–724, 1993.
14. Morrell, S., Taylor, R., Quine, S., Kerr, C., et al. A cohort study of unemployment as a cause of psychological disturbance in Australian youth. *Soc. Sci. Med.* 38: 1553–1564, 1994.
15. Jahoda, M. *Employment and Unemployment: A Social-Psychological Analysis.* Cambridge University Press, Cambridge, 1982.
16. Warr, P. *Work, Unemployment and Mental Health.* Clarendon Press, Oxford, 1987.
17. Frank, R. Organized delivery systems: Implications for clinical psychology services, or, we zigged when we should have zagged. *Rehabil. Psychol.* 44: 36–51, 1999.
18. Bandura, A. *Social Foundations of Thought and Action.* Prentice Hall, Englewood Cliffs, NJ, 1986.
19. Lorig, K. Chronic disease self-management: A guide for tertiary prevention. *Am. Behav. Sci.* 39: 676–683, 1996.
20. Murphy, G. *Predicting Vocational Achievement Following Spinal Cord Injury.* La Trobe University Rehabilitation Research and Training Unit, Bundoora, Australia, 1999.
21. Murphy, G., and Reid, K. Chronic illness, disability and rehabilitation: The nature and role of personal control variables. *Aust. J. Prim. Health,* 2003. In press.
22. Devins, G., Cameron, J., and Edworthy, S. Chronic disabling disease. In *Cognitive Behavioural Therapy for Persons with Disabilities,* edited by C. Raduitz, pp. 105–140. Jason Aronson, Northvale, NJ, 2000.
23. Fordyce, W. *Behavioral Methods in Chronic Pain and Illness.* Mosby, St. Louis, MO, 1976.
24. Klaphow, J., Fillingim, R., and Doleys, D. Pain management. In *Sourcebook of Occupational Rehabilitation,* edited by P. King, pp. 369–388. Plenum, New York, 1998.

25. Mahoney, M. *Cognition and Behavior Modification.* Ballinger, Cambridge, MA, 1974.
26. Mahoney, M. Minding science. Constructivism and discourse. *Cogn. Ther. Res.* 27: 105–123, 2003.
27. Chambless, D. In defence of dissemination of empirically-validated treatments. *Clin. Psychol. Sci. Pract.* 3: 230–235, 1966.
28. Kamen, L., and Seligman, M. Explanatory style and health. *Curr. Psychol. Res. Rev.* 6: 207–218, 1987.
29. Taylor, S., and Brown, J. Illusion and well-being: A social psychological perspective on mental health. *Psychol. Bull.* 103: 193–210, 1988.
30. Trieschmann, R. *Spinal Cord Injuries: Psychological, Social and Vocational Rehabilitation.* Demos, New York, 1988.
31. Affleck, G., Tennen, H., and Apter, A. Optimism, pessimism and daily life with chronic illness. In *Optimism and Pessimism,* edited by E. Chang, pp 147–168. APA, Washington, D.C., 2001.
32. Devins, G., and Shnek, Z. Multiple sclerosis. In *Handbook of Rehabilitation Psychology,* edited by R. Frank and T. Elliott, pp. 163–184. APA, Washington D.C., 2000.
33. Gillham, J., Reivich, K., and Shaffé, A. Building optimism and preventing depressive symptoms in children. In *Optimism and Pessimism,* edited by E. Chang, pp. 301–320. APA, Washington D.C., 2001.
34. Australian Institute for Health and Welfare. *Australia's Health 2002.* Author, Canberra, 2002.
35. World Health Organization. *The World Health Report 2002.* WHO, Geneva, 2002.
36. Thune, I., and Furberg, A. Physical activity and cancer risk. *Med. Sci. Sports Exerc.* 33: 5530–5550, 2001.
37. Kelley, D., and Goodpaster, B. Effects of exercise on glucose homeostasis in Type 2 diabetes mellitus. *Med. Sci. Sports Exerc.* 33: 5495–5501, 2001.
38. Green, R., Malcolm, S., Greenwood, K., and Murphy, G. Impact of a health promotion program on the health of Primary School principals. *Int. J. Educ. Manage.* 15: 31–38, 2001.
39. Petajan, J., and White, A. Recommendations for physical activity in patients with multiple sclerosis. *Sports Med.* 27: 179–191, 1999.
40. Murphy, G., and Young, A. Contradictory effects of social support. *Aust. J. Prim. Health* 4: 8–17, 1998.
41. Cobb, S. Social support as a moderator of life stress. *Psychosom. Med.* 38: 300–314, 1976.
42. Cohen, S., and Wills, T. Stress, social support and the buffering hypothesis. *Psychol. Bull.* 98: 310–358, 1985.
43. Schwarzer, R., and Leppin, A. Social support and mental health. In *Life Crises and Experience of Loss in Adulthood,* edited by L. Montada, S. Filippo, and M. Lerner, pp. 435–458. Lawrence Erlbaum, Mahwah, NJ, 1992.
44. Ajzen, I. *Attitudes, Personality and Behaviour.* Open University Press, Milton Keyes, 1988.
45. Vinokur, A., Price, R., Caplan, R., van Ryn, M., and Curran, T. The jobs. 1. Preventative intervention for unemployed individuals. In *Jobs Stress Interventions,* edited by L. Murphy, J. Jurrell, S. Sauter, and G. Keita, pp. 125–138. APA, Washington D.C., 1995.

46. Wanberg, C. A longitudinal study of the effects of unemployment and quality of re-employment. *J. Vocat. Behav.* 46: 40–54, 1995.
47. Levi, R. *The Stockholm Spinal Cord Injury Study.* Karolinska Institut, Stockholm, 1996.
48. Gutmann, L. Statistical survey of one thousand paraplegics and initial treatment of traumatic paraplegia. *Proc. R. Soc. Med.* 47: 1099, 1954.
49. El Ghatit, A., and Hanson, R. Variables associated with obtaining and sustaining employment among spinal cord injured males. *J. Chron. Dis.* 31: 363–369, 1978.
50. Krause, J. Employment after spinal cord injury. *Arch. Phys. Med. Rehab.* 73: 163–169, 1992.
51. Stapleton, D., and Burkauser, R. (eds.). *The Decline in Employment of People with Disabilities.* Upjohn Institute, Kalamazoo, MI, 2003.

CHAPTER 11

Before the Epidemic Strikes: Identifying Warning Signs of an Emerging Epidemic and Conducting Baseline Empirical Studies in Industry

Claire Mayhew

As discussed in a number of earlier chapters, the internationalization of the business environment has had significant flow-on effects on the hazards and risks faced by workers. Sometimes completely new work-related injuries and illnesses result from radically changed working environments. For example, the emergence of the SARS virus in early 2003 provoked widespread panic in some sectors of the population (resulting in a significant downturn in the airline and tourism industries), intense pressure on epidemiologists to identify transmission mechanisms, and a marked increase in morbidity and mortality among exposed workers in affected geographical areas (particularly health care workers).

Yet theorists had been warning for years—if not decades—that such epidemics were long overdue, and early SARS cases had been extant for months. Why were OHS and healthcare workers so unprepared? Why were symptoms, transmission mechanisms, and core preventive strategies unknown for so long? Arguably, if the early warning signs had been heeded and a baseline "grounded" empirical study conducted, preventive interventions could have been implemented long before the full force of the epidemic struck.

In this chapter, the author analyzes scenarios where the early warning signs of an emerging epidemic are extant and where baseline OHS empirical studies in industry are warranted. Detailed guidance is also provided on how to go about conducting such "grounded" empirical OHS research when the first "sentinel" cases of an emerging epidemic are identified.

INTRODUCTION

There are a range of reasons for conducting research studies, and a series of publications are available on scientific research design, hypothesis generation and testing, formatting of questionnaires, sample selection, and statistical analysis of data. For example, hypotheses are usually generated when there is an amount of unexplainable data or a pattern of associations that existing theory or knowledge cannot fully explain.

However, the steps that need to be taken before hypothesis generation can occur are rarely aired. Even in the social sciences—where qualitative research methodologies are most commonly utilized—the need for a scientific basis to hypothesis generation processes is rarely elaborated. The need for substantive data on which to base hypotheses is most acute where the range of variables is unknown, the problem is potentially acute, and the existing data are particularly poor. Such scenarios are, arguably, common in emerging areas of OHS research.

In this chapter, it is argued that large-scale baseline empirical studies can be of enormous utility in the hypothesis generation process in the social sciences if data are collected in a "scientific" manner. Further, the collation and analysis of extensive qualitative and quantitative data gathered during empirical studies, and any subsequent objective interpretations, are likely to be accepted by the broader research community if some basic "scientific" principles are followed. In short, this chapter is designed to provide guidance on the design, implementation, and conduct of large-scale empirical studies so that the findings are likely to be accepted by the broader research community of physical and social scientists working in OHS.

All the research study examples discussed in this chapter were based within an OHS/industrial sociology paradigm. The common theme in each of the 14 studies discussed below is that key people recognized that there was a problem of some sort but had no idea of the parameters of the OHS issue, were unable to identify the influencing factors or causative mechanisms, the likely contexts when the problem was most likely to occur were unknown, it was not possible to articulate correlations between specific actors and the probability of particular outcomes, and researchers *could not generate a hypothesis for testing*. That is, the traditional epidemiological mechanisms used in scientific research into epidemics could not be adopted because the identification of the specific patterns of morbidity and mortality had *not yet* progressed sufficiently. Yet, as has been demonstrated throughout history, the nature of most epidemics is that they start with a few sentinel cases prior to widespread affliction. The central argument underlying this chapter is that large-scale empirical studies that are conducted within a "grounded" theoretical paradigm are an important (and frequently overlooked) tool for establishing baseline indices about emerging epidemics. The discussion concludes with a detailed description on the scientific methodology adopted in one recent large-scale empirical research study in the Australian health care industry.

BACKGROUND: A BRIEF REVIEW OF METHODOLOGY

The reason for a scientific research project is to generate knowledge about a particular problem or issue in a way that provides reliable data or information, or to establish an objective basis to a body of knowledge through facts and reason and not through feelings, beliefs, traditional thoughts, or intuition. The scientific basis to the conduct of research can be accomplished by a range of methods, all of which are more appropriate in some enquiries than in others. For example, physical scientists may rely to a greater extent on laboratory analysis than do social scientists. Just as in the natural sciences, there are a range of different methodologies that can be adopted in social science research. Whatever scientific methodologies are adopted, objective investigative methods are needed in the collection of information, analysis of data, interpretation of findings, and during the write-up. Because of the wide variety of methodologies used by different disciplines—and which vary according to the problem under investigation—it is impossible to preview them all in this chapter. There are, however, three guiding principles that most scientific researchers aim to achieve:

• Validity (the study actually measures what it is purported to measure);
• Generalizability (the findings are applicable to similar populations/ situations); and
• Replicability (if study is repeated, the same or similar findings are likely to be identified).

Statistics will usually be gathered during research studies, including those using an interview process, postal surveys, historical reviews, laboratory-based studies, and during secondary data analysis. *Descriptive* statistics concentrate on the influence of particular variables, central tendencies, and correlations. Statistics are also useful to identify whether the population sampled is representative of the population from which they are drawn (e.g., on the basis of age or gender), or the extent to which findings are consistent between studies. Where an analysis is made between two or more variables, the process is called *inferential statistics,* which may identify the probability of a particular event or association occurring.

Because there are constraints in every research process, many researchers will adopt *"triangulation"* of data during the analysis phase and bring together data from a range of different sources or from disparate perspectives. For example, in the author's area of research—OHS—she will often collect primary data about a particular problem from a large number of interviewees, collate workers' compensation claims data from that particular occupation/industry group of workers from state or national databases, and/or examine hospital treatment data. Subsequently, the separate sources of data will be compared in some way and if the findings concur, the validity of findings is likely to be higher. However, all researchers need to be aware that most of us have a conscious or unconscious tendency to a "self-fulfilling prophecy" where we tend to analyze data or interpret findings to fit our prior beliefs and/or support an underlying hypothesis and to ignore findings that conflict with this primary (perhaps unconscious) belief.

The majority of research studies go through a series of steps, usually including:

- Hypothesis development, or identification of the core research question;
- Review of the relevant scientific knowledge about the research problem (which may form the literature review chapter of a subsequent research report);
- Identification of the most appropriate methodology to assess the research question;
- Gaining funding for the study (i.e., convincing others of the worth of the study);
- Gaining ethical approval for the study;
- Collection of new relevant data, possibly through participant observations, a postal survey, face-to-face interviews, health measurements, laboratory experiments, physical science measures, etc.; and
- Analysis of data, critical review of prior assumptions, interpretation of data, identification of relationships, synthesis of associated patterns between variables, resolution of differences identified during previous related studies, write-up, and subjecting the findings to the peer-review process.

However, *what happens when the basis for hypothesis generation (or setting of the primary research question) is too thin? How does a researcher go about identifying potential factors where the core variables are unknown?*

In the case of emerging epidemics, the traditional "scientific" techniques (such as hypothesis generation and testing, primary or secondary data analysis, or scrutiny of organizational records) are clearly insufficient because the basic nature of variables and relationships between employment-related factors is unknown. In such a scenario, *deductive* scientific methods *cannot* be utilized, but yet the design of preventive interventions *requires* use of a scientific research design to ensure validity, generalizability, and reliability of the findings and recommended actions. The remainder of this chapter focuses on the need to conduct grounded empirical studies in a scientific manner where baseline information about phenomena is unknown, and where even the core variables are yet to be identified.

CONDUCTING A BASELINE EMPIRICAL STUDY

The starting point for a baseline empirical study is an understanding of *inductive* research processes. With inductive research, theory is built from the ground up following the gathering of extensive empirical evidence (1). This process is in marked contrast to *deductive* studies which start with a hypothesis based on extant data.

Research studies based on inductive approaches aim to develop theoretical explanations of why phenomenon occur, and support these assertions by logical, evidence-based arguments. In an ideal situation, the developed theory will also allow for some prediction about future phenomena. Inductive methodologies are frequently chosen when baseline information on which to base hypotheses are not available. This approach to research is also often referred to as "grounded" research as inductive studies set the groundwork, or baseline, for future, more positivistic studies which may use the findings from these preliminary studies to form hypotheses for testing. Thus, the findings from inductive studies identify basic problem characteristics and may indicate the direction of cause-effect relationships, whereas more positivistic studies start from a premise or hypothesis about causation direction. For example, in inductive studies, occupational violence may be identified as commonly associated with perpetrators having a particular characteristic, or in explicit high-risk scenarios. Similarly, with emerging epidemics, unusual features may be identified as frequent, or particular sets of symptoms may occur in a specific time order. Or, participants may identify that preventive interventions do not work effectively under a particular set of circumstances. Nevertheless, as with more traditional study designs, in inductive research *temporal-order* logic requires that the cause must come before the effect, *associations* between variables are identified, and potential causal relationship are identified. Thus, "good causal explanations identify a causal relationship and specify a causal mechanism" (2).

Inductive research methodologies are essentially linked with what have become known as *interpretive social science* methodologies and ideas, including hermeneutics (theories of meaning), ethnography (cultural understandings), and phenomenological and symbolic interactionist (subject and researcher influence each other in a dialectical fashion) ideas. All of these methodologies adopt participant observation or field research that involves close contact between researcher and subject so that the social reality under study is understood from the standpoint of the participants, usually within a practical orientation. Further, those who adopt a critical approach to inductive research will have a systematic (3):

> . . . critical process of inquiry that goes beyond surface illusions to uncover the real structures in the material world in order to help people change conditions. . . reveal the underlying mechanisms that account for social relations . . . social research uncovers myths, reveals hidden truths. . . .

Getting the Best of Both Worlds:
Combining Different Sources or Types of Data

Qualitative data gained from such inductive studies are a very rich source from which to identify the *context* under which particular events occur. In contrast, quantitative data provides an improved understanding about the *extent* to which such incidents or associations happen. In the past, many researchers assumed qualitative and quantitative research processes were almost mutually exclusive.

Today, this breach is lessening and innovative methodologies are continually being devised. Ideally, researchers will try to take "the best" from all potential methodologies. Hence, when designing a new research study the author will typically aim for:

- A research problem area that is relatively unknown;
- A small "executive committee" to help with critical early review—and who are likely to ensure that, whatever the outcome, the findings are made public (arguably an essential pre-condition for those working as civil/public servants);
- Use of scientific selection procedures to gain access to a representative sample of workers for a semi-structured interview;
- A process that includes face-to-face interviews with a relatively large sample;
- Development of a semi-structured questionnaire that includes a number of open-ended questions as well as some quantitative measures of the scope of the problem;
- An instrument where the questions asked—and data gathered—allow for comparisons with either qualitative or quantitative data gathered during other studies and/or secondary data collections (to enhance triangulation); and
- A final write-up that involves a peer-review process.

Each of the research studies listed in Table 1 was essentially designed within an *inductive* approach because the available baseline data were insufficient for hypothesis generation, and yet circumstances had arisen that indicated major OHS issues were being experienced that might, or might not, be indicative of an emerging epidemic or significant OHS issue. Many of the 3,339 people interviewed in the 14 separate studies fall within the definition of *precarious* workers, i.e., they were self-employed, casual, in micro-small businesses, or employed on short-term contracts. The precarious nature of the employment of many workers across the industrialized world is, arguably, an increasing phenomenon which will provide a rich source for future baseline empirical studies in different industry sectors and occupational groups. Many of these studies were conducted with colleagues—whose contribution is evident in the publications listed at the end of this chapter—and to whom an enormous sense of gratitude is due.

When the first study was conducted 12 years ago, there was no premonition that this would form the basis for a series of studies, or indeed that subsequent studies would even be funded. Nevertheless, in different employment situations, roles, and environments, distinct research studies were commissioned. Because the future is unknown for all of us, as a guiding principle researchers should allow for the *potential building of composite data banks through comparable data across different studies.* Hence,whenever possible, data should be collected and collated in such a way that information from future studies will be able to be compared. This requirement means that even basic questionnaire coding categories for primary data should remain the same wherever possible across subsequent studies. When deciding on coding categories, it may also be useful to consider existing secondary collations of data. For example, age of respondents can be coded within similar age groupings to that used by the OECD or the statistics department of the country's civil service. This means that if something unusual is found and there are insufficient numbers for validity, the findings may be comparable against secondary data, for example in census data or through community profiles as shown in the *ABS Social Atlas* for a particular period of time.

These 14 separate studies are briefly summarized below.

1. *Maritime:* This research study was initiated to provide baseline data on the incidence and severity of occupational violence *between* individual seafarers employed on the same vessel. Indicators of the incidence and severity of what is known as "internal" violence in this working population had not previously been reported in the scientific literature. The pilot study found that the international seafaring labor force exhibited all the core characteristics of a precarious labor force: their labor market position was weak; hours of labor were long; and pay was comparatively poor. In addition, occupational violence was relatively common, with 19.4 percent verbally abused in the immediately previous 12 months, although threats (5.5 percent), physical violence (1 percent), and sexual assault (1 percent) were less common (4). That is, this grounded empirical study identified that low-level occupational violence was endemic among this population of international workers.

2. *Tertiary education:* This study assessed characteristics of the "work environment" at an Australian university, including identification and evaluation of threats, aggression and bullying between staff members, and of the risks posed by students. One hundred people employed in the tertiary education/university sector were interviewed face-to-face and completed a semi-structured interview schedule focused on bullying/occupational violence (5). Again, there was insufficient extant scientific literature for hypothesis generation, and grounded research was necessary for identification of the core variables and estimation of the potential risks.

3. *Healthcare:* This inductive study was initiated to provide baseline indices on patterns of occupational violence experienced by a range of health occupational groups, including medical officers, allied health, ancillary staff, ambulance officers, and nurses (6). It was found that low-level aggression was in epidemic proportions among specific health workers, including ambulance officers and those in emergency departments (see later discussion).

4. *Retail:* This empirical study was commissioned to provide baseline data on crimes experienced by small retail business owner/managers (particularly armed hold-ups), prevention strategies adopted, and to evaluate the

Table 1

Overview of 14 empirical studies involving 3,339 face-to-face interviews

	Industry sector	Year completed or published	Number of face-to-face interviews	Geographical area	Title of study
1	Maritime	2001–2003	108	Australia, Malaysia, and Sweden	Occupational Violence in the Australian Maritime Industry
2	Tertiary education	2003	100	Queensland	The Work Environment at [named] University
3	Health care	2002	400	NSW	The Occupational Violence Experiences of Some Australian Health Workers: An Exploratory Study
4	Retail	2001	50	Tasmania	Pilot Evaluation of the Small Business Self-Audit Checklist in Tasmania
5	Long-haul transport	2000	300	NSW	Occupational Health and Safety amongst 300 Long Distance Truck Drivers: Results of an Interview-Based Survey
6	Fast-food	1999/2000	304	Queensland, NSW, and Victoria	OHS Issues for Young Workers in the Fast-Food Industry
7	Clothing manufacture	1998	200	NSW	Outsourcing and OHS: A Comparative Study of Factory-Based and Outworkers in the Australian TCF Industry

8	Building contractors, cabinet-makers, and demolishers	1997	331	Queensland	An Evaluation of the Impact of Targeted Interventions on the OHS Behaviours of Small Business Building Industry Owners/Managers/Contractors
9	Garage, café, newsagent, and printing	1997	248	Brisbane	Barriers to Implementation of Known OHS Solutions in Small Business
10	Childcare, hospitality, transport, and building	1996	205	Brisbane	The Effects of Subcontracting/Outsourcing on OHS
11	Indigenous labor market	1996	257	Queensland	Aboriginal & Torres Strait Islander OHS: A Pilot Study of Hazard Exposures, Patterns of Work-Related Injury and Illness, OHS Information Provision, and Injury Reporting Behaviours in Queensland
12	Building	1994/1995	600 (Queensland 500; U.K. 100)	500 in Queensland; 100 in U.K.	An Evaluation of the Impact of Robens-Style Legislation on the OHS Decision-Making of Australian and United Kingdom Builders With Less than Five Employees
13	Taxi	1993	100	Brisbane	Taxi Drivers: The Extent and Impact of Violence of Work
14	Building and transport	1992	136	Queensland	Work-Related Injuries: A Comparison of Employee and Self-Employed Transport Workers *and also* Building
	Total interviews		3,339		

utility of a self-administered self-audit checklist that was designed to reduce vulnerability (7). This grounded research study identified that victimization of small business workers in the retail industry was in epidemic proportions. However, violence association with armed hold-ups was less common than were shoplifting, break-ins while closed, or even credit card fraud.

5. *Long-haul transport:* This baseline empirical study was initiated to identify the OHS risk factors experienced by 300 long-haul truck drivers. It was found that economic stress was the underlying cause of excessive hours of work, fatigue, stress, and poor OHS indices. Self-employed owner/ drivers were identified to be at significant risk of exposure to a range of OHS hazards, but had very limited ability to control their exposures to risk factors (8).

6. *Fast-food:* This grounded empirical study assessed OHS among 304 young casual workers across three states of Australia: 50 percent worked in company-owned and 50 percent in franchised outlets of an international fast-food chain. The inductive study identified that a stringent OHS management system could be an effective mechanism to improve OHS outcomes, enhance levels of knowledge about injury prevention, and to reduce the risk of work-related injury and illness (9).

7. *Clothing manufacture:* This inductive empirical research project involved comparison of OHS indices between 100 factory-based employees and 100 outworkers who manufactured clothes from home in two Australian states. It was found that outworkers were experiencing an epidemic of work-related injury and illness, with an incidence ratio three times that of factory-based workers, predominantly due to their low rates of pay and extended working hours (10).

8. *Building contractors, cabinet-makers, and demolishers:* This large-scale grounded research project evaluated the relative effectiveness of three different OHS preventive interventions among 331 self-employed and micro-small business owner/managers: an intensive mailed OHS campaign, on-site visits by an inspector; and a regulatory change (11).

9. *Garage, café, newsagent, and printing:* This inductive empirical study focused on evaluation of understandings of three key OHS areas: manual handling; OHS legislation; and hazardous substances. The grounded study involved interviews with 248 owner/managers of micro-small businesses. A significant level of exposure to OHS hazards and risks was identified, with a resulting extensive burden of acute and chronic illness. However, a very limited understanding of injury and illness prevention strategies was identified among this population (12).

10. *Childcare, hospitality, transport, and building:* This baseline comparative study involved face-to-face interviewing of 205 workers: approximately half were employees, with the rest matched by industry sector but

employed under outsourcing arrangements. The empirically gathered data identified that the primary determinant of injury risk was the hazard exposures associated with particular industries/occupations, but that precarious employment was an important subsidiary risk factor that contributed to the burden of injury and illness (13).

11. *Indigenous:* This study was commissioned to provide substantive baseline data on the work-related injury and illness profile of Australian Indigenous (Aboriginal) workers (which, somewhat surprisingly, had not previously been assessed). Overall, the data identified that indigenous workers were at increased risk, reflecting their generally poor labor market positions. In addition, a concerning level of work-related stress was identified among those who worked at the interface between western and traditional societies, including police liaison officers, health, and social service workers. The research process involved face-to-face interviewing of 257 indigenous workers in the state of Queensland (14).

12. *Building:* This empirical study was commissioned to establish the baseline OHS indices of small-scale builders. A high level of chronic morbidity, poor OHS preventive knowledge, low levels of regulatory understanding, and long hours of labor were widespread. The research process involved face-to-face interviewing of 500 self-employed builders in Australia and a matched group of 100 in Britain (15).

13. *Taxi:* This grounded inductive study was commissioned to estimate the baseline incidence of occupational violence experienced by taxi drivers. It was found that 81 percent had been verbally abused, 17 percent threatened, and 10 percent assaulted in some way over the immediately previous 12-month period. The research process involved interviewing 100 randomly selected taxi drivers who worked out of the four major taxi depots in the city of Brisbane (16).

14. *Builders and transport:* This study was designed to elucidate any variations in OHS data recorded by workers' compensation, hospital records, ambulance treatments, and healthcare providers. Individual worker experiences were also compared with the secondary data through face-to-face interviews with self-employed builders and transport owner/operators working in rural and urban areas. It was found that there were significant, and largely non-overlapping, indices of work-related injury and illness in the separate databases (17–19). That is, the study identified that sentinel "flags" about emerging epidemics may show up in some data sets but not others.

Each of these 14 studies involved face-to-face interviews with workers. In all cases, the available data were insufficiently reliable *prior to the study* to conduct traditional hypothesis-based studies. Each study also involved practical difficulties at some point or another.

SOME PRACTICAL TIPS

The conduct of large-scale empirical studies is not easy, and there are a number of potential pitfalls. The most crucial aspect is that the key researcher should thoroughly understand the topic, research process, and resulting data. Ideally, the key researcher will conduct all or most of the interviews. In grounded research, there is no place for token and distant chief investigators—although the temptation to appoint well-published senior staff often arises when research funding is sought! A second core—and often overlooked issue—is to ensure the safety and security of field workers, particularly those conducting interviews in remote or isolated sites, or working in evening or night hours.

Yet even when the best possible research methodology has been designed, the process of conducting a research study is seldom straightforward and sometimes variations in methodology will have to be adopted "in the field" as problems arise. The way in which a researcher deals with these problems and openly admits to weaknesses in their methodology is usually an indication of the conceptual abilities and level of commitment to scientific research principles. A good scientific researcher will always keep in mind the need to ensure the research methodology is not compromised, and ensure objective mechanisms to gather data are always adopted if the original methodology has to be adjusted. Some further pitfalls and potential solutions are detailed below.

Getting Access to the Population: The Role of the "Intermediary"

Before the fieldwork starts, background briefings are essential. Expending effort on this stage of the research project is likely to result in far easier future access to interviewees and better-quality data. In most worksites, this process includes ensuring the personnel manager, the trade union delegates on site, and any relevant professional group know what the research is about, who is in charge, and contact phone numbers for members of the Ethics committee overseeing the study. The names and contact details of field researchers also need to be provided (e-mail is probably the most appropriate medium, as phone calls will disrupt interviews). These background briefings also allow any one of the key people to double check on any concerns. For example, on a university site the student union and any other key student organizations may be briefed.

Getting Interviewees to Discuss Sensitive Topics

Experienced interviewers—particularly those probing sensitive and confidential topics—do everything that they can to ensure that the person being interviewed feels relaxed, comfortable, and not afraid to speak freely about a range of factors that they *perceive* to be related to the problem under investigation. There are a number of aspects that contribute to this ambience.

Interview site or room: The field researcher should try to select a site where the interviewer will be alone with each interviewee and cannot be overheard. The interview place should be one where the person feels very comfortable and at ease. Because many of the topics that may arise during face-to-face interviews are very private, a wise precaution is to conduct all interviews in the garden of a worksite, in a café/tea room out of normal use hours, or in the on-site union delegate's office (when he or she is absent). As a guiding principle, a manager's office should *never* be used because of the potential for misconceptions. It is quite amazing how often people ascribe ulterior (and quite incorrect) motives to particular research projects or individual researchers.

Wherever possible, the interviewer should arrange the furniture in an interview site so that the interviewee becomes dominant and the interviewer is in a less-dominant position. For example, if there are two chairs in an office (and one chair is large and the other a small one), the person being interviewed should be encouraged to take the larger or higher chair. Similarly, if there is a rectangular table in an office, it is wise to have the interviewee placed at the head or top of the table. This process may subconsciously encourage the interviewee to take charge, and even the most timid may feel compelled to talk.

Each interviewer needs to ensure that she or he has adopted an objective mindset. It is crucially important that s/he recognizes any bias in her/his own opinions or preconceived ideas. We are all affected by these assumptions about individual characteristics, behaviors, or abilities based on gender, race, age, educational levels, or even sexuality. The best example of an ideal interviewer is that they should *try to become as much like a good vacuum cleaner as possible!* A good vacuum cleaner picks up absolutely everything, makes very little noise, is inconspicuous, the color blends in with the room, and when it is finished the task (vacuuming) nothing is left behind.

It is also crucially important that the interviewer has no real or *perceived* power relationship over the interviewee. Appearance and language are of crucial importance. The interviewer should ensure that their dress, forms of language used (avoid long words or complicated phrases), and tone of voice blend in with the audience being interviewed. Thus, if interviewing shopfloor workers, an interviewer might wear jeans, but if the population under study is business executives, a suit and tie would be more appropriate. The interviewer should also have some knowledge of body language, and ensure their *tone* of voice is soft (while ensuring those with hearing loss are not excluded in any way).

The beginning of the interview process: People taking part in research projects often have incredible misconceptions about the purpose of interviews. Many are frightened about potential impacts on their employment security. Hence, it is appropriate to repeat the assurance that comments are confidential and that the names of individuals and the companies for which they work are never recorded. It may also be appropriate for the interviewer to stress that there are no "right" or "wrong" answers to any questions. Interviewees who are illiterate will frequently say they "left their glasses at home" or something like that. In such cases the interviewer should be sensitive and never comment, but just read the questions out to the interviewee and fill in forms for them (where appropriate).

Each interviewee should be provided with a one-page information sheet to take away with them that provides an overview of the purposes of the study, key questions, contact points to access the findings of a study, and the name(s) of independent research ethics people who can be approached if participants have any concerns about the conduct or purpose of the study. During the early explanatory stage of each interview, the researcher should answer any immediate questions or concerns raised by the participants. It should be stressed that participation is voluntary and that participants may withdraw at any time. Ideally, the participant will sign an Informed Consent form at the beginning of the interview process.

The whole purpose is to get the interviewee's ideas, perceptions, and interpretations. After all, those who fund the study do not want to know the interviewer's views. Hence, an interviewer should *not* talk very much after the initial introductions. On some occasions there will be a long, blank pause in discussions; the interviewer should keep his/her mouth shut to encourage an opinion or comment from the interviewee.

The interviewer should have memorized most of the questions to be asked, their sequence, and to have read all the background material for the study. With experience, the interviewer will be able to sense when an interviewee is troubled about a question, and it may be appropriate to stress again that the survey is confidential. After a few trial runs, the interviewer may feel comfortable laying a semi-structured questionnaire on a table partially in front of an interviewee, but filling the questionnaire out for the participant. This process of assisting interviewees will reduce the time required for completion and is more likely to ensure that the written words will be able to be correctly transcribed (a not uncommon problem).

Scheduling and Coping with Personal Exhaustion

Social science research studies are almost always conducted under significant time and financial constraints. Further, most research granting bodies require regular updates and production of objective markers of progress (e.g., journal articles accepted in peer review journals). Further, sometimes Ethics Committees spend lengthy periods of time adjudicating over topics and procedures. As a result, field researchers may find that their proposed timelines are contracted sharply. As one example, in one of the author's recent large-scale studies, the project had to be approved by five separate Ethics Committees (study 3 in Table 1). With inevitable questions to be answered and adjustments made, in the end it took longer to proceed through the various Ethics Committees than it did to conduct 400 face-to-face interviews.

In the field, this author usually draws up a daily schedule with a maximum of around 10 interviews a day scheduled on a single site. Even when interviews are only expected to take 20 minutes or so, hourly timetabling allows for interviewees being unavoidably delayed, for movement between different offices or buildings (such as on a hospital site), to accommodate interviewees who are upset when remembering and discussing prior experiences, in case the researcher becomes lost, or if prior participants "bail up" the field researcher and ask a question about the study in a public area. As a general rule, a one-hour lunch break is left free (which may be used to catch up on rescheduled appointments). Intermittent rescheduling should be regarded as a normal expectation whenever interviews are being conducted at workplaces.

Even experienced and dispassionate interviewers can become emotionally drained if conducting interviews on distressing topics (such as bullying or sexual assault). For example, in the recent study on bullying within a University (study 2 in Table 1), it was decided to conduct interviews on only three days each week to ensure continuation over a period of months. A similar level of emotional exhaustion resulted during a study of coronial files into the work-related fatalities of seafarers (20).

A more detailed explanation of the rationale for conducting an inductive research study, the way scientific principles were integrated into the research design, the sample selection process, and the conduct of one large-scale empirical study is provided below, together with a brief outline of the findings.

CONDUCTING AN INDUCTIVE EMPIRICAL STUDY IN THE HEALTH INDUSTRY

In 2002, a substantive empirical research study was commissioned to assess the extent and severity of occupational violence experienced by health workers in Australia. This study involved 400 face-to-face interviews with nurses, medical officers, allied health, ambulance officers, and ancillary staff (6). The study was necessary because there were no substantive scientific studies in Australia that included a range of health occupations, various sites, and which included prevention strategies. Only small-scale, single occupation, or site-specific studies had been published in the scientific press; for example, the second Work Related Fatalities Study (WRFS2) identified that around one health worker a year was murdered in Australia (21). International studies had suggested that while the *incidence* of occupational violence might be high for health workers, the *severity* was not (in comparison with other occupational groups) (22, 23). Further, there were very few substantive violence prevention guidelines in existence at that time (24, 25). Thus, baseline data were required on estimates of incidence and severity, risk factors, perpetrator characteristics, higher-risk contexts, and levels of awareness of basic prevention strategies.

Further, without baseline data, hypotheses about cause and effect relationships could not be generated, and the relative effectiveness of preventive interventions could not be evaluated.

This empirical study was linked with a concurrent international joint program on occupational violence involving the International Labour Office (ILO), International Council of Nurses (ICN), World Health Organization (WHO), and Public Services International (PSI). A report summarizing studies of occupational violence across the health industry in a number of countries was subsequently published (26). The ILO/ICN/WHO/PSI also released *Framework Guidelines for Addressing Workplace Violence in the Health Sector* (27). The ILO subsequently developed a Code of Practice, titled *Code of Practice on Workplace Violence in Services Sectors and Measures to Combat this Phenomenon* (28).

Methodology

The stated *aims* of the health violence research study were to establish baseline estimates of occupational violence among the public health workforce, including

- Estimates of *incidence* and *severity* for the different *types* of violence (verbal abuse, threats, assaults, bullying, etc.);
- Identification of any variations in estimates of incidence between the various health occupational groups (nursing, medical officer, etc.);
- Identification of any variations between rural and urban areas, and between geriatric, mental health, and emergency departments, etc.; and
- Identification of characteristics of perpetrators, "hot spots," and key risk factors (6).

This research study was essentially designed within an *inductive* approach. Face-to-face interviewing was the preferred option as many people will not divulge personal information through a mailed questionnaire, and probing on sensitive issues is far more difficult through the more anonymous telephone. Face-to-face interviewing also ensured good response rates (only one refusal) and high-quality contextual data.

It was not feasible to conduct the study across all geographical areas of the country and state. Hence, the study was conducted in four geographically distinct regions: two rural and two urban. It was assumed that these four localities represented a demographic cross-section of patient socio-economic and industrial profiles. The research proposal was reviewed by five separate Ethics Committees (the central departmental Ethics Committee, plus one in each of the four geographical areas where the study was conducted).

The Sampling Frame and Sample Selection Process

The aim in this research study was to interview a representative sample (based on the available data on workforce demographics) of the public health workforce who had regular face-to-face contact with patients/clients. Hence, those who worked in offices, kitchens, or facilities with no face-to-face contact were excluded (e.g., payroll staff). From the overall population of 100,000 public health system employees in this organization, it was estimated that a minimum of 400 workers were needed to take part in the research study. These 400 interviewed healthcare workers were based in 45 different hospitals and 14 ambulance stations, in addition to a number of other linked community health sites and clinics (6).

The occupational breakdown of interviewees was 40 allied health, 40 operational ambulance officers, 40 medical officers, 80 ancillary staff members, and 200 nurses. These five broad occupational groups included people in a range of jobs; for example, nursing staff (enrolled, registered, and assistants in nursing), physicians (registrars, medical officers on rotating rosters, and visiting medical officers), allied health (social workers, psychologists, dieticians, occupational therapists, speech therapists, etc.), and ancillary staff (wardpersons, community aids, admissions officers, security, hospital assistants, and others who had contact with members of the public). Because of the sampling selection process, health workers at all levels of hierarchies in different occupational groups participated; for example, assistant in nursing to director of nursing, and registrars to newly graduated medical officers (6).

Workers in all *employment status* categories were included: permanent staff, short-term contract, part-time, casual, and agency staff members. Permanent staff were those with on-going positions either as full-time or part-time workers; short-term contract and casual workers were hired for a set period of time; and agency staff were contracted via a private employment business for one shift at a time. For those not familiar with the term "casual pool," these are workers who are hired in a general capacity and may be sent to any ward within a healthcare complex depending on needs on a particular day (e.g., staff absence through illness) and skills required.

All hospital-based or linked community (e.g., aged care and disability services) interviewees were selected from employment payroll records held separately in each region utilizing a numerical selection process. For example, if 100 allied health members were on the payroll in a region and 10 were required, every 10th person listed was chosen. The very mobile ambulance officers were selected on the basis of availability on a range of sites at random times. The selected health workers were usually interviewed at work during rostered shift hours. With repeated visits to health care sites at different times of the day, evening and night, and over weekdays and weekends, it was usually possible to interview most of the selected shift workers. Access to casual staff sometimes proved to be difficult;

for example, if they were still listed on the payroll but had not worked a shift for a period of months.

Strengths and Weaknesses in Research Methodology

Based on the best available demographic data, the sample population interviewed appeared to match the public health workforce as a whole (except that rural employees were over-represented). Thus, the findings were likely to represent the experiences of occupational violence across this workforce, although it must be recognized that (since the population interviewed consisted of a sample of only 400 workers) some of the patterns identified may have been marginally skewed. For example, the inclusion of casual workers who were on the job and exposed for fewer hours per year may have resulted in lowering of the overall estimated incidence ratio. (It was not possible to adjust for this source of bias as many casual workers held more than one job.)

Information Collected and Research Instrument

A standardized, semi-structured questionnaire that required both quantitative and qualitative responses was devised, pilot-tested, and refined. The questionnaire was formatted in such a way that the gathered information could be compared against other occupational violence data; for example, information on assault convictions as well as data from previous empirical studies conducted by the principal researcher. The questionnaire was revised marginally during pilot testing after the ILO/ICN/WHO/PSI comparative study research questions became available (26). As a result, some questions were *identical* to those used in the other country studies (e.g., procedures for reporting of violence); in other cases the Australian data were *comparable,* for example, on the extent of bullying and witnessing of violence on others (6).

The data collected included number of violent events experienced over the immediately previous 12-month period, witnessing of violence on other staff members, perceived high-risk places and perpetrators, violence prevention strategies in place, recommendations to improve violence prevention efforts, and other employment-linked violence issues. Interviewees were also asked to describe the contexts/scenarios of violent events. The *severity* of each violent incident was estimated by interviewees separating events into verbal abuse, threats, assaults, bullying, or "other" activities, e.g., spitting. The quantitative questions allowed calculation of incidence ratios for the different types of violence, and the qualitative data elucidated the contexts under which violent events most frequently occurred. The data were also collected in a way that information could be separated by type of ward or service (e.g., mental health, community, etc.), by urban/rural areas, and by occupational group (e.g., medical officer, allied health, etc.).

It was hypothesized that there were likely to be some emotional injury/stress repercussions following violent events, in addition to any physical injuries. An objective but simple instrument to measure these stress outcomes was required. The General Health Questionnaire (GHQ) is an instrument that has been repeatedly used and validated across a range of Australian and international studies to measure levels of stress (29–32). The GHQ has pre-set questions with numerical scores allocated for each response; these are then totalled to give an overall score. The abbreviated GHQ-12 was selected and attached to the semi-structured questionnaire. Use of the GHQ-12 also allowed comparisons with the findings from some other studies conducted by the principal researcher, particularly the previous long-haul transport research project (study 5 in Table 1), and the more recent tertiary education empirical work (study 2 in Table 1). Past studies have indicated that, when using the Likert scaling method, a GHQ-12 score of between 8 to 10 is relatively normal with a threshold of around 11 or 12; a person with a score greater than 14 probably requires urgent assistance (31, 33). The threshold score has been defined as ". . . the number of symptoms at which the probability that an individual will be thought to be a case exceeds 0.5" (34). Nevertheless, there are concerns about the ability of the GHQ to detect long-latency conditions; for example, post-traumatic stress disorder may remain undisclosed in the short term (29, 35).

Research Process

The broadly representative sample of 400 employees was interviewed face-to-face over the period October 25, 2001 to March 3, 2002 (100 in each of the four regions where the study took place). All 400 interviews were one-on-one, with the exception of three dual-person interviews conducted with ambulance officers (because they work in teams and stopping work for an interview required both officers to be absent from their tasks). The semi-structured questionnaire was used as the basis for all interviews, with responses checked off by the researcher. Only around 5 percent of interviewees asked to fill in the questionnaire themselves. In no cases did anyone either take away a questionnaire or undertake the exercise without the researcher overseeing the whole process. All interviewee identifiers were destroyed immediately afterwards and no record of names was retained.

Findings in Brief

The incidence of violence was found to vary across health occupational groups. Violence was clustered around "hot spots" (e.g., emergency departments) and "hot tasks" (for example, when at-risk children were taken into care), and was disproportionately perpetrated by "hot people" (e.g., drug and alcohol clients) (6, 36). Broadly speaking, ambulance officers appeared to have the highest incidence of victimization and ancillary staff the lowest (with the important exceptions of security officers and admissions staff). An analysis of variance (ANOVA) found the relationship between exposure to violence at work and elevation of GHQ score (emotional injury/stress) was significant at the 0.0001 level (1 df, standard error 0.21331, t-value 4.56) (6). This finding is highly significant. As in a number of other studies into violence in the community, the perpetrators of "client-initiated" violence were disproportionately male, younger, affected by alcohol or illicit substances, with the additional risk of aggression from those suffering from dementia (6).

That is, the fundamental rationale for commissioning the empirical research study was met: baseline *incidence* ratios were calculated for the public health workforce; the *severity* of each violent incident was estimated (by interviewees separating events into verbal abuse, threats, assaults, bullying, or "other" activities); and the higher-risk contexts identified.

CONCLUSION

In this chapter it was argued that *baseline* large-scale *inductive* empirical studies are an under-utilized method to identify indices associated with a range of problems faced by working populations. Further, the findings from such studies—even those based on qualitative data—are likely to be accepted by the broader research community if key scientific principles are followed when the data are gathered. These grounded empirical studies are likely to be of enormous utility to the working population when sentinel cases indicative of an emerging epidemic are diagnosed; for example, with an entirely new ill-health condition. Unfortunately, few textbooks discuss appropriate methodologies to be adopted during such large-scale baseline empirical studies.

This chapter was concerned with detailing some ways by which large-scale empirical studies could be reasonably conducted, and to identify some pitfalls, with the hope that these methods will be more widely accepted. A series of 14 empirical studies that involved face-to-face interviews with 3,339 workers were described in brief to highlight the types of problem areas that could be reliably researched using these methods.

One of the studies was described in depth to highlight the depth of insights that can be gained through the use of large-scale empirical studies. The large-scale empirical study conducted among the public health workforce allowed for baseline incidence ratios to be estimated, for the identification of characteristics of perpetrators to be determined, and for the contexts when violence most commonly occurred to be highlighted. The baseline data and findings from this study have been accepted by the international community, OHS and health professionals, and even by epidemiologists. The study therefore achieved the basic aim of producing baseline estimations, identifying key variables, and providing a basis against which the effectiveness of interventions to reduce the risk of occupational violence can be judged.

In sum, while on their face value large-scale empirical studies based on inductive methodologies appear to be time-consuming and expensive, the reverse is generally the case. When scientific principals are used during the design of empirical studies and while gathering data, inductive research can provide a rich source of both qualitative and quantitative data on relatively unknown problem issues. The end products of such large-scale empirical studies are likely to have a high level of validity, to be generalizable to the broader industry sector/occupational group, and to be repeatable. Further, when the emergence of a distinctly new ill-health condition is suspected, large-scale empirical studies designed within an inductive paradigm provide the most reliable mechanism to identify the characteristics of an emerging epidemic in a timely fashion.

REFERENCES

1. Neuman, W. *Social Research Methods: Qualitative and Quantitative Approaches,* p. 41. Allyn and Bacon, Boston, 1994.
2. Neuman, W. *Social Research Methods: Qualitative and Quantitative Approaches,* pp. 45–46. Allyn and Bacon, Boston, 1994.
3. Neuman, W. *Social Research Methods: Qualitative and Quantitative Approaches,* p. 67. Allyn and Bacon, Boston, 1994.
4. Mayhew, C., and Grewal, D. Occupational violence/bullying in the maritime industry: A pilot study. *J. Occup. Health Saf. Aust. N.Z.* 19: 457–463, 2003.
5. McCarthy, P., Mayhew, C., Barker, M., and Sheehan, M. Occupational violence in tertiary education: Risk factors, perpetrators and prevention. *J. Occup. Health Saf. Aust. N.Z.* 19: 319–326, 2003.
6. Mayhew, C., and Chappell, D. The occupational violence experiences of some Australian health workers: An exploratory study. Special issue of *J. Occup. Health Saf. Aust. N.Z.* 19: 3–43, 2003.
7. Mayhew, C. Getting the message across to small business about occupational violence and hold-up prevention: A pilot study. *J. Occup. Health Saf. Aust. N.Z.* 18: 223–230, 2002.
8. Mayhew, C., and Quinlan, M. *Occupational Health and Safety amongst 300 Surveyed Truck Drivers.* Research study conducted as part of the *Safety Inquiry into Long Haul Trucking Industry,* formal inquiry set up by the Motor Accident Authority of New South Wales under M. Quinlan, 2001.
9. Mayhew, C. Occupational health and safety management systems (OHSMS) impact on OHS performance in the franchised outlets of a large fast-food chain. Paper presented at the Voluntary Guidelines for Management Systems for the Working Environment Workshop, Brussels, June 14–16, 1999.
10. Mayhew, C., and Quinlan, M. *Outsourcing and Occupational Health and Safety: A Comparative Study of Factory-Based and Outworkers in the Australian TCF Industry.* Industrial Relations Research Centre, University of New South Wales, Sydney, 1998.

11. Mayhew, C., Young, C., Ferris, R., and Harnett, C. *An Evaluation of the Impact of Targeted Interventions on the OHS Behaviours of Small Business Building Industry Owners/Managers/Contractors.* Division of Workplace Health and Safety (Queensland) and National Occupational Health and Safety Commission, AGPS, Canberra, Australia, 1997.
12. Mayhew, C. *Barriers to Implementation of Known Occupational Health and Safety Solutions in Small Business.* National Occupational Health and Safety Commission and the Division of Workplace Health and Safety, AGPS, Canberra, Australia, 1997.
13. Mayhew, C., Quinlan, M., and Bennett, L. *The Effects of Subcontracting/Outsourcing on Occupational Health and Safety.* Industrial Relations Research Centre Monograph, University of New South Wales, Australia, 1996.
14. Mayhew, C., and Vickerman, L. Aboriginal and Torres Strait Islander occupational health and safety: A pilot study. *Aust. Aboriginal Stud.* 2: 61–68, 1996.
15. Mayhew, C. *An Evaluation of The Impact of Robens-Style Legislation On The OHS Decision-Making of Australian and United Kingdom Builders With Less Than Five Employees.* Report to NOHSC, Sydney, 1995.
16. Mayhew, C. Occupational violence: A case study of the taxi industry. In *Occupational Health and Safety in Australia: Industry, Public Sector and Small Business,* edited by C. Mayhew and C. Peterson, pp. 127–139. Allen and Unwin, Sydney, 1999.
17. Mayhew, C. Identifying patterns of injury in small business: Piecing together the data jigsaw. In *Occupational Health and Safety in Australia: Industry, Public Sector and Small Business,* edited by C. Mayhew and C. Peterson, pp. 105–115. Allen and Unwin, Sydney, 1999.
18. Mayhew, C. The endangered proletariat: Occupational injury amongst subcontractors and consultants. *Labour Indust.* 7: 149–164, 1996.
19. James, C. (Mayhew). Self-employed and employee transport workers: Labour process determinants of occupational injury. *Labour Indust.* 5: 75–89, 1993.
20. Mayhew, C. *Work-Related Traumatic Deaths of British and Australian Seafarers: What are the Causes and How Can They Be Prevented?* Seafarers International Research Centre, Cardiff University, Cardiff, 1999.
21. Driscoll, T., Mitchell, R., Mandryk, J., Healey, S., and Hendrie, L. *Work-Related Traumatic Fatalities in Australia, 1989 to 1992.* National Occupational Health and Safety Commission, Ausinfo, Canberra, Australia, 1999.
22. Chappell, D., and Di Martino, V. *Violence at Work,* Ed. 2. International Labour Office, Geneva, 2000.
23. Mayhew, C. Occupational violence in industrialised countries: Types, incidence patterns, and "at risk" groups of workers. In *Occupational Violence in Industrialised Countries,* edited by M. Gill, B. Fisher, and V. Bowie, pp. 21–40. Willan Press, London, 2002.
24. CAL/OSHA. *Guidelines for Security and Safety of Health Care and Community Service Workers.* Division of Occupational Safety and Health, Department of Industrial Relations, San Francisco, 1998.
25. Mayhew, C. *Preventing Client-Initiated Violence: A Practical Handbook.* Research and Public Policy Series No. 30, Australian Institute of Criminology, Canberra, Australia, 2000.

26. Di Martino, V. *Workplace Violence in the Health Sector Country Case Studies, Synthesis Report.* ILO/ICN/WHO/Psi, Geneva, 2002. www.ilo/public/english/dialogue/sector/papers/health/violence-ccs.pdf or www.icn.ch

27. ILO/ICN/WHO/PSI. *Framework Guidelines for Addressing Workplace Violence in the Health Sector.* ILO, Geneva, 2002.

28. ILO. *Code of Practice on Workplace Violence in Services Sectors and Measures to Combat this Phenomenon,* ILO, Geneva, October 2003.

29. Chapman, S. The use of the general health questionnaire in the Australian Defence Force: A flawed but irreplaceable measure? *Aust. Psychol.* 36: 244–249, 2001.

30. Goldberg, D., Gater, R., Sartorius, N., Ustun, T., Piccinelli, M., Gureje, O., and Rutter, C. The validity of two versions of the GHQ in the WHO study of mental illness in general health care. *Psychol. Med.* 27: 191–197, 1997.

31. Goldberg, D. *The Detection of Psychiatric Illness by Questionnaire.* Oxford University Press, London, 1972.

32. Graetz, B. Multidimensional properties of the general health questionnaire. *Soc. Psychiatry Psychiatric Epidemiol.* 26: 132–138, 1991.

33. Goldberg, D., and Williams, P. *A User's Guide to the General Health Questionnaire.* NFER-Nelson, Windsor, United Kingdom, 1988, reprinted 1991.

34. Goldberg, D., and Williams, P. Op cit, 1991, p. 3.

35. Goodchild, M., and Duncan-Jones, P. Chronicity and the general health questionnaire. *Br. J. Psychiatry* 146: 55–61, 1985.

36. Brookes, J., and Dunn, R. The incidence, severity and nature of violent incidents in the emergency department. *Emerg. Med.* 9: 5–9, 1997.

CHAPTER 12

Conclusion: Models of Epidemics

Chris L. Peterson

Over the past century there have been many epidemics in occupational safety and health (OSH). These identified epidemics have been associated with working in mining (such as asbestosis), heavy manual handling (e.g., back strains and injuries), in keyboard work (e.g., RSI), through exposure to a range of noxious substances (resulting in cancers and other diseases), and reactions to working in very competitive environments. In some cases, epidemics have been associated with new products and new production processes that over time have proved to be detrimental to health. Others have resulted from the uptake of new technologies where ergonomic and workflow designs have not been sufficiently developed to produce safe working conditions. The latest of the recognized epidemics (stress) has been associated with increased competition among companies, work intensification, greater tension in workplaces, and longer hours of work, all of which have placed greater physical and mental strain on employees.

According to Takala (1) there has been a significant increase in the levels of many work-related cancers, circulatory diseases, occupational injuries, and communicable diseases transmitted at work. One core reason for this increase is that databases now include conditions that were not always previously counted, for example, communicable diseases. Similarly, some circulatory diseases are now included in counts when previously they were excluded; for example, following a coronary attack at work.

Nevertheless, there are a range of incidents that are excluded from OSH injury/ill-health databases in most industrialized countries. For example, changes in the labor market have resulted in greater proportions of self-employed and contract workers, whose work-related injuries and illnesses are almost always excluded from organizational records and formal injury databases. Similarly, workers who have retired and who subsequently develop long-latency diseases (such as cancers from exposure to hazardous substances at work) are highly unlikely to have their ill-health indices recorded as work-related (unless the disease is specific to particular agents, e.g., mesothelioma). Further, as processes

211

of production have changed, the hazards and risks workers are exposed to have also altered. In the early stages of emerging epidemics from new production processes, the "sentinel" injuries and illnesses (and sometimes even fatalities) are likely to be excluded from databases. For example, the emotional trauma from extensive bullying at work is only just beginning to be recognized, and hence *may* be recorded on internal organizational records—but is unlikely to make the official governmental databases.

There is no "one best "model for explaining epidemics in OSH. Rather, there are a number of models available that are based on the nature of the problem behind the epidemic, and provide explanations of the social, psychological, and political processes that surround an epidemic, the level of acceptance in the broader community, and the continuity or cessation of the epidemic. There are critical questions that need to be asked about epidemics in OSH:

- First, what constitutes an epidemic compared with an up-surge of cases?
- What were the predisposing factors to the epidemic?
- Were the new epidemics the result of a particular cause, or were there numerous contributors?
- What other factors or pressures (e.g., social or political) can explain why an epidemic occurred (beyond biomedical, medical, and legal interpretations and rulings)?
- What is the role of research, pressure groups, and particular "test cases" in uncovering or identifying an epidemic?

To answer these questions, broad understanding of the full context is required, including ideological, biopsychological, ergonomic, and social and political explanations.

This final chapter summarizes the various OSH epidemics detailed in this book, and presents model explanations based on three core approaches to OSH issues: (a) biological and biomedical; (b) psychosocial; and (c) sociocultural/ socio-political. Finally, an analysis is presented of the economic, social, and political environment within which epidemics occur and are (or are not) recognized.

FRAMEWORKS FOR ANALYZING EPIDEMICS

Wainwright and Calnan's (2, p. 161) analysis of the epidemic of stress centered on factors that may be common to many OSH epidemics. That is, while an epidemic may be due to changes that have occurred in the way that work is done over the previous two to three decades, ". . . it is the broader socio-cultural changes . . . that account for experiences at work being interpreted through the medicalised prism of epidemic and disease." Further, any epidemic in the workplace may be conditioned by factors that occur outside of work. Wainwright and Calnan (2) argue that there are a number of competing perspectives that contribute to the construction of an epidemic, including litigation, the government policy framework, the trade union view, employees' perspectives, management interpretations, and the lay approach. Each of these approaches will be detailed below.

The Contribution of Litigation to Recognition of an Epidemic

A *litigation* approach helps to identify factors that are important in shaping public consciousness about an OSH epidemic. For example, a basic Web search using the word "mesothelioma" results in a listing of multiple sites for lawyers advertising the best options for pursuing litigation following diagnosis of mesothelioma or other asbestos-related diseases. One such site (3) claims to have settled a large number of cases for over U.S. $1 million (including a Vermont pipe fitter with mesothelioma who was awarded over U.S. $13 million). Many of these sites also contain extracts of confidential correspondence where managements had either sought to deny the problems of asbestos or to have significantly downplayed the risks. Similarly with occupational stress, Wainwright and Calnan (2) draw attention to British experiences where employees have received compensation payments for stress-related incidents with claims pursued under the *Management of Health and Safety at Work Regulation* (1992) or the *Health and Safety at Work Act* (1974).

Publicity about litigation in the national press may significantly increase public awareness of specific OSH risks. Where media campaigns are sustained about particular OSH risks, the general public may become aware of specific work-related epidemics. Willis (5) cites the fuelling of recognition of repetitive strain injury (RSI) as an epidemic through media reports and through the publicity given to the first employee in Australia, Susan Davis, to be awarded compensation for RSI.

As detailed in Chapter 3 of this book, occupational violence may be the most acute of the "emerging" work-related epidemics of the 21st century. Arguably, violence at work will be recognized as an OSH epidemic more quickly than previous injuries and illnesses because many of the acts are included within the *criminal codes* of nation states, as well as under the OSH *Acts*. For example, in the U.S., under Section 654(a) of the *Occupational Safety and Health Act*, under the general duty clause, employers may be subject to Occupational Health and Safety Administration (OSHA) penalties if violent acts endanger employees. Employers willfully violating the act can incur a penalty of between U.S. $5,000–U.S. $70,000 (4).

The Contribution of Government Policy to
Recognition of an Epidemic

The strength of government policy reflects the extent of jurisdictional interest in emerging OSH issues, and is evident through the potency of *Acts*, the level of enforcement of regulatory regimes, and timely support for preventive strategies. For example, the British Health and Safety Executive is responsible for OSH policy, but there have been examples where this was exceedingly slow and not developed until long after the signs of epidemics were evident through extensive litigation. For instance, stress was absent from the Health and Safety Executive's agenda as late as 1992 (2). In Australia, the National Occupational Health and Safety Commission provides a national forum for policy development, but has no enforcement powers. Here, enforcement and prevention are under State control through the various OSH agencies.

However, not all governments in all nation states have taken sufficient action to control recognized epidemics where cause-effect relationships are clear. For example, it is still legal to incorporate asbestos in a number of consumer products in a number of countries. Asbestos is found in some garden products, clutches, car brakes, and roofing materials. Further, asbestos may be a hazard in existing buildings and homes containing shingles, insulation materials, cladding in many factories, and tiles. Hence, when renovations or demolition work is in progress, workers and nearby residents can readily be exposed if extensive preventive strategies are not enforced. While some nation states have moved to enactment of a total ban on asbestos mining, importation, and use, others have prevaricated. Countries totally banning use include China, Denmark, Norway, Sweden, the Netherlands, Germany, Britain, France, Belgium, Austria, Poland, Switzerland, the Czech Republic, Slovania, Luxembourg, Saudi Arabia, Italy, and the Emirates (6). Until such appropriate action is taken at the government level in all nation states, it is difficult to prevent on-going exposure and hence on-going epidemics of asbestos-related disease.

The Contribution of Trade Unions to Recognition of an Epidemic

The trade union movement has historically acted to protect the safety and health of members, even when other agencies (such as governments) responded inadequately to risks. Nevertheless, even trade unions sometimes prioritized other issues (such as job protection) over OSH. For example, in Australia, it was relatively recent (the early 1980s) when the trade union movement showed strong support for specific OSH issues across a number of epidemic threats. For instance, in the late 1990s, the Australian Council of Trade Unions led a national stress campaign to heighten awareness of an epidemic that government authorities were slow to respond to and even denied (particularly employers) (7). Similarly, 200,000 health and safety representatives in Britain addressed the breach left by the Health and Safety Executive regarding stress. In 1998, a British trade union congress passed a number of agreements and resolutions about the emerging risks from bullying in the workplace (8). In Australia, the union movement has also been proactive about violence and bullying in the workplace. Nevertheless, the influence of the union movement has subsided in many countries due largely to decreasing membership, rising levels of precarious employment, more fragmented workforces, and less unified approaches to industrial relations. If the union movement regains strength, their role in OSH epidemic identification and action will undoubtedly increase.

The Contribution of Employers to Recognition of an Epidemic

Managerial perspectives on OSH are important for both the recognition of epidemics and their denial/suppression. The epidemic of work-induced stress during the 1990s provides a useful example. Chandler, Berg, and Barry (9) argue that British employers were relatively slow to acknowledge the epidemic of stress. Peterson (7) argues that, in Australia, many employers emphatically denied an epidemic of stress and questioned whether stress among employees even existed. Nevertheless, Calnan and Wainwright (2) report that while in a survey of 500 members of the British Institute of Directors 40 percent regarded stress to be a big problem, many quibbled with the conceptualization of stress, and numerous respondents regarded it as an individual phenomenon. Employer responses to violence in the workplace have varied significantly according to the *type* of violence. Those events that come under criminal justice systems tend to be widely accepted (e.g., armed hold-ups); in contrast, "internal" violence/bullying tends to be discounted (see Chapter 3). In the U.S. employers have been urged to take action to prevent overt violence in the workplace (4, 10). However, because it is often the organizational industrial relations environment that is the precursor to "internal" violence/bullying, many employers are keen to individualize the problem and blame particular employees rather than see it as one of many outcomes from workplace arrangements. Hence "external" occupational violence may be recognized as a "new" epidemic, but "internal" aggression is unlikely to be (see Chapter 3).

The Contribution of the Population at Large
to Recognition of an Epidemic

The lay population—or anecdotal approach—can also exert significant influence of whether an OSH epidemic is recognized or not (2). Some issues, such as fatalities, hold-ups, and mesotheliomas have been presented by the media as issues of concern, and have been accepted by the wider population as important. Hence, such risks may be widely acknowledged through lay understandings as important OSH issues. Changes in the public consciousness are a core feature among those OSH conditions accepted as epidemics.

Hence, the extent to which the media picks up on OSH risks, the penalties levied on liable employers following litigation, the level of influence of pressure groups, and the strength of independent research findings (particularly dissemination to the wider public) are all important precursors to widespread lay recognition of OSH epidemics.

Each of the chapters in this book focused on a different OSH epidemic and elaborated the contexts where the hazards arose, the characteristics of the resulting injuries/illnesses among the exposed workers, the approaches taken to control the risks, and the ways by which the epidemics were finally recognized (often after initial denials). Detailed review of the content of these chapters in this book reveals that increased pressures from globalization, enhanced productivity demands, and changes in operating environments underpin many of the work-practice changes that are associated with the "new" epidemics.

THE EXTANT AND EMERGING EPIDEMICS FROM WORK-RELATED CAUSES

Internationalization and Epidemics

David Walters maintains that epidemics arise due to a constellation of factors. He argues that they are due to structural changes in work and the labor market, as well as deregulation and the withdrawal from inspection control and resourcing of the state. In addition, there are the effects of globalization, and social and political factors on OHS. Social and economic paradigms need to be employed to understand the effects of internationalization. David Walters also points to the effects of neo-liberalism on deregulation in OHS.

He identifies that up to 2.3 million workers may have been victims of work-related deaths in 2000. This represents both long-latency disease conditions and traumatic fatalities at work. Market globalization, production pressures and footloose capital, have consequences for the organization of work and the labor market and are defining features at the end of the 20th century which continue to be important. In addition, direct management-labor relations have been replaced by networks of workers which make the basis of negotiating work-related conditions more tenuous than previously. Further, there has been the decline of manufacturing, and increased growth of small business, again making the boundaries between employer and employee negotiations less well-defined than previously. Coupled with this, the decline in strength of the trade union movement has meant that employee rights and perspectives are less strongly represented and pursued. In all, changes to work regulation and structure have meant that increased deregulation has been a pervading influence over the past decade or so. All these factors contribute to the "new" emerging epidemics in one way or another.

Occupational Violence

Chapter 3 focuses on the most severe emerging epidemic of the 21st century. Claire Mayhew argued in Chapter 3 that there has been an upsurge of interest in occupational violence across the industrialized world. In the U.S., occupational violence is a significant OSH risk with around two million workers a year reporting incidents, including a high rate of occupational homicide. In Europe, about 10 percent of workers report incidents of violence at work, and in the U.K. the incidence has increased markedly in recent times in the services industries. Mayhew reports that violence is most likely to occur in jobs which involve dealing with cash, and also extensive face-to-face contact with clients. She also notes research evidence that males tend to experience more physical abuse while females have proportionately more verbal and sexual abuse. Mayhew also assessed the evidence and concludes that there is significant under-reporting of violence at work on official data bases. Claire Mayhew concludes that the ILO *Code of Practice* is an essential precursor to both reduction of the incidence of occupational violence and to widespread recognition of this risk as the most significant emerging OHS epidemic in the 21st century.

Precarious Employment

Michael Quinlan maintains that one of the most pervading influences over the past two decades has been the growth of insecure and precarious employment. In Australia, for example, about 46 percent of workers are part-time, temporary, or in other ways precariously employed. Michael Quinlan argues that there is a growing body of scientific evidence showing the poor health effects of insecure and precarious employment. Reviews of studies have shown that inferior OHS outcomes have been associated with precarious employment, and have been increasing over the past two decades. These have included poorer quality work practices, higher injury rates, increased exposure to hazards, diseases, and stress. Seventy-four of 188 studies review reported negative OSH consequences from precarious employment. Tele-workers are one specific category that have particular OHS problems associated with their work.

Michael Quinlan argues that more research is required on home-based and temporary work, leased labor, small business, part-time work, and multiple jobholding and downsizing. Further research is also required on the social implications of precarious employment for cost, regulatory frameworks, and OHS systems. In addition, precarious employment and its health effects pose a number of challenges for traditional data collections and data sources.

Long-Latency Disease

Chapter 5 focuses on well-known occupational diseases that have been in epidemic proportions for some decades. Jim Leigh identifies that while the original conception of epidemic was in relation to infectious disease, the term is now more generally applied to environmental and occupational causes of diseases of both long- and short-latency. Starting with Thomas Arlidge in the British

Staffordshire potteries, a series of diseases are analyzed from his perspective as an epidemiologist. Jim Leigh reports that all occupational diseases are experienced within a political context, and as a result, results of studies can be delayed or other means used to circumvent conclusions, such as with long-latency conditions that employers may not want brought to light. In addition, because of the variable economic consequences associated with litigation and compensation, long-latency conditions such as coal workers' pneumoconiosis can be compensated in some countries and not others. Jim Leigh argues that the history of long-latency epidemic recognition is an essentially political process: first there is public recognition of the condition by attention being paid to diseases or deaths. The second stage usually involves employers downplaying the significance of the OSH events or even denying their existence. The third stage usually involves persistent efforts by often isolated scientists and investigators who identify cause-effect relationships for particular diseases. Fourth, depending on the socio-legal and socio-medical context, the condition may become accepted as a legitimate disease and be controlled through legal OSH regulations. However this whole process usually takes some time and involves conflicting relations between employers, scientists, and other investigators and medical and legal representatives. Meanwhile, until control strategies are implemented, further workers are put at risk, which extends the epidemic across additional members of the working population.

Child Labor

Chapter 6 focuses on a largely *non-reported* epidemic. Claire Mayhew argues that child labor is extensive across the developing world, with one child in eight performing work that could cause mental or physical damage, including prostitution, construction, mining, and deep-sea diving. Within industrialized countries, extensive employment of adolescents occurs, often encouraged by parents and/or in family businesses, in industry sectors (such as fast food) where emerging epidemics are more common (such as occupational violence), or in more hazardous jobs (such as illegally in the construction industry or in farming). The consequences of child and adolescent labor are visible through a range of different epidemics, according to the specific hazard and risk exposures. Mayhew argues that the true extent of work-related epidemics among child/adolescent workers is largely unknown because their employment is likely to be highest in countries which under-report OSH incidents, and in informal sectors of the economy.

Stress

Chapter 7 focuses on an epidemic blamed on the victim. Chris Peterson reports that work-related stress is at epidemic levels, due to work intensification, the pressures of open market competition on businesses, rational economic management principles, longer working hours, and working environments conducive to creating high levels of stress. U.K., U.S., and Australian evidence on compensated stress are presented that show the incidence has been sustained at high levels for the past decade. Coupled with this has been a decrease in unionization levels and presence in large numbers of organizations. As a result, stress has become an established expectation for many employees in the 21st century. There are a number of reasons why stress has become formally accepted as part of the OSH agenda. First, there is an extensive psychobiological literature, which shows that stress has important consequences for health. Second, the psychosocial literature argues that stress is increasing due to greater competition between organizations and deregulation of work practices. Third, the extensive cultural and political literature argues that stress occurs largely as a consequence of management-employee relations and effort/reward imbalance. However, counter-balancing arguments have been facilitated by psychological interpretations that focus on individuals and their susceptibility. Hence, management often retreats to this *individual* causal explanation for stress. The result is that stress from work is an established epidemic which is frequently blamed on the victim.

Standing at Work

In Chapter 8, Karen Messing, Katherine Lippel, Ève Laperrière, and Marie-Christine Thibault present evidence of the increase in standing on the job and the negative health consequences. However, they argue that demonstrating a link between exposure and injury can be problematic, and has important implications for compensation. The authors argue that "silent" pain may also be contributing to the rise in musculoskeletal disorder, and that any conditions which depends on waiting for epidemiological data will lead to an epidemic. The authors maintain that over the past two decades there has been extensive deregulation of work which has led to the proliferation in some cases of more dangerous working conditions. In the case of excessive standing at work, this has precipitated an epidemic.

Pain in the back is almost twice as likely to occur among those standing for excessive periods at work. In addition, standing at work is associated with excessive pain in the lower limbs. In Canada, for example, 59 percent of workers stand for lengthy periods, and this figure increases to more than 80 percent for younger workers. There are no strong reasons why many workers who stand for long periods could not sit doing the same work, for example among supermarket checkout workers. The authors observe that in some countries such as Thailand, workers sit performing tasks that are routinely carried out in a standing position in North America, the U.K., and Australia.

The Discourse of Abuse in Return-To-Work:
Iatrogenesis in Occupational Health

The focus of Chapter 9 is the epidemic associated with return to work programs and the sometimes harmful effects that these may have on employees. Joan Eakin argues that many OHS programs themselves have some harmful effects on employees, and these are related to some labor laws and their policing, and also to the harmful effects of many employer-employee relationships that place limitations on workers' participation. Return-to-work in countries such as Canada is a complex process that often leaves employees severely disadvantaged, particularly those who are not able to return to the workforce. Many of the reasons for this are socio-political in nature. Part of the reason for the growth in the discourse of abuse has been, for example in provinces in Canada, the shift of responsibility for return-to-work programs from government to employers and injured worker. In Ontario, for example, the government mainly now sets the ground rules but not the process and procedures for return to work. Thus, the author argues that there has developed an epidemic of abuse associated with return-to-work programs.

Occupational Health and Safety,
and Occupational Rehabilitation

Chapter 10 focuses on the rising costs and reduced effectiveness of rehabilitation programs over recent years. Greg Murphy argues that, in a number of countries, regulations were developed because rehabilitation was a very costly exercise. In Australia, for example, a no-fault compensation scheme was introduced to curtail costly legal proceedings over the cause of illness and injury. However, a major threat emerged as these schemes did not produce expected return-to-work rates and reduce absences significantly. Consequently, the no-fault compensation systems became financially threatened due to the continuation of long absenses from work by claimants. Greg Murphy argues that a key to the problems associated with rehabilitation was that much of the decision-making power about rehabilitation had been taken out of the hands of organizational decision-makers and placed in the hands of external agents such as doctors, providers of services, and insurance companies. Consequently, the problem associated with the epidemic of spiraling costs of rehabilitation services have both socio-legal (changing regulation to reduce legal claims) and socio-structural causes (that is a shift of decision-making power to expert professional groups and out of the organization).

Recognition of Emerging Epidemics

In Chapter 11, Claire Mayhew analyzes the risks when the first "sentinel" cases of a possible *new* epidemic are identified. She provides examples of scenarios where baseline OHS empirical studies in industry are warranted, details guidance on how to go about conducting "grounded" OHS research, and argues that if scientific principles are used throughout the conduct of inductive empirical research, rich qualitative and quantitative data on relatively "unknown" problem issues can be gathered. The end products of such large-scale empirical studies are likely to have a high level of validity, to be generalizable to the broader industry sector/occupational group, and to be repeatable. Further, when the emergence of a distinctly new ill-health condition is suspected, large-scale empirical studies designed within an inductive paradigm provide the most reliable mechanism to identify the characteristics of an emerging epidemic in a timely fashion.

These different perspectives provided by different authors on epidemics show some similarities in causative agents for epidemics. However there are also global theoretical perspectives that explain epidemics and these will be investigated in the next section of this chapter.

THREE PERSPECTIVES ON
THE EMERGENCE OF EPIDEMICS

There are three levels of explanation relevant to describing the causes of epidemics in OSH and how they are responded to. These are the biological or bio-physiological explanation, the psychosocial explanation, and the socio-cultural and socio-political explanation. Each of these has a well-developed theoretical, scientific research and empirical base. Each provides different but overlapping levels of explanation, rather than competing discourses. These three approaches have been variously adopted by management, insurance companies, and the proponents of labor as explanations for OSH problems and epidemics.

Biological and Bio-Psychological Approaches

Historically, biological approaches were the first explanations for OSH problems, and subsequently became tools by which management and insurance companies could strongly argue limited liability for injury and illness. House (11) maintains that up to the 1950s, health and illness were shaped almost entirely by the paradigms of medical care and biological processes. The infectious disease model was as prevalent in OSH as it was in public health, and was based on assembling sufficient scientific and objective data to demonstrate causation. Hence, epidemics were explained in biological terms with approaches such as virology and immunology being important. During the late 1960s and beyond, the work of bio-psychological researchers such as Mason (12) made important links between factors such as a lack of control and bio-psychological processes which could lead to hormonal effects and tissue damage which initiated the onset of disease. In certain areas of OSH, these bio-psychological approaches provided important insights into causal factors for the onset of disease.

However, the political climate associated with compensation and the increasing costs associated with epidemics led to biological and bio-psychological approaches being less frequently directed to of work as a cause of illness and disease. The biomedical model's tenants provide a good example: when questions of developing epidemics associated with workplace practice change arise, the biomedical approach can be a lever used by employers and insurance companies to narrow the focus of association between work and disease. Consequently, in times of developing epidemics the biological approach can be a tool firmly wielded by employers and insurance companies to stem the tide of claims.

Biomedicine uses demonstrable patho-chemistry, patho-physiology, and diagnosis through extant pathologic signs and symptoms (13). Biomedicine has been practiced widely throughout most of the 20th century with the clinical encounter organized around taking patients' symptom histories by the clinician who attempts to translate this into a diagnosis. Thus, the biomedical approach is based on identifying a malfunction in the body and assigning a diagnosis for that malfunction, together with a treatment to deal with the break down. Clinicians purport to base their diagnoses on proven data, with scientific literature assumed to be an accurate representation of reality. Lax (13) maintains that occupational medicine has shared this biomedical approach with other branches of medical practice. In the process of identifying disease causation, methods are borrowed from infectious disease. For example, asbestos exposure has been identified as the cause of lung cancer, asbestosis, and mesothelioma. Consistent with the biomedical model, exposure and dose should ideally be demonstrated by quantitative methods such as air monitoring and biological monitoring independently of the worker/patient's signs and symptoms (13, p. 518). The corporate drive behind occupational medicine in the U.S. has increased the push for more objective measures of scientific validity, and insurers' and employers' demands for increased objectivity have led to less reliance on the accounts of patients. Consequently, fewer ill workers/ex-workers are recognized as suffering from occupational diseases. Lax (13, p. 516) argues that illnesses due to poor air quality, work-related musculoskeletal disorders, stressful working conditions, and multiple chemical sensitivities are emerging in complex ways. In this context "clinicians in the United States are being increasingly pressured by workers' compensation insurance carriers and employers to use only traditional and narrowly focussed diagnostic, treatment, and functional assessment tools to characterize these conditions" (13, p. 516). Therefore, if tests do not show physiological derangement, for example, then etiology, diagnosis, and disability is not possible to be established. This, according to Lax, significantly diminishes employer responsibility.

In sum, the biological and bio-psychological approach tends to focus on narrow testing and conceptualization, and relatively straightforward cause-effect relationships. Yet, occupational physicians are being increasingly pressured to rely on this biomedical model: ". . . the problem is essentially one of inadequate knowledge and the need is for the development of more powerful tools to accurately assess exposure, risk, effect, and impairment/disability" (13, p. 516). The editors of this book consider that the biomedical model only partially recognizes causation of many work-related injuries and illnesses, and places ill and injured workers at a considerable disadvantage.

Psychosocial Approaches and Perspectives

The psychosocial perspective emerged toward the middle of last century and essentially linked work practices and psychosocial states of workers. Today, however, the psychosocial approach is more frequently used to individualize OSH problems, direct attention to "poor" individual traits, and absolve employers from responsibility.

According to House (11), developments in medical sociology and social epidemiology transformed popular understandings of the nature and causes of illness. Health and illness are now much more understood as shaped by social, behavioral, and psychological factors. Stress at work is a case in point, where House argues that social epidemiology has identified a range of factors that contribute to ill health. These are: event-based or acute stress; supportive social relationships; psychological disposition including hostility and anger, pessimism, a lack of self-efficacy; and chronic life and work stress. Research has also shown that socio-economic status and position predisposes certain people to be at greater risk of many biomedical and environmental risk factors (11). There have been numerous contributors to the development of psychosocial approaches. While traditional psychological approaches to OSH have tended to individualize the process of illness and injury (which can lead to blaming the victim), social psychology and psychology of the emotions have focused on specific impacts from the work environment and work processes on psychological health. Nonetheless, an important conclusion has been that not all employees respond the same way to work environment issues.

The danger, of course, is that this knowledge base can be used to remove those who are seen as having an inappropriate disposition or capacity. For example, employment screening checks that have been proposed in Australia and other countries are based on the premise that if susceptible employees are not hired in the first place, then the chances of developing an OSH epidemic for some type of work-related illness or injury can be minimized.

The research on extent of work demands (14, 15) and "control" at work (16) is important in psychosocial approaches to understanding employee susceptibility. Variables that may be studied include hours of work, inappropriate supervision, or pace of production on assembly lines. The research into teamwork composition, membership, and functioning has also been an important focus, with many employees engaged in more flexible working arrangements over the past decade.

According to Takala (1), possible psychosocial contributors to stress at work include smoking, workplace violence, and alcohol and drug problems.

Psycho-social aspects are often behind the development of health promotion programs, where individual behavior change is the focus. However, there are also important structural factors beyond individual behavior, and this is where the focus of some health promotion programs may not be as effective.

One particular problem associated with U.S. employers and insurers' pressure to focus on psychological and genetic factors associated with occupational illness and injury is that this approach shifts the causal problem from work to the employee (13). Similarly, job satisfaction and locus of control factors can be argued to have an individual base where employees should improve through learning a new set of coping mechanisms. This approach presumes that workplace change need not adequately address the problems of employees who are individually susceptible to occupational illness and injury. The development and acceptance of this approach by corporate interests results in decreased environmental monitoring and preventive efforts, disenfranchises individual workers, diminished preventive efforts, and fewer illness claims being supported.

Lax (13) argues that understanding the psychosocial dimensions of illness greatly expands on the biomedical model and approach. Clinicians can better see the extent to which symptoms link with a disease process, including why the person decided to become a patient and other factors shaping the person's illness experience. The argument goes that by using this approach an occupational physician is more easily able to interface with the work environment to see what aspects of the job are contributing to the condition, and which needs changing in the event of a return to work. Similarly, in an OSH change program, certain job features can be identified as contributing to illness and injury. Thus the psychosocial model is a substantial advance over the perspective of a narrow biomedical approach.

Nevertheless, there are a number of significant critiques. Allvin and Aronsson (17) debate the utility of the psychosocial approach, and argue that neither subjective nor objective concepts were very successful. Their subjective psychosocial work environment assessments focussed on the social relationship in and between groups, and found practices such as inadequate social relationships, poor quality supervision, and sexual and social harassment. However, their diagnosis and recommended changes were often regarded by management as an unwelcome intrusion into the workplace. Allvin and Aronsson (17) also identified that workers sometimes had difficulty in recognizing risks, that preventative measures often required complete organizational overhauls, that senior management needed to foster changes, and that many change programs actually lost sight of the individual workers whose health they were supposed to support and protect.

In sum, psychosocial process models have added much to the biomedical approach and at least have fostered a focus on work environment factors that contribute to OSH risks. Thus, the psychosocial approach can recognize and respond to OSH epidemics related to work-organization risk factors, but it does not provide an adequate explanation of why they emerge.

Socio-Cultural and Political Approaches

The socio-cultural/socio-political perspective is a much broader approach that can link the broader political environment, neo-liberal policies which shape the relations between management and labor, and complex power relations and negotiations between various parties with OSH indices. The core parties whose contribution is analyzed in this perspective include employers, employees, trade unions, insurance companies, the medical profession, and the legal profession. Thus, the socio-cultural/socio-political approach to analysis focuses on OSH and labor/management relations. Hence, from this approach, OSH epidemics result from broader political/economic relationships.

Figlio (18) was one of the earlier writers to develop a socio-cultural and socio-political framework for examining the emergence of new OSH conditions. In his analysis of conditions such as miners' nystagmus, he identified the processes involved in the legitimization of a condition for compensation, including key stakeholders in the socio-legal, socio-medical, and socio-political environment. He argued that for an illness and injury to be acceptable to courts for compensation, the medical profession needed to identify a set of symptoms with specific causes in the workplace. These cause-effect relationships were central explanations why some conditions became accepted for compensation and others did not. Thus, from this perspective, the recognition of an epidemic is largely the outcome of a bio-medical plus a socio-political process.

Willis (5) further developed Figlio's framework while examining the causes of repetitive strain injury (RSI), and its passage in becoming acceptable as a compensable injury. In doing this, he further developed Figlio's socio-political perspective and argued that RSI (like miner's nystagmus), started as distress associated with dehumanizing work practices, was created by new technology and poor workflow with poor management organization of work, and yet became a legitimate condition acceptable for compensation. Willis described three proc-esses that caused RSI to gain this socio-political meaning: observers instigated various medical mechanisms; medicine constricted the scope of the disease; and compensable aspects were restricted. Therefore, social aspects mediated diagnosis, there was a negotiated meaning for the illnesses, and socio-economic and political aspects influenced the scope. Other writers in this book to adopt a socio-cultural and socio-political explanation for the development and acceptance within the OSH arena for specific conditions were Mayhew (19), with her analysis of occupational violence and bullying, and Peterson (20), with work-related stress.

Lax (13) argues from a critical theory and post-modern perspective that several studies have demonstrated "the effects of social factors on the recognition, treat-ment, and prevention of occupational diseases such as pneumoconiosis, silicosis, and radium and lead poisoning" (13, p. 528). Another study that focused on musculoskeletal disorders, hearing loss, and back pain showed how the interplay of factors (including financial compensation, labor activism, economic instability, and new technology) shaped ideas and conceptions about occupational illness and injury. Lax (13) maintains that occupational illnesses can be understood as social constructs reflecting the balance between political, scientific, cultural, and economic factors at their time and in their environment. Further, the interplay between medical officers and patients in occupational health encounters are influenced by clinicians' cultural experiences that are often shaped by beliefs that being in the workforce is better than being out of it, that somehow workers might be wanting to rort the system, and that more highly educated employers must be trying to do the "right thing." These socio-cultural assumptions provide a strong framework within which many OSH medical encounters are carried out.

In sum, a political economy of OSH perspective comes closest to describing the interplay of social and political processes that occur as specific illness are identified, defined, categorized, and considered for compensation. In an historical analysis of political parties' involvement in social inequalities and health, Navarro and Shi (21) point out that it is the more conservative governments that support open-market competition and neo-liberal policies, that have the weakest record of policies which redistribute wealth, and arguably the strongest record in maintaining resources in the hands of power-holders. A social-construct analysis applied to many occupational illnesses enables an unlocking of the biases inherent in biomedical and psychologically based decisions for compensation following a work-related injury or illness. In some cases the process may be fairly cut and dried, but with conditions such as asbestosis and even more straightforward musculoskeletal injuries, the processes are far more social and political.

CONCLUSION

There are a number of useful frameworks for analyzing OSH epidemics. The discussions above were informed by insights from earlier chapters in this book, and highlighted the significant influence of pre-existing paradigms among OSH researchers and writers. It was argued that a range of disciplinary, power, and lobby groups control recognition of work-related injuries and illness (particularly those which are apparently in epidemic proportions), including litigators, government authorities, trade unions, and management interests, and the extent to which the lay population is exposed to media coverage. Clearly, different perspectives give different—but still valuable—insights into when work-related illness and injury reaches an epidemic state.

The different chapters in the book identify a range of social, economic, governmental, and regulatory factors that have contributed to different epidemics. The explanations of the different epidemics reported in the book are varied, but the theme of globalization, the development of neo-liberal policies, and internationalization all feature strongly in the development of OSH epidemics. The authors indicate that the epidemics reported today are in most cases different to those of a century ago, but nonetheless, many are as potent in their negative effect on the health of working populations.

This chapter has posited that three particular models are relevant for understanding the identification of OSH conditions which develop into epidemic proportions. These are the biological or bio-physiological, the psychosocial, and the socio-political and socio-cultural approaches.

The biological or biomedical approach to epidemics offers a clear-cut analysis as to when an epidemic occurs. It ignores social, economic, and political processes in the definition of illness and questions about the "objectivity" of markers that are used. The biomedical model developed from the initial biological classifications of infectious diseases, but more recently is an approach welcomed by managements and insurance companies in order to dissuade claims for compensation. This approach also tends to ignore many facets of illness and injury-causation processes, such as shopfloor exposures. Thus, on its own, the biomedical approach is the most conservative.

The psychosocial perspective usually focuses on a worker's experience of occupational illness or injury, and includes the response of workers to working conditions that may affect their health. In this sense, the psychosocial perspective provides a broader explanation of the emergence of OSH epidemics and their causes. Nevertheless, this approach has led to programs of change in workplaces that have not always been accepted by employees, as many recommendations (such as pre-employment genetic screening) are not always in the best health interests of workers.

The socio-political and socio-cultural perspective offers a much broader understanding of the roots of epidemics in workplaces across the developing and industrialized world, including the contribution of management/employee relations to unhealthy work environments. The socio-political approach also allows an improved understanding of the broader medio-legal, economic, political, and social processes that occur between the major proponents in OSH. Hence, while biological and bio-physiological and psychosocial approaches offer important insights, socio-political approaches are the most comprehensive explanation of how OHS epidemics have achieved that status.

In sum, there have historically been a series of OSH epidemics. Many of these have had direct cause/effect relationships, but many result from multifactorial exposures. Through the evidence presented in the various chapters, it is clear that some well-known hazards continue to cause epidemics, and that as work processes alter, "new" epidemics emerge—and may continue to emerge over this century.

REFERENCES

1. Takala, J. Introductory report: Decent work, safe work. Paper presented at the XVIth World Congress on Safety and Health at Work, Vienna, May, 2002.

2. Wainwright, D., and Calnan, D. *Work Stress: The Making of a Modern Epidemic.* Open University Press, Buckingham, 2002.
3. The David Law Firm. www.mesotheliomia-legal-services.com/main/successful.html
4. Antonetti-Zequeria, L. F. Workplace violence: Its legal aspect and socioeconomic consequences. *Bull. Newslet.* 2 September 10, 2002. www.ag-internet.com/bullet_iln_two_one/goldman.htm
5. Willis, E. RSI as a social process. *Commun. Health Stud.* 10: 210–219, 1986.
6. Asbestos Network. www.asbestosnetwork.com/news/nw_081301-senatehear.htm
7. Peterson, C. *Work Stress: Studies in the Context, Content and Outcomes of Stress: A Book of Readings.* Baywood, Amityville, NY, 2003.
8. McGrillen, H. Trade unions environment and health. www.unedforum.org/health/EHMagazine/Magazine9/tunions.htm
9. Chandler, D., Berg, E., and Barry, J. Stress in the UK. In *Work Stress: Studies in the Context, Content and Outcomes of Stress: A Book of Readings,* edited by C. Peterson, pp. 33–52. Baywood, Amityville, NY, 2003.
10. Why some employers are caught in the middle. www.cpmy.com/articles/viol.htm
11. House, J. S. Understanding social factors and inequalities in health: 20th century progress and 21st century prospects. *J. Health Soc. Behav.* 43: 125–142, 2002.
12. Mason, J. W. The scope of psychoendochrine research. *Psychosom. Med.* 30: 565–575, 1968.
13. Lax, M. B. Occupational medicine: Towards a worker/patient empowerment approach to occupational illness. *Int. J. Health Serv.* 32: 515–549, 2002.
14. Karasek, R. A. Job demands and job decision latitude and mental strain: Implications for job redesign. *Admin. Sci. Q.* 24: 285–304, 1979.
15. Karasek, R. A. Job socialisation and job train: The implications of two related psychosocial mechanisms for job design. In *Working Life: A Social Science Contribution to Work Reform,* edited by B. Gardell and G. Johansson, pp. 75–94. John Wiley and Sons, New York, 1981.
16. Aronsson, G. Dimensions of control as related to work organization, stress, and health. *Int. J. Health Serv.* 19: 459–468, 1989.
17. Allvin, M., and Aronsson, G. The future of work environment reforms: Does the concept of work environment apply within the new economy? *Int. J. Health Serv.* 33: 99–111, 2003.
18. Figlio, K. How does an illness mediate social relations: Workmen's compensation and medico-legal practices 1890-1940? In *The Problem of Medical Knowledge: Examining the Social Construction of Medicine,* edited by P. Wright and A. Treacher, pp. 174–224. Edinburgh University Press, Edinburgh, 1982.
19. Mayhew, C. Occupational violence in industrialized countries: Types, incidence patterns, and "at risk" groups of workers. In *Violence at Work: Causes, Patterns and Prevention,* edited by M. Gill, B. Fisher, and V. Bowie, pp. 21–40. Willan Publishing, Cullampton, U.K., 2002.
20. Peterson, C. *Occupational Stress: A Sociological Perspective.* Baywood, Amityville, NY, 1999.
21. Navarro, V., and Shi, L. The political context of social inequalities and health. *Int. J. Health Serv.* 31: 1–21, 2001.

Contributors

JOAN M. EAKIN is a Professor in the Department of Public Health Sciences in the Faculty of Medicine at the University of Toronto, and an Adjunct Senior Scientist at the Institute for Work and Health in Toronto. She is a sociologist by background, and has had long-standing research interest in issues of social etiology and prevention and change in work health and safety, particularly in relation to small workplaces.

KAJ FRICK is senior researcher at the National Institute for Working Life and professor of Work Environment management at Lulea Technical University in Sweden. He studies various aspects of OHS management, including in small firms, through worker participation, regional safety representatives, national and international governmental policies and regulations, and also the discourse of economic OHS arguments. He also promotes research in this field, including internationally. With Jensen, Quinlan, and Wilthagen, he edited *Systematic Occupational Health and Safety Management—Perspectives on an International Development,* Elsevier 2000. At present he heads a Swedish evaluation of the implementation of the regulation on OHS management.

ÈVE LAPERRIÈRE is employed at CINBIOSE and Department of Biological Sciences, Université du Québec à Montréal, Montreal.

JAMES LEIGH (MB BS MD Ph.D. MA MSc (Syd) BLegS (Macq) CEng FAFPHM, FAFOM) has been carrying out research and tertiary teaching in occupational medicine and epidemiology for 38 years. He is currently Senior Lecturer and Director of the Centre for Occupational and Environmental Health, School of Public Health, University of Sydney. From 1988-97 he was Head of the Epidemiology Unit at the National Occupational Health and Safety Commission and from 1998-2000 Head of the Research Unit in the same organization. He has published over 200 papers in this field and has held consulting positions with WHO, WTO, ILO, CNRS France, and the Finnish Institute of Occupational Health.

KATHERINE LIPPEL is a full Professor of Law at the Faculty of Law and Political Science at the University of Québec in Montréal and a member of the Quebec Bar. She specializes in legal issues relating to occupational health and safety and workers' compensation and is the author of several articles and books in the field. She currently directs three multidisciplinary research teams on the following themes: Health effects of compensation systems; Policy, precarious employment and occupational health; and interactions between law and medicine in the field of occupational health and safety. She also co-directs, with Karen Messing, the research group *l'Invisible qui fait mal*, a partnership with three Québec unions oriented towards improvement of women's occupational health.

CLAIRE MAYHEW (B.Admin (hons), Ph.D.) is a Visiting Fellow in the Department of Management at Griffith University in Brisbane, Australia. She has worked in the healthcare system in Australia and Africa, as an academic in commerce, environmental science, and behavioral science faculties, and in the Australian civil service. Claire has a PhD in occupational health and safety and has published widely in the Australian and international scientific press on a range of issues, including OHS risks in micro-small businesses and the prevention of occupational violence.

KAREN MESSING is an ergonomist and full Professor in the Département des Sciences Biologiques of Université du Québec à Montréal. With Katherine Lippel, Dr. Messing co-directs the research group *l'Invisible qui fait mal*, a partnership with three Québec unions oriented towards improvement of women's occupational health. She is the author of numerous articles and of *One-eyed Science: Occupational Health and Working Women* (Temple, 1998) and editor and co-author of *Integrating Gender in Ergonomic Analysis* (1999) published by the Trade Union Technical Bureau of the European Trade Union Confederation. Her current research focuses on the effects of prolonged standing among workers in the service sector, on ergonomics of work usually done by women, and on application of gender-sensitive analysis in occupational health.

GREGORY MURPHY (Ph.D.) is an Associate Professor in Rehabilitation Psychology at La Trobe University in Melbourne and Director of the Rehabilitation Research and Training Unit within La Trobe's School of Public Health. Greg's major research interests are in the areas of work motivation and community re-establishment following serious injury. Greg has consulted to both government and private-sector occupational rehabilitation agencies and has published over 100 articles in scientific and professional journals in the areas of organizational behavior and rehabilitation psychology. He is a past National President of the Australian Association of Cognitive and Behaviour Therapy.

CHRIS PETERSON (BA, Ph.D.) is a senior research fellow in the Faculty of Medicine, Nursing and Health Sciences at Monash University, Australia. He is a health sociologist with a long term interest in occupational health and safety and work related stress. He has a number of books including *Stress at Work: A Sociological Perspective* (Baywood) and edited *Work Stress: Studies of the Context, Content and Outcomes of Stress: A Book of Readings* (Baywood). He is also the author of a number of national and international articles on stress and occupational health and safety.

MICHAEL QUINLAN (B.Ec. (hons), Ph.D.) is a Professor in the School of Industrial Relations and Organisational Behaviour at the University of New South Wales. He is the author of articles on occupational health and safety as well as author/editor of a number of books, including *Managing Occupational Health and Safety* (Macmillan 1991 and 2nd edition 2000), *Work and Health* (Macmillan 1993) and *Systematic OHS Management* (Elsevier, Oxford, 2000). A particular focus of his research has been the effects of institutions, regulation, and employment status on OHS.

MARIE-CHRISTINE THIBAULT is employed at CINBIOSE and Department of Biological Sciences, Université du Québec à Montréal, Montreal.

DAVID WALTERS is TUC Professor of Work Environment at Cardiff University. He was formerly Professor of Occupational and Environmental Health and Safety at South Bank University. His main research interests are in the social relations and regulation of the working environment in the UK and the European Union and he has published widely on these subjects. He is also the editor of the international academic journal *Policy and Practice in Health and Safety*.

Index

Peterson, Chris, 10, 11, 218–219
Peto, Julian, 84
Pittsburgh Corning, 82
Pneumoconiosis, coal workers', 77
Poland, 214
Policy and recognition of OHS epidemics, government, 171, 213–214
Political economy of OHS perspective, 225–226
Pollution, fatalities caused by, 3
Posture and prolonged standing, 143–144
Poverty/poorer communities, 3, 99
    See also Developing countries
Precarious employment
    adolescents/children and work-related injuries, 101
    categories of work included in, 53
    conclusions/summary, 69–70
    mobility of labor, 6
    overview, 217
    regulatory challenges
        enforcement, 67
        other effects, 69
        overview, 62–64
        prevention, 64–67
        workers' compensation claims, 67–69
    research/studies on, 55–62
    structure/organization of work, changing, 18
    surveys charting, 53–54
Prescriptive vs. process regulation, 23
Price, C. W., 79
Privatization, 61
    See also Deregulation
Process vs. prescriptive regulation, 23
Production structures, changing. See Organization/structure of work, changing; Precarious employment
Psychology, health and rehabilitation, 179
Psychosocial harm and return-to-work, 170
Psychosocial risk factors perspective for new epidemics, 7–8, 223–224, 227

Public confidence in government/decision makers, 19
Public-sector managerialism, 26

Quinlan, Michael, 9, 217

Raybestos Manhattan, 82
Reasoned action, theory of, 182
Recognition of new forms of work-related injuries/illnesses, 2
    See also Empirical studies, large-scale inductive
Regulation, state involvement in engagement of
    international controls/developments, 21–23
    recognizing OHS epidemics, 213–214
    right-to-work, 171
    standing, prolonged, 148–152
    See also Deregulation; regulatory challenges under Precarious employment
Rehabilitation, occupational
    advances in, 177
    conclusions/summary, 182–183
    exercise enhancement, 181
    explanatory style, 180–181
    mental health benefits of work, 178–179
    overview, 220
    pain behavior management, 180
    psychology, health and rehabilitation, 179
    safe practice, workplace, 177–178
    social support, 181–182
    workers' compensation claims, 175–177
    See also Return-to-work
Repetitive strain injury (RSI), 2, 128, 213
Replicability and inductive empirical studies, 189
Reporting, reduced/under
    adolescents/children and work-related injuries, 103, 104–105, 107